STEPHEN O'BRIEN

'Dubbed the heir to Doris Stokes' crown . . .'
Woman

'Stunning clairvoyance . . . superb mediumship'
Psychic News

'Britain's brightest young medium . . . Power seems to
radiate from his fingertips. These eyes can see beyond
the grave'
Daily Star

'It's hard to be sceptical of the psychic world when a
stranger tells you precisely what you were doing that
morning, and even days before. I was startled, almost
shocked'
Liverpool Echo

By the same author

VISIONS OF ANOTHER WORLD
The Autobiography of a Medium

VOICES FROM HEAVEN
Communion with Another World

ANGELS BY MY SIDE
The Psychic Life of a Medium

IN TOUCH WITH ETERNITY
Contact with Another World

Stephen O'Brien

BANTAM BOOKS
TORONTO · NEW YORK · LONDON · SYDNEY · AUCKLAND

IN TOUCH WITH ETERNITY
A BANTAM BOOK 0 553 40534 9

First publication in Great Britain

PRINTING HISTORY
Bantam Books edition published 1992
Bantam edition reprinted 1993
Bantam edition reprinted 1994

Set in 10pt Linotype Century Schoolbook by
Falcon Graphic Art Ltd, Wallington, Surrey.

Bantam Books are published by Transworld Publishers Ltd,
61–63 Uxbridge Road, Ealing, London W5 5SA,
in Australia by Transworld Publishers (Australia) Pty Ltd,
15–25 Helles Avenue, Moorebank, NSW 2170,
and in New Zealand by Transworld Publishers (NZ) Ltd,
3 William Pickering Drive, Albany, Auckland.

Printed and bound in Great Britain by
Cox & Wyman Ltd, Reading, Berkshire.

To the Everlasting Love
that will not let us go . . .

Acknowledgements

I wish to express my deepest thanks and gratitude to all my friends, in both worlds, whose continuing warmth and encouragement has supported me while giving the Message of the Spirit to millions of souls in need.

You'll never know how much your love strengthened and healed me through some of the most difficult times of my life.

At my journey's end, when I finally return Home, if any soul claims a measure of knowledge or comfort from my work, then know I couldn't have done it without you.

What we share is something very special.

You know who you are.

Thank you for being there when I needed you.

Contents

PART THREE
Life in the Beyond

Truth builds her Nest
only in the Branches of an Open Mind . . .
and as a Gift to those who Love her
she will set their Spirits Free.

Stephen O'Brien

Prologue

Tonight at 7.30 while happy music plays, backstage
I will walk through a rabbit warren of dimly lit
corridors leading from my dressing-room, up onto
a short flight of stairs and out into the wings of
another big theatre. And in the semi-darkness,
I will patiently wait behind the closed, red velvet
curtains . . .

Tonight has now come – and I am here, standing
backstage.

Beyond the lighted drapes, hundreds of people are
seated in the buzzing crowd; each face, a stranger;
each soul speaking to his neighbour, or silently
waiting, hoping, or praying that the man about to
make his entrance will make contact with his dear
ones who have, perhaps, suffered some dreadful pain
or tragedy, and then passed out of this world and into
an invisible place Beyond . . .

Backstage, in the semi-darkness, my heart is
thudding against my chest, while my mind spins like
radar. I'm desperately seeking the sound of voices not
of this world: gentle, still small voices. I want to hear
the tones of souls whom I sense standing close to me,
spirit people who want me to tell their loved ones
tonight that their lives didn't end when they 'died',
that they're still conscious beings in Eternity, still

caring for, and visiting, their families each day.

Suddenly the music stops, and the seconds are quickly ticking away towards the start of another evening of mediumship . . .

Stealthily, I position myself at the centre of the curtains, and I'm aware of the announcement introducing me to the crowd. Having heard it countless times before, my silent prayers start rising to the Great Spirit . . .

'May I be of service to the people. May I help them realize that Love is the Greatest Power in the Universe – even stronger than death.'

Beyond the curtains, the once-noisy public voices are now stilled. They're eagerly awaiting my entrance. Hope is rising in their breasts because they've seen my picture, read my books, witnessed me on television or in their favourite magazine and radio features, and now they are actually here, tonight, sitting in the meeting place and waiting, clutching their tickets like passports to hope.

Silently, they're willing me to succeed, and their inward joy can be felt, sensed and known. They're very happy to be present.

But I, the medium, am standing alone in the shadows with a heavy, broken heart. I'm in danger of losing my home; my body is tired and my soul needs rest. My mind is stung with the news of my elderly father lying far away on a bed of pain, close to death. But I must be here, tonight, not there beside him.

(I, too, am just a man who laughs and weeps, a being whom the sting of life has often touched; and I've known public ridicule because of my mediumship, sometimes being all but pilloried, just because I wanted to share my gifts with others.)

Deep down, my heart is weeping. But I must fight back my tears, deny my own hurt, and somewhere from the depths of my spirit I must dredge up a smile and place it on my face.

'God, who dwells in silence, knows I've always tried my best. He will send me His strength. He will not let me down.'

The public don't want to know my personal troubles. And I will never show them, for tonight they're hoping some of their own will be solved.

Suddenly my thoughts are shattered:

'Ladies and gentlemen, would you please welcome the man who hears voices from heaven – Mr Stephen O' Brien.'

My name has been called, and in an instant the flower-decked stage is flooded with brilliance as the big curtains sweep aside and my form is picked out in the bright spotlight.

Hundreds of people are applauding in the darkness: some are cheering and whistling in their seats; seas of smiling strangers are all focusing their full attention upon me. Through the noise, a few who've travelled hundreds of miles are waving in the hope I'll see them, despite the powerful lights.

I do, and my eyes sparkle in return, especially for them, and I wave back.

It has begun.

Raising my hands, I acknowledge the public and step towards the microphone, my heart much quieter now as a warm expression rises to my face from deep within me, responding to their sincere love and welcome.

My vision blurs behind a wall of gratitude, as the noise gradually fades and dies ...

Then, just before I speak – for a fleeting moment only – suddenly my own hurt flashes again before my gaze, intense in its private pain.

But I, the medium, must cast it aside and smile

while my heart is weeping; for now I am the servant and these are my public. I have donned the cloak of service to work for them, these hundreds who are eager to hear the great news of *Eternal Life for All*.

There can be no time now for myself – the medium must shore up his feelings, rise above them, and try to mend the sorrowing hearts of those before him.

In the silence, I take a deep breath, compose myself and I'm ready to begin – for the public are waiting, and so are the people in the Next World . . .

PART ONE
A Bridge Between Two Worlds

1

A Young Boy's Blue-Sky Days

The little girl with wispy blond hair suddenly appeared at the side of the stage, surrounded by a silver-blue light. I was right in the middle of delivering a spirit message at the time she caught my eye, but I knew no-one else in the packed theatre was aware of her presence – only me, so I sent out a silent thought to the beautiful child:

'I'll be with you in a minute, my darling,' I said. 'Make yourself comfortable and be patient, there's a good girl.'

She wrinkled her nose with a smile and flounced her ringlets with slim hands as she contentedly sat down on the front of the apron, very pleased I'd noticed her. Then, with legs dangling over the side of the stage she gazed around the huge theatre, thoughtfully peering into the dim auditorium. Even in the flash of a second, I particularly noticed the sky-blue ribbons among her locks, perfectly matching her sparkling blue eyes which twinkled bright with fun as they scanned the rows of occupied seats.

As I finished one spirit message from the Other Side and the audience applauded, I re-established my link with this child, who was now sitting upright and pointing an eager finger out into the darkness.

'My Mum!' she said excitedly, attracting my attention. 'My Mum's out there! Up in the gallery with Nana!'

Shading my eyes with a hand I peered through

3

the dazzling spotlights as best I could.

'There's someone in the balcony who's lost a little girl about six years old,' I said. 'She's got blonde bouncy ringlets and blue bows in her hair, and she's wearing a blue gingham-check party-dress. "It's my birthday today," she says.'

Immediately an arm started waving back and forth in the shadows – in the very area the child had indicated – and suddenly a young woman's voice called out from the midst of the crowd:

'Yes Stephen! Here I am!'

And just as soon as this was said the spirit girl sprang to her feet and immediately started jumping up and down with glee – so I knew I'd found the right person.

'You're her mother, and you have family connections with America. And Nana's up there with you, too.'

'Yes!' said a kindly older woman sitting next to the recipient, 'I am.'

'Will you step to the microphones so I can hear you properly?' I asked. 'Please don't be shy, come forward and have a few words with me. Your daughter's here and she's so excited to see you.' So they did, Nana supporting Mum who was already so overcome in anticipation of a contact from her special 'lost' child that I could see her shivering with emotion.

'Don't be nervous,' I said gently, 'just try and relax and I'll do my best to link you all together. Your girl's getting really excited here; but I'll see what we can do . . . '

Fortunately the youngster had tuned into my mental wavelengths very well, making it one of those delightful occasions when I could hear spirit voices quite clearly.

'She was only six, but she says: "They've let me come

4

to see you, Mummy, because today's my birthday! I'm seven!"'

The two women were instantly dumbstruck and could only stare at me, open-mouthed. They were so totally overwhelmed they could only just about manage a nod in agreement.

'The poor little mite passed over into the spirit world with chest pains,' I continued, 'it was a congenital heart problem.'

'That's right,' said the quiet ladies in unison.

'And she remembers going over just before Christmas. "I didn't get to open my presents, Mummy," she says.'

'No she didn't . . . we lost her two days before . . . ' said the tearful young mum, now gripping tightly onto her mother's strong arm as she remembered her daughter's precious last moments on Earth.

'Well, she's not lost now,' I smiled, 'she's full of beans here and skipping about beside me – brimming with mischief and kisses; "and don't forget my Daddy," she says with a wink.'

By now my two recipients were weeping with joy, but this clever child had another surprise in store for us, more unusual evidence to deliver – further facts known by no-one but her mother and herself, not even her Nana would be aware of them. After transmitting all her love, there then came a very simple yet profoundly clever memory which convinced her grief-stricken family that she was indeed very much alive in another world beyond death:

'She's holding up some items for me to see,' I relayed, trying to focus my psychic vision to discern them more clearly. 'Ah! She's got a yellow toy duck with an orange beak, and over her other arm is a pair of faded blue denim dungarees. Do you know why she's brought these?' I asked.

There was a slight pause while the whole theatre quietened, eagerly awaiting an answer. Nana looked puzzled, but Mum started sobbing and dabbing her eyes, able only to speak in snatches, softly through tears:

'Yes . . . nobody knows . . . except me, but . . . I've just cleared out her old things; clothes and toys . . . I gave them all away, but I just couldn't part with everything; so . . . I kept her yellow toy duck and her favourite pair of dungarees.'

For one brief moment there was an eerie stunned silence hanging over the crowd, while a lump came into my throat and I felt a film of water building in my eyes – then spontaneous applause burst out through the hundreds of people, in full realization that death's silent door had been flung wide open by an innocent child of six.

We breathed in shallow emotional gasps as, through the noise, I gazed out across the sea of strange faces shrouded in semi-darkness: here and there I saw women wiping away tears, men sniffing quietly and hoping their wives or girlfriends hadn't seen them; shining eyes were twinkling in reflected light all around, all focused directly on me and my two overjoyed recipients.

Instantly, as though a bolt of lightning had struck my senses, I immediately knew again that my work meant something special to these people. It had somehow touched their souls, some hidden part of themselves which often lies buried deep beneath thick layers of a work-a-day materialistic world.

Though for me this was just another one of the many hundreds of spirit messages I deliver each year, for these folk I was witnessing it opening up a whole new world of thought. I'd been so accustomed to giving spirit messages that I'd almost forgotten what a mind-shattering effect that first contact with the next world could have; that first thunderflash when the truth of another existence beyond death dramatically lights up the soul.

Through the applause ringing around the theatre I remembered once again just how much power to change lives mediumship possesses. It confers comfort, hope and knowledge on all those it touches, and somehow makes greater sense of the meaning and purpose of life on Earth.

After the meeting my two recipients, who stood at the end of a long line of patient people waiting for autographs, were so profuse in their thanks, so genuinely grateful, clasping my hands and smiling and brimming with tears, that the young mum even gave me a cuddle.

'You'll never know how you've transformed my life tonight, Stephen,' she said, her own mother nodding in agreement and blinking back her tears. 'You see, after I lost my little girl, life for me was over. It got so bad I even contemplated suicide . . . but your message from my daughter's changed all that. It's restored my faith in God, and people – and living again.'

What could I say?

Nothing.

I couldn't speak; there was a lump as big as an apple in my throat and I could feel my lips quivering with the utter joy this woman so plainly projected. I was especially moved because I'd recently been moaning to myself about how tired and stressful my public life was, mainly because of my mediumship, and now here I was confronted again with the very heart-rending reasons for doing it.

In just a few moments I felt all at once humbled, re-kindled to carry on with my calling, and also thoroughly ashamed of my selfishness.

'God bless you both, and your daughter,' was all I could manage.

But something else was stirring within me too, something wonderful; in that dark theatre I could once more plainly see how a single communication from the next world can work its silent miracle – the true test of a spirit message is how much it changes lives for the better. Like thirsty watered flowers, the happiness of the two ladies before me had been visibly quenched: it was now blooming and growing again, plus they'd also added to their store of spiritual knowledge. Beyond any shadow of doubt, their souls had been touched. They would never be the same two people again; and so my job, as a medium, was done . . .

Since the publication of my first two books, *Visions of Another World* and *Voices from Heaven*, I've travelled many thousands of miles throughout Britain bringing messages like this from the next world to countless people in huge theatres and city halls, meeting folk from all over the world; sometimes household names and media 'stars', as well as mere ordinary mortals like you and me. Over the years I've got used to people's thanks, too, however embarrassed I might feel at the time. My answer to praise has always been the same: 'Thank your loved ones; they did all the hard work, I only delivered it.'

I'm very proud of the work I do, but there's a price to pay, and there have been many setbacks. As a very private man, one of the biggest problems I've had to learn to cope with is being a familiar public face, caused by guest appearances on British TV shows like *Wogan*, *Daytime UK*, *Gloria Live*, *This Morning* and others, plus national radio programmes like Radio One's top show *Steve Wright in the Afternoon*. Television is a very powerful medium, bringing you right into millions of living-rooms and at once making you part of the viewer's family. This has produced a regular prolific postbag: sometimes hundreds of letters a week. (It's not been unknown for me to scream at the sight of yet another sack of mail to be answered!)

People's letters are usually serious, funny, cheerful, sad and revealing or deeply tragic. Sometimes they're also desperately personal. (How people can confide such intimate details in me, I'll never know: subjects can range from nervous depression, rape, psychosis or even sexual abuse in childhood.)

But many contain profuse thanks for my being able to shed a little light into cruelly darkened lives, and I must confess, at the end of the day, a sincere 'thank you' does mean a lot because it shows I've done my work properly. Yet so much of my 'acclaim' is owed to the dedicated, compassionate spirit people who have relinquished their right to live in higher worlds in eternity to stay close to Earth and help me with my calling.

Granted, as a team, we aren't always as successful as we'd like to be – not all spirit messages are as clear or detailed as the young girl's I've just mentioned – but we always try our best, and often under very difficult circumstances.

In spite of this two-worlds effort, it is me whom the media have made 'a celebrity'. Interviews are still frequently requested and I've done so many now that I've lost count! I'm also quite choosy now about what engagements I'll accept. Though I've got an excellent and wicked sense of humour, the other day I turned down a TV show requiring me to be hit over the head with a sugar-glass bottle by the host while he joked: 'You may be clairvoyant, Stephen, but I bet you didn't see *that* coming!'

Even so, it's still a big surprise for a small-town boy

like me to see photographs of myself in public places. After filming for one TV programme in Manchester my train was delayed at Crewe (no surprises there from British Rail!) and so I sauntered into the station bookstore only to be confronted by both my books with portrait-shots staring down at me. 'Over 50 million people have witnessed his amazing psychic powers,' said the card. I was taken aback.

'Will you sign them, please?' asked the assistant.

'Certainly,' I replied, regaining my composure and squeezing out a red-faced smile as I dumped three heavy bags onto the floor, just missing the pour soul's feet.

'They're bestsellers you know, Stephen. Your first book's been out for two years – re-printed four times in the first year and it's still selling. That's quite a feat in these days of recession, if I might say so,' she gushed enthusiastically. 'Seen you on the telly. You look much nicer on the box.' (!)

We shook hands warmly as I thanked her and slithered quickly outside onto the cold platform. Being such an intrinsically private man I still find being recognized a trial. (I'm sorry, but I do. And it's no use people pretending they haven't seen me if they *have* – I can always tell: they display a peculiar 'Isn't that "what's-his-face" ? ' grimace!)

How I'd like to tell them that when the day comes for old 'what's-his-face' to pass over – back into his true spirit home – believe me he won't be pulling such a wrinkly disgruntled face: he'll go without hesitation! I shan't be one of those hysterical folk who at the last moment hang on to the bedposts with whitened fingers screaming blue-murder to stay!

I'm not afraid of death.

I know I'll pass into another dimension where I'll more than likely glance back at my life and sigh:

'Well, Stephen, whatever they say about you now, my old son, at least you tried your best to help a few souls along the way; God knows.' Up yonder I'll probably wonder how many people truly understood what I tried to achieve, what everyone in the spiritual fields hopes to accomplish? Will they have realized that a medium's work is filled with deeper spiritual purpose and implications? Will they have known that mediums aren't seaside fortune-tellers, or will they still confuse the two?

Mediums consciously co-operate with spirit people to join two worlds together in an effort to prove the continued survival of the soul beyond death. And because of our contacts with progressed minds we're able to share their wisdom, knowledge, philosophy and way of life which – they hope – will help to spiritualize humanity and the planet on which it lives. 'We are trying to raise man morally, emotionally, mentally and spiritually,' says my spirit guide, loyal friend and teacher, a splendid but ancient North American Indian whose tribal name is White Owl.

After I'm gone I'll no doubt smile, as I often do now, at the way some folk expected me to be strange, weird or mysterious, when all the time I was just an ordinary man expressing the powers of the spirit. The world wrongly labels these 'supernormal', but mediumistic abilities are perfectly natural functions of the mind and soul. One day everyone will regain these talents to see, sense and hear people in the Beyond, just as our ancestors did in antiquity before the worship of materialism suppressed such gifts.

But all this, as yet, lies ahead of us.

I've come a long way since my birth into a poor Welsh family during a thunderstorm, thirty-seven years ago. I was brought up in a humble working-class council house. Everyone on our shabby estate barely scraped a living to survive from day to day, working very hard for every penny they got. As I remember their struggles many other memories also flicker onto the screen of my mind; elusive butterfly days of childhood: those bright-eyed seasons when everything was sunny and carefree and nothing really mattered, even though we were poor. Everything looked so big then, and I was so small and painfully thin. But I cared nothing for worldly pressures and I was carefree, and free: free as the sea-birds rising on hot thermal breezes high above the bays of my small home-town, Swansea in South Wales.

In those glorious, endless summer days I could run where I liked, be what I liked, and do what I wanted. The whole wide world and everything in it was mine. Oh, how much happier I'd be today if I could only fully recapture this innocent childhood wonder. If only I could experience again a young boy's amazement as he discovers a hidden nest of starling's eggs, or hears for the very first time the distant jangling sounds of a gypsy funfair with its pungent smells of toffee-apples and candy-floss and the chiming music of merry-go-rounds; the whirring of the big wheel and noisy dodgem cars. Or re-live his wide-eyed wonder as he looks up through young eyes at a brilliant sun in cloudless blue skies and, instead of it, sees a swaying Spanish galleon in full sail, burning seas of yellow beaches as it goes. It seemed to me then that problems just didn't exist, and life was good.

Even now, the taste of sticky toffee-apples lingers with me still, and the pure joy of knowing that I was King of the Stars for a day: nobody told me what to do with the sky or cliffs; the entire planet was mine, as small as I was. The trees, the sky, the creatures in the fields – they belonged to me, and I belonged to them. We were all a part of one another: brothers

12

and sisters every one, and if someone hurt them – they also hurt me.

Glancing back, I can still visualize myself when a boy: that small-framed lad with a sometimes serious expression, unless he smiled, when hazel-green eyes twinkled. Full of vibrant life, his high-spirited nervous energy rushed him through his youth at whirlwind speed, or else so terribly exhausted him that he felt he couldn't move. And although he was 'a proper little chatterbox', expressing thoughts fearlessly, at other times he was such a painfully silent child: introverted, completely engrossed in his painting, drawing, reading or thinking. In a way, he was strangely lost, and standing utterly alone.

But he loved his mother more than words could ever say, plus his closest childhood companion – a docile cat named Tibby, on whom he lavished untold affection. I can still see before me his surprised eyes widening at the incredible miracle of birth as Tibby's five or six shaky wet kittens stumbled blindly into a newspaper-lined cardboard box beneath his awe-struck gaze. The joy on his face at the sounds of delighted purring and licking as his faithful companion proudly washed her children's fur will remain with him forever.

Many times this youngster dreamed in the stillness: he loved his own company; but then he'd suddenly want to run, skip and jump through the sunshine or sit by a blazing coal fire in the humble kitchen on freezing winter nights, cuddled into the crook of his mother's arms, with Tibby purring in his lap.

Sometimes now, in the quiet of an adult evening, just at sunset, my mind can still feel the hot golden sands under this boy's young feet, or know again his perceptive eyes as they search for sea-polished green glass thrown up onto the beach; or sense again the glow of warm bricks in a high sea wall as he strove to climb it, just for the joy and challenge of it. Mighty in his success, I watch him stand upon the summit – his face wreathed in smiles – and with a cry of triumph, arms outstretched to the sky, he shouts to the world: 'I *made* it! *I did it!*'

As a youngster, something wonderful was moving through his dream-like days; something so vibrantly real yet strangely intangible: it was a glorious silver thread of careless freedom. And oh, how I loved it! I wallowed in joyous ecstasy as I followed the wind wherever she led, dancing through my green years like the flat throwing-stones which first skimmed the foaming waves, then sunk into silent graves, like my innocent dreams and hopes . . .

A Young Boy's Blue-Sky Days

A barefoot boychild skips through yellow sands
    Like a pony in the meadow,
    Joylight dancing in his hands;
Greengrassed laughter sings across the bay:
'An endless summer of blue-sky days'.

Shining like a brightstar, he's piercing the haze,
    Running through the sunshine
    And scattering its rays;

    Laughing at flatstones skimming the waves
    Dancing on the waters way out far,
    Then smuggling gold in hidden caves,
    And lying on the night cliffs, counting stars . . .

    Spreading rainbow gossamer-wings,
    He's flying fast through sapling years
    So careless, wild and free –
'Ere manhood brings its midnight-blue
Through a door marked 'dull-dark key'.

Yet still he dreams of preserving his Now
    To breathe it again in unborn years,
    Like the perfumed scent of sweet bouquets,
    Filling his future with youthful pleasure
    And joylight mem'ries that will ever measure
A young boy's glorious blue-sky days.

At dusk, even now my mind sometimes projects
haunting voices from the past; groups of children's
voices long since gone, yet strangely still alive:

    'On the mountain
    Stands a lady,
    Who she is we do not know,
    All she wants is gold and silver
    All she wants is a nice young man . . .'

'*Stephen*! *John*! Come on you two boys! Your dinner's
been on the table for half an hour! Come *in*! It'll be
freezing cold!'
    'In a minute, Mam!'
    'A minute's not quick enough! It's on the plate
for thirty seconds – *then it's in the fire*!'
    'Oh, Mam!'

    'Good King Wenceslas looked out
    On the Feast of Stephen;
    When the snow lay round about,
    Deep and crisp and even . . .'

'Mam! Mam, look! He's been! He's *been*! Look what
he brought me. *Look, Mam*!' And I shook her awake
at 4 a.m. to see the toy she'd secretly placed at my
bedside just two hours earlier on Christmas Eve.
'Look, it's a fireman! See! You turn this key and
he walks up the big yellow ladder by himself: *see*!'
    Click, click, click:
    'Look: there he goes!' and the cheap clockwork

fireman obliged, jerkily lifting his legs as the key in his side jiggered and spun around.

There was a film of sleep over my mother's green eyes.

'Oh yes, son; lovely. Now go back to bed, there's a good boy . . . it isn't dawn yet . . . ' And she turned over, burying her tiredness under the sheets, as my father snored and I dashed back to my bedroom to wake my only brother:

'John! *John*! Look at my fireman!'

But John, true to form, was completely unconscious . . .

> 'The big ship sails down the ally-ally-oo
> Ally-ally-oo,
> Ally-ally-oo,
> The big ship sails down the alley-ally-oo
> On the last day of September . . .'

'This boy is sick,' said Dr O'Kane's deep voice. My mother looked anxiously across at him as he shone the bright torchlight into my dilated eyes.

'He may have scarlet fever.'

Through delirium I twisted my aching head back and forth, and just for that moment nothing mattered. Filled with a great and drowning helplessness I only remember thinking, 'If I'm going to die, please God – let it be quick.' And I flapped my weakened arm around outside the makeshift bed on the sofa until my mother grasped it lovingly in her own. Then I felt safer, as the doctor's voice snapped me back to reality.

'What have you been doing, young man?'

'I was only . . . playing . . . '

'Who with?'

'My little . . . friends . . .'

'Oh; I forgot about those,' frowned my mother, hand to mouth.

'Me and Leighton collected bluebottles . . . in a jar. We were going to let them go, honest we were . . .'

My mother looked embarrassed, as the doctor said:

'That's where he caught it. Being kind to animals is one thing, Stephen, but you've been a silly boy; they carry germs, you know.'

Two full-mooned adults glowered down at me, faces pale and gaping, as I uttered weakly:

'But they're my friends . . . the animals are our friends . . .'

And the last thing I remember was my mother's soft kiss planting itself on my burning-hot forehead, as I fell into a deep and swimming sleep . . .

Isn't it odd how some memories float back, yet others remain buried away, somewhere secret, never to return? Or *are* they completely gone and lost forever, I wonder? Perhaps not; at least, not psychically.

In the 1970s, when in my twenties, I awoke one morning from a haunting 'dream' which had stirred my soul and profoundly moved me. My childhood days – and my wonderfully kind mother with them – had long since vanished, but on that strange night I found myself fully conscious having been somehow transported back into former years when I was a boy and she was still alive. It was an unforgettable experience which has remained with me to this day, even though it occurred while I was physically sound asleep.

In my 'dream', I was amazed to find myself becoming aware of standing in the centre of our old humble kitchen where I'd lived as a lad in the late 1950s. Everything around me was so vividly clear and real:

17

the old threadbare matting on the lino floor, the coal fire with its smoky smell and crackling sticks burning in the grate. Each detail, without exception, was exactly as it had been twenty years previously; even the faded wallpaper which had hung on the wall since long before my birth; and the quaint and battered brass candlesticks on the mantelpiece, next to the clockwork timepiece which always ticked too slow. And there behind the small television table was the big sash-cord window which overlooked a raised concrete yard with a steep drop onto our grassy weed-bound garden. How big and tall that window had looked when I was a child, and how small and insignificant it seemed to me now.

Through it shone a sun-kissed day with a gentle breeze outside, swaying our rickety washing-line back and forth in the back-garden, at the bottom of which was another garden: rows and rows of back-to-back terraced houses trailing away; old houses, badly repaired and poorly furnished – like our own – full of working-class folk who scraped together a few shillings to feed hungry mouths. Money was tight in those days, and my parents did backbreaking work for very little pay.

At the foot of the garden was our tumble-down outside toilet, just as I remembered it: a tin-sheeting and brick affair which froze you half to death in the winter when cold December snows whipped in through gaps in its old battered door.

I sighed deeply as I positively absorbed all these poignant sights and sounds of yesteryear, wonderful moments seldom recaptured by any adult mind. But on *this* night – as my physical body lay fast asleep – here was I *right in the middle of the moving pictures, sounds and feelings of my boyhood*; and this marvellous experience compelled me to cry in gratitude for the wonderful memories strangely mine again. But I held back my tears, for fear of breaking this magical psychic spell.

Everything before me was so incredibly tangible and real: I could breathe in the musty smells of the coal fire as it crackled in the grate, and the wafts of cooking passing through the rooms from our humble scullery watered my mouth. These 'living' things would have seemed more at home in some faded sepia picture . . .

Then I turned and faced the dusty, threadbare, two-seater settee, for there was a bustling sound nearby. Motionless and completely at a loss to describe my amazement, I silently stood and watched as my dear mother fussed in from the tiny scullery. Here she was, before me, my own mother – but young again, as she'd been in my youth. Wearing a bright blue-and-white, flowery-print, short-sleeved 1950s dress, belted at the waist and full-skirted, she walked across to the small mirror over the fireplace and pushed her fingers through her dark thick springy hair. Her clear bright eyes and high cheekbones were glowing with radiant health as she then pottered around the small kitchen, tidying things up, unable to sense or see me.

It was all so miraculous, so breathtakingly vivid: she was actually present, and everything was fantastically clear. Yet I couldn't speak; I could hardly breathe . . . My mother – 'Mam' – was living once more, passing before me in a waking dream: moving, existing, breathing – *alive again*.

Fully conscious of every tiny detail, powerful emotions began to rise within me, almost to bursting point; I wanted to speak with her. I wanted to say how much I'd loved her, how much I'd missed her since she'd 'died' of agonizing cancer at forty-nine years old. I wanted to tell her how wonderful she'd been and what marvellous love, trust and loyalty she'd given her children. How I wished I could have moved my mouth and said 'Mam – it's me; Steve. Mam, I love you . . . It's so good to see you again.'

But nothing would come; not one single word . . .

Just then, a scuffling of footsteps clattered down the long passageway leading from the green front door, past the tiny parlour, and into our small kitchen – and a moment later a spritely young boy arrived in the sunny room, panting and wiping the sweat from his brow with a bare arm: he'd been running like fury down the street.

Instantly I was thunderstruck as I beheld the form of my own former self – me, as a boy of six years old.

Disbelievingly, I shivered as I leaned forward and searched the young lad's face: his sad green-brown eyes, his features, the shape of his head, the sloping round shoulders covered by a yellow, loose, open-necked summer shirt, and his thin bare legs lost inside wide short trousers – and my heart stopped beating and I remember thinking: 'My God, it *is* . . . It's *me* . . .'

Fixing my stare much harder on the youngster's eyes and the freckles on his glistening skin, I marvelled at his slender form. Here was another living person, breathing, present – not a shadow, but a real little boy. Yet how could this be? My mind couldn't comprehend the immensity of what was happening, when suddenly these thoughts were broken by my mother's familiar voice:

'Stephen, wash your hands now, there's a good boy. Your dinner's nearly ready.'

'What is it, Mam?' said the child brightly.

'Beans on toast. I haven't had time to go to the shops yet.'

'Oh great!' And then the little body dashed out into the scullery, leaned up and drew some water from the big tap and fumbled with a large bar of green household soap while my mother puckered up settee cushions with sharp, dusty slaps.

Meanwhile my adult self, half-afraid to breathe, moved cautiously across to the scullery door and peeked inside, just to gaze in wonderment at the slim young lad stretching up on tiptoes and making a clumsy job of washing his small hands over the metal sink. It *was* me: young again – six years old and pressing my lips together deep in concentration and splashing water everywhere as I always did.

But how could I be living *now* as a lad, when I was already an adult in my twenties? Both this 'ghost' of my younger self and my mother had long since vanished from Earth. So what was happening?

Though deeply confused and lost for an answer, I consciously stopped myself wondering and then just accepted the simple beauty of it all, savouring forever the images being strangely granted to me. However they were occurring didn't matter now – I just immersed myself in them with deep gratitude and relished every moment of the unfolding scene through misted eyes; and for the first time in many years I felt the warmth of happiness inside.

As powerful emotions rose in my breast while the little boy before me – totally unaware of the presence of his larger self and the big wide world awaiting him – wiped his young hands, I had an overwhelming desire to stretch out my arms and touch him. I wanted to embrace myself. I wanted to hold him close and plant a gentle kiss upon his brow and tell him about what, as yet, lay ahead of him on life's road: the griefs, the joys; his writings brought about by links with minds beyond death; the clamouring journalists and media people; the press and the derisive sceptics; and years of national touring, declaring the message of the spirit to millions of people; and all this counterbalanced by floods of sincere affection and love from the public, and so much laughter and very many tears, all waiting to be shed.

I wanted to tell him he'd been chosen to be a medium, to prepare him for his difficult future life; but I knew the time for such knowledge wasn't yet right.

And I longed to make him promise with all his heart that he'd always love and cherish his mother, all his days, and never say one unkind word to her (as I knew full well he often would).

But how I ached to press the young lad next to my thrumming heart and kiss the fresh face, as if to soothe away all the troubles he was yet to know, every sorrow he would experience, and for the cruel battering many would inflict upon his spirit.

All these things I wanted, but I could have none of them, for my time amongst these thrilling images was quickly dissolving away; it was spent, and – without warning – this unforgettable psychic journey was over all too soon.

The scenes quickly shifted and faded out into blackness as I lost touch with my visions, my feelings, and my past. Suddenly the kitchen and everything in it had gone.

Everything was silent; and I remembered not another thing . . .

2

A Little Child Shall Lead Them

Dreamily, in a semi-tranced state, I was standing on the windswept street, swaying gently while distant muffled voices floated past me. I was mentally so far away that all my thoughts centred on 'How on earth will I get through this entire day without collapsing of exhaustion?' I'd been on my feet since 4 a.m. and had already driven hundreds of miles and was now in the middle of a filmcrew briefing session at two o'clock in the afternoon on a damp and blustery Manchester street – barely conscious, for I'd already been working ten hours and the day wasn't even half over yet.

Suddenly the director's voice shattered my thoughts:

'*Stephen*!'

I blinked, uncomprehendingly, then stretched the tension from my neck and faced him with full attention.

'Sorry, Peter,' I said, 'I was in a little world of my own then . . .'

'As I was saying,' he resumed, 'once the camera's running, drive the car down the road, around the corner, then stop outside the guest-house, ring the bell and go inside, and we'll shoot everything.'

This was how the London-based filmcrew started recording its special documentary on my work, and I did as I was instructed – *four times*! But then, filming is always a long and tedious process; they took shots of us arriving, entering the hallway, outside on the steps, and heaven knows where else! I was already dog-tired and still had a meeting to take at the Queen Elizabeth Hall in Oldham that night. Earlier, I'd been interviewed on Greater Manchester Radio and when we got to the digs the filmcrew were already anxiously awaiting us: me, Jeff and Graeme (our helping hand for this tiring stretch of my 1991 nationwide tour).

'Now look, Stephen,' said Peter, whose director's tone smarted me back to reality again, 'we don't want to get in your way but we'll follow every move all day long – so just be normal and we'll trip along behind with the camera.'

'But how can I be when there's a camera running, a great big boom with a microphone stuck on the end of it swinging over our heads or wiggling under our noses, and a lighting man with his assistant flitting in and out, plus yourself? It's hardly natural, is it?'

'Just forget us, and it's business as usual.'

So we did. Mind you, we kept bumping into them every five minutes or sauntered into shots we weren't supposed to be in, plus getting under their feet all day. At one point, at the hall, I'd been on stage chatting in an interview to camera and then I'd walked off to change, but quickly bounced back on asking loudly: 'Was that OK then?'

'*Get off! We're still filming!*' they shouted. So I duly blushed and sneaked away like a naughty schoolboy who'd just raided the tuckshop and had been caught red-handed pinching a sticky bun! Well it isn't easy to be on your best behaviour all day!

In the end they also filmed a business meeting between Jeff and myself, plus arriving at the venue, setting up lights and sound, more intimate interviews (in and out of dressing rooms, at one point while I put on my trousers!), unloading books and luggage, preparations before the performance and even the 'show' itself (as they called it), with some snippets of my spirit messages forever preserved on celluloid.

The film was supposed to be a sort of 'Day in the Life of' documentary, introducing the kind of work I do to a wider public, with its pressures and stresses, as well as the education, comfort and joy I try to give people across the nation. This meeting was just one venue out of forty-five during 1991 to promote my second autobiography, *Voices from Heaven, Communion with Another World.*

The producer said from the start: 'I'm not making a promotional film Stephen, it's a balanced view of one of your days,' and this meant that a handful of Christian Fundamentalist picket-line protestors, who thought my work was 'evil'(!) and who were gathered outside the hall, also got a chance to air their views.

But without doubt, one of the most amusing episodes was when Jeff wittily said on stage, before the meeting started, in a private chat to camera that, 'Stephen can be very difficult to work with because he's such a perfectionist, you see.' He then proceeded to arrange various white potted flowering plants around the stage, while delivering a caustic aside to the camera: 'You watch now, I bet when he comes down he changes all these around!' And, true to form, *I did*! It was so funny!

My only disappointment with recorded shows is that the TV people never transmit my messages in full, but rather in piecemeal clips. How can people ever hope to judge life's vital issues from an incomplete picture? Nevertheless, I suppose even one tiny ray of light is precious to those who stand in spiritual darkness and are searching. The spirit world certainly brought light and hope to one couple in the crowd that night.

One of the most moving messages was delivered

by a little boy from the Other Side of Life to both his parents who were called forward to the microphone. I'd heard a spirit voice saying 'Taylor' and 'Jean', and assumed my communicator may have been called 'Jean Taylor'; sometimes the conditions for contact aren't ideal and voices are faint or not as clear as I'd like them to be. However, Jean said she'd brought 'a little boy who'd died from heart difficulties; he'd passed over after some surgery'. His Mum stood up and I called her forward, but before she moved I knew the boy also wanted his Dad:

'Is his Dad there? Let's have his Dad, please. He's calling for him, too.' As the young couple stepped to the front of the stage the look of hope on their expectant faces moved me. What then followed was a most touching, emotional, and exceptionally poignant message. I thought I heard the little boy say something which sounded like 'Adam and Eve' and, even though it seemed like nonsense, I've worked with the spirit people long enough to know that when they really want to communicate they'll use any means at their command. So I repeated the phrase, which brought an immediate response from his Mum:

'*Adam was his name!*'

Then the young lad mentioned another name and his mother confirmed it was the surname of Adam's first hospital consultant.

Little Adam joyously called out to me:

'I'm six!'

His Mum said he was five when he'd 'died' and that his sixth birthday was approaching in just over a month's time.

'Buy him a birthday cake, Mum,' I said, 'and put six candles on it and light them, because he'll be there and it'll mean the world to him to know you've not forgotten.'

26

By now they were so tearful, it was plain to see their souls had really been touched. But young Adam went on to describe further details, including how his Dad had held his hands as he lay in the hospital bed. Both parents were obviously moved, and I nearly added my own tears when I felt a powerful wave of love from Adam towards them, then back again from them to him. Caught in the middle of it, it took all my self-control not to break down and cry. It was such a wonderful contact.

Adam's parents, Karen and Aiden, were enthralled with their son's message and delighted to receive a large bouquet of flowers which I presented to them from the stage-set, afterwards.

At the end of the meeting the filmcrew recorded queues of people clutching books, souvenir programmes, audio cassettes and inspirational greeting cards to be autographed, plus enthusiastic people wanting a few words and a handshake. I also noticed the director filming an interview with Adam's parents. When they'd finished, I joined them and instinctively gave Karen a kiss on the cheek and hugged Aiden; they were two such lovely people. I shook their hands and just felt I needed a chat about their little boy.

They were delighted I'd made the effort and Karen produced two photographs of her son, one of which he'd already said during his message that he didn't like. He was pulling a face on it, not like the other one where he was smartly dressed in his football gear, holding up his Dad's trophy, pleased as punch. Through tears Karen unfolded their sad story, and what the contact had really meant to them:

'We saw an advert in the *Manchester Evening News* which mentioned your book, *Voices from Heaven*, and I immediately bought it in W.H. Smith's, plus your first book, *Visions of Another World*, and then we decided to come.

'This is the first time we've seen you, and we'd hoped so much to get a message from our son tonight – and we got it.' Her voice broke and faltered, and while she dried her eyes her husband spoke:

'More importantly, you see, tonight it's eleven weeks to the day that Adam died.' And his tears, too, could not be contained any longer. I looked across at him and clasped the young couple's hands in sympathy.

'Never think of your boy as "dead",' I said, 'because he's not. He's still very close to you, so why not visit local Spiritualist churches and give him further opportunities to contact you again? I'm only here for one evening, but now that he's managed to get through I'm sure he'll want another chance.'

A flicker of wariness moved across their eyes at my suggestion, but it soon dissolved away.

'Spiritualists are quite friendly folk, you know,' I said. Then after half an hour we parted amicably with Karen donating to me the photograph of her young son Adam, dressed in his football togs, which, with their kind permission, I've reproduced in this book.

'Don't think your link with me is finished because your son's message is over,' I said. 'Write and let me know how you get on.' Then I gave them some of my inspirational cards: one called 'The Greatest Power' (Love), and the other with my poem about a special life, taken from *Voices from Heaven*, called 'Do Not Forget Me' on it.

After they left, now much happier beings and more at peace with themselves, one of the stewards told me they'd thought of placing the bouquet I'd given them on Adam's grave, but this helper had suggested, 'Why not take them home and put them in a vase next to his picture, because he'll often pop in and see you? Much better.' And I wholeheartedly agreed.

Sometimes hard-nosed sceptics hurl public condemnation at me, and my fellow mediums, wickedly alleging we mislead grieving people by deploying 'trickery', 'practising fraud', or other nasty-minded claims, which are unfounded and are their weak excuses for rejecting the fact of life after death – even when startling evidence for it stabs them in the face.

These cynics rarely accept my challenge to 'ask the people I've helped what their spirit messages have meant to them'. So let's try and re-adjust the balance now. Setting aside my embarrassment and risking the unsightly label of 'arrogance', here are two personal letters (combined into one for reasons of space) which I received from Karen Taylor about her son's message on that night.

Sceptics please note that the Taylors and I had never met; they were strangers in a large crowd, and even though, at the time of writing, they cannot place the spirit name of Jean Taylor (the communicator who'd brought their son to greet them from the Other Side) they do share the same surname, one which I'd also taken great pains to spell out, letter by letter, during the link. I think 'Jean Taylor' might well be a distant relative of theirs.

Here's Karen, young Adam's Mum:

Aiden and I went to your public meeting at Oldham on 30 April. We were both in deep despair and were searching for hope and proof of Life after Death. We lost our youngest son, Adam, on 12 February 1991 after open heart surgery. Adam was only five years old and we love him so much; he always was, and will be, our Special little boy. He was born with a very serious and rare heart defect and we knew that he would need high-risk surgery when he was about four or five (he had lots of chest infections and a few spells in hospital) – but as he was such a character, so determined and such a fighter, we were convinced he would get through it all right, but he didn't.

After surgery he clung to life for twelve days following a cardiac arrest and two very serious drops in his blood pressure, and after receiving kidney dialysis and liver massage, Adam wasn't responding at all and was put on a life-support machine. He'd also had a lot of fluid in his body and the doctors were worried that this had gone to the brain. They told us that even if he ever got off the machine and could breathe again for himself, he would almost certainly be blind, deaf and very handicapped indeed.

They said the kindest thing we could do was to allow them to switch off his life-support machine.

What a terrible decision to have to make and live with; words cannot describe our horror and how we felt. The tests they performed gave us no hope of just a slight handicap – they said we would basically just have a body to feed. What were we to do?

We went along with their advice, and our son Adam died in the operating theatre, and they removed his organs (which we felt he would have wanted to have been donated to help someone else), and I think, really, we died with him.

When we saw him later, he looked so peaceful, but how terrible we felt.

We love him so much and we're a close family, but now we're just existing, caring for our two other boys. We're so unhappy and the hurt inside is too much to bear. Our life has really ended: we both feel we have lost everything, our family is torn apart in grief, never to be the same again.

Then I saw an advertisement in the *Manchester Evening News*: you were appearing in Oldham, and we were interested now in learning as much as we could about life after death, seriously, for the first time.

We got tickets, never expecting to get a message from Adam.

That evening we went to see you, you gave us hope. Thank you, Stephen, you gave us a message that provided us with proof that Adam continues to live in another place. You said 'I have a lady called Jean Taylor here and she has a little boy with her.'

You said, 'The little boy had something wrong with his chest' – my heart was beating so fast, being a very shy person I was so frightened of standing up and putting my hand up, but I was so desperate and I'd so strongly felt I had to go and see you on that evening.

I put my hand up, I couldn't let it go if it was Adam.

Then you said to me, 'I'm getting "Adam and Eve".' And I said 'His name was Adam,' and you asked us to come to the front.

We were both so nervous and I felt so shocked as the message that came through was so clearly for us: I couldn't describe how I felt. My husband, Aiden, got very emotional.

About my son's illness you said that 'a valve was blocked and there was a hole in the heart, and the lungs were involved'. All exactly correct.

You went on to further describe Adam's heart condition, and other details, all so accurate and only we knew them. Thank you so much, Stephen.

You then said Adam was saying 'Happy Birthday' to someone. It was my Dad's birthday on 7 May, but also on that day his brother's friend had a birthday and Adam used to play with them both.

You mentioned 'white flowers', and we said that we'd got Adam a lot of red and white flowers for the funeral – but later we learned that his grandad was growing all white chrysanthemums for Adam's grave.

You also said my son mentioned to Aiden, my husband, 'Two hands!' What Adam meant was two hands saving goals: saving shots from his Dad. Adam had some junior goals set up in the garden and he would have stayed there all day if we had let him.

Plus, on Adam's gravestone we have had a special picture done of a goalkeeper making a 'save' on one side, and a footballer kicking the ball on the opposite side, all in gold gilt.

You said that his birthday was coming soon and he would be six and that he wanted us to get him a birthday cake with six candles. It was his birthday on 14 June, we did what he asked, but what a sad day it was: no present to give, no little head to kiss. How terrible we felt on that day; so sad.

Adam was only a few weeks old when his first hospital consultant diagnosed what was wrong with him but, quite remarkably, he gave you his name.

You said, quite correctly, that we both carried Adam's picture on us and that Adam didn't like the picture that his Dad had.

You said we got a sudden call to go to the hospital; this was also true – we got the phone call on the day before.

You also said, quite correctly, that I had something wrong with my foot. I saw you lift up your right foot and touch it – and it was my right foot that I had had trouble with for weeks. Only Aiden and I knew that.

You also said there was a grandad there too, but didn't mention him again. Both my grandads were shy personalities.

After investigation, we don't know who the Jean Taylor is; but the people next to us claimed Jean Taylor. Maybe their Jean Taylor helped our Adam to make contact. Perhaps we were all together in the hall and she met Adam and offered to help him. But whoever she is we're so grateful to her.

We have (since) been to the Manchester Spiritualist Church a few times, to the special demonstrations with a guest medium. So far, unfortunately, we have had no (further) contact. If you are ever in the Manchester area again, we will certainly come to see you. You are such a good medium. I get the *Psychic News* now to see if you are on tour anywhere near us. I have received a lot of comfort from your books and tape.

As you will recall at the end of the evening we gave you a picture of our Adam in his football kit, holding his Dad's trophy. Also the cameramen interviewed us; they were very nice. Do you know if the programme will be shown? I hope so, we want to tape our message to keep forever and show his elder brother, when we think he will understand. A programme showing your mediumship, which is so outstanding, can only help other people like us in grief.

Thank you, Stephen. Please write back. Every day I go over that evening. You don't know how much you helped us that night.

I don't suppose we will ever have personal contact with a medium as good as you, unfortunately, but we thank you from the bottom of our hearts for the comfort we have received by getting the proof that our son lives on.

> Yours sincerely,
> God Bless and Take Care,
> Karen Taylor

Placing aside my obvious embarrassment at some of Karen's glowing remarks, I have to say that her letter isn't by any means unique, for I've received thousands of similar ones over the years, mostly from people who've seen me on the media, live at meetings, or who've read and enjoyed my books, been intrigued, or simply wanted to know more about life's deeper issues.

If I've been able to help them, I couldn't have done it without the love and support of my compassionate spirit friends.

Adam's link, of course, was emotionally very touching, but not all spirit messages are so serious; in fact there have been countless amusing ones and some hysterically funny messages, too, because people don't change immediately on 'death' – their character and sense of humour stays with them, thank God.

I've found that positive, cheerful attitudes and laughter in an audience actually lifts the psychic vibrations and helps good communication to take place; laughter is a burst of high-frequency energy which gives the Other Side a power boost and makes it easier for them to transmit clear, detailed evidence.

One night, when conditions for contact in a southern meeting were particularly good owing to the audience having built up the psychic power by reacting favourably to witty communicators, I was then able to receive specific facts for a woman in the crowd:

'Elizabeth Johnson from the Other Side sends her greetings.'

'I'm Mrs Johnson and Elizabeth is my daughter, though she's still alive on Earth.'

'But she's named after Elizabeth Johnson in the spirit world,' I said.

'No.'

'Oh, but it must be right; I heard it so clearly! And she says she's watching over her namesake – your daughter. I can tell you that this Elizabeth died in 1902.'

Then, just as my recipient was about to open her mouth and refuse again, her eager husband – two rows back – leaned forward, took the microphone and announced:

'That's perfectly correct, Stephen. I've been researching our family tree and Elizabeth Johnson was born in 1848 and died in 1902, just as you said.'

There was spontaneous applause; a common occurrence when the spirit people are able to get such clear messages as this through to us.

But detailed evidence can also be delivered wrapped in folds of love and powerful emotion, too, as in the case of a lad of thirteen who, during a Wiltshire meeting, reminded his sister of his unusual passing:

'He was just a youngster,' I said, 'and he was hit in

the neck by something hard ... something like glass
– no wait a minute, it wasn't glass, it was a *snowball*.
Does Robert mean anything?'

'That's him,' the astonished girl replied. 'He's my
brother, and that's how he died.'

'He was catching his breath; he says, "I choked
on my food".'

'Yes, he did.'

At this point, loud sobbing came from the lady next
to her. 'That's my Mum,' said Robert; and indeed she
was. The microphone was passed to her but she was
much too overcome to speak, so his sister continued
until Mum could catch her breath again through
her tears. Robert went on to mention 'John', and
'standing on the touchline watching the lads playing
football and having a marvellous time, and shouting
them on to win!'

'John was his football team coach,' she smiled.

'And Mum, Robert says you've had his football
jersey in your hands this week. Have you?'

'Yes,' she whispered, barely recovering from the
overwhelming joy her 'dead' son's message was
bringing her. 'I've been cleaning out his room this
week, and sorting through his things.'

'Well he knew because he's been close to you
all, and he's telling me to say: "Please will you give
my football jersey to John, Mum? I like him such a
lot."'

Sympathetic sighs murmured through other parts
of the hall as his final phrases broke through the
silence:

'I'm fine, Mum ... Please don't worry about me:
I love you ... I love you; I love you ...'

Such messages are so terribly moving, and when
they're delivered you can usually hear a pin drop in
the hall. But, the mood and style can quickly change

when a new communicator's personality is felt. Each link is different, and Robert's contact was immediately followed by a humorous, whimsical grannie on the Other Side who brought forward some delightfully comical memories. I began with:

'There's a lady here with me who says she was "a char – I worked for Mr Pilkington, and he didn't pay much either!" ' When I described her and then relayed she'd 'met up with Mrs Stevenson, and we've had a good chat about old Pilkington,' a woman in the back of the stalls quickly responded.

'Yes, I know her. She worked for the Pilkingtons: they were wealthy landowners and Mrs Stevenson was her friend – she lived a few doors up.'

Our bubbly char then delivered more clear facts:

'He was a (bloody) difficult man,' she announced, 'and *very* mean too! (I didn't say "bloody" in public, or repeat some of her other choice language!) And I remember the time,' she went on, 'when he left a few pounds on the sideboard to *tempt* me! He wanted to see if I'd pinch it! (Bloody cheek!)'

'That's quite correct,' said my recipient, 'I remember her telling me.'

'That *really* hurt me,' said grannie, 'so I got my own back on him. I wanted to leave the (bloody) job but I needed his reference, see – so one day, I told him a story about his daughter that he wouldn't forget.'

'That's right,' said the smiling woman.

'And it worked a treat! He fired me *and* I got my reference!'

There were gasps from some of the audience because she was such a good communicator, who finished up making us laugh with: 'Pilkington's over here with me now, and I've given him what for and told him *exactly* what I thought of his (bloody) job, where he could (bloody) stick it, and my pittance of a wage!'

Hundreds in the crowd had a good belly-laugh at her comments, probably because they'd like to have done the same thing to some of their own employers!

And I'll never forget what happened at another meeting, this time in Wales, where an audience member's innocent remark caused hysterical laughter: it was such a memorable experience! I'd just started a very serious message from the next world and the crowd was wrapped in deep concentration and attentive silence; I could practically hear them breathing.

'There are two gentleman with me,' I said quietly, 'two brothers called William and George Griffiths. Someone here knows them.'

There was no answer.

'Let me have a voice,' I said, 'it's George and Willie Griffiths.'

Utter silence once again; absolute peace, until it was suddenly snapped by a teenage girl's loud and squeaky voice blurting out:

'Well, *I* can take a Willie!'

There was only a moment's pause – then hundreds of people burst into instant hysterics! They were rocking back and forth in their seats, gasping for air and holding on to each other, as the full realization of her unfortunate remark hit home. Tears streamed down faces and I've never seen an audience enjoy themselves so much – not before or since. There must have been a good minute's laughter before I weakly quivered back: 'Pardon?'

And the girl, gasping for air herself, wheezed out again through strangulated chuckles: 'I said *I* can take a Willie!'

'Well, I don't think we'll go into that!' I replied,

which further delighted the audience, pleased to know that laughter is still the best tonic!

But not all my messages are transmitted in such a light vein, thank goodness, and neither are they all given in public. Some are received privately when I'm by myself, or else in small circles of psychic friends who sit especially to contact the next world.

Over the years I've been given numerous messages by spirit people from all walks of life. These have included quite memorable words transmitted by some well-known figures in our world. Whenever I get a link from such people I'm always reticent to publish, unless, of course, they ask me to do so. Dr Martin Luther King was no exception to my rule.

This remarkable man led a Civil Rights Movement for black people from the mid-1950s up until his death on 4 April 1968, when he was shot by an assassin in Memphis, Tennesee. Dr King didn't seem bitter about his passing, a quality which seems to link admirably with the Nobel Prize for Peace which he was awarded in 1964. Martin maintained, preached and propounded the noble doctrine of non-violent protest to gain relief from the cruelty of racialism.

He was, and still is, a very great man; and it seems his fight to free people from oppression is continuing from his new world, as he reveals in his contact, the words of which are an inspiration to peace-loving souls everywhere:

Dr Martin Luther King

I was only a young man when the call came for me to leave and go to the Promised Land.

Those who should have been helping me, hurled me into in the next world, but I'd seen over the mountain tops and I knew where I was going.

Through the great love I have for my own people, and all other races, creeds and colours, I tried my very best to show a way of brotherhood, a way of peaceful cohabitation between all kinds of people in all different kinds of social and racial structures.

Looking back upon those hard and difficult years – difficult for me and my dearly loved family, especially my children – I think I can say a measure of success was ours.

But the battle is not yet over.

There is more work yet to be done.

My brothers and sisters in other lands, as well as in America, are crying out 'Freedom!'

They're calling out 'Justice!'

They want the bonds and shackles of oppression to be cut away from them so that they can breathe the pure air of freedom of expression.

So I shall not cease from my fight.

I have never, no not for one moment, given up my goal: that of freeing my people, and any others bonded by slavery of one form or another.

The world is a beautiful place.

The souls of men and women are beautiful. If we can encourage this great beauty forward then all the ugliness will be purged away, as the sunlight bleaches the scorching lands of Africa.

I pray for peace and love, one towards another.

I have not rested; I shall not rest. No: I shall inspire and send my strength to everyone still engaged in the great march forward, toward the lights of freedom, truth, peace and love.

3

Soul Powers

Peace, Love, Truth and Freedom are just some of
the many qualities of the soul, and being a medium
builds up psychic sensitivity to such a degree that I
can often 'feel' or sense these intangible attributes in
other people.

I'm often aware of impressions reaching me from
this world, and not the next, like the time when private information was revealed to my soul-perception:
I didn't know it was a secret, and I certainly didn't
mean to embarrass anyone. My natural soul powers
were working quite freely one day when I was introduced to a friend's young boss:

'This is my manager,' she said, as we shook hands
– and I immediately picked up his illness: it was an
instantaneous thought, an inner knowing, but I didn't
mention what I'd psychically received, not until the
following Sunday when I confided in my friend:

'By the way, did you know your boss has something
wrong with his chest?'

She nearly dropped her teacup.

'Yes, I do actually,' she said, interest flickering
in her eyes. 'Go on, Stephen: tell me more,' and she
leaned forward in her chair, eagerly listening.

Well, I'm afraid he's got a heart murmur: a small
hole in the heart.

With that, she plonked her cup down noisily and
dropped her jaw onto her chest.

'You're absolutely right. But he never speaks about

it, he's only ever told one person: *me*. How did you know?'

Fidgeting with my biscuit I stirred my coffee and explained:

'When I shook his hand I just immediately "knew". Perhaps it's been worrying him or he's been thinking about it recently.'

'But *how* did you know?'

'My soul registered it.'

'Stephen, you're *uncanny*,' she said, eyes lifted to the heavens.

Well, I've been called worse things so I expect that's a compliment!

Her boss, like every other life-form, is surrounded by swirling fields of electro-magnetic activity – auric fields – and a part of my own power mingled with his, instantly conveying his problem to my mind. Reading the aura is a very skilful art, a useful soul-ability which takes years of careful practice to perfect, and one of the easiest auras to sense is the physical aura which contains a complete 'picture', or matrix, of a person's health problems and true character.

When developing sensitivity we become aware of other fine vibrations belonging to *this* world and not necessarily the next. Auric awareness conveys an instant and stunningly correct 'picture' of someone's personality. All living things, even seemingly 'dead' objects, carry their life stories around with them. These impressions are alive in the mind and electro-magnetic fields. Once you're sensitive, you can register them – and that's that; it's as automatic as breathing.

I vividly recall one man whom I can only describe as a devious, wealthy 'sceptic' who offered me thousands of pounds to submit myself to be 'scientifically tested' by him. (Scientific, *my eye!*)

How naive of him not to realize I could see right through the open secret in his heart. As far as I was concerned he might as well have been completely transparent; the true motivation behind his smiling façade stood out a mile, my psychic awareness having clearly revealed his lies as if they were an active volcano. Why didn't he speak the truth?

'Let me publicly ridicule you by twisting results and explaining away any shred of evidence you offer. Submit yourself to me and make me famous.'

(Fancy thinking I could be lured by money and deceit. What a cheek!)

Millions of people have experienced this basic form of extrasensory soul-sensing, with the obvious exception of our sceptical friend, for it's quite a common occurrence. Many folk meet a perfect stranger for the first time and though, at first, they might seem happy-go-lucky characters, underneath 'something' isn't what it seems; and they later prove to be quite unpleasant individuals.

All mediums are naturally sensitive, but in varying degrees. We can't help it; it's part and parcel of our psychic awareness. But we're not alone in possessing these abilities. I've often watched folk on street corners shaking hands: 'Oh, how *lovely* to see you,' they say. But as the person turns away they pull an horrendous face at what they'd *really* felt when contact was made.

Countless women have this ESP, sometimes calling it 'feminine intuition', and my mother was no exception. I don't know about yours, but mine could spot a lie at thirty paces! And there's plenty of evidence, too, indicating that psychic power frequently runs in families. My mother certainly passed hers on to me: I can recall numerous occasions when this sixth sense functioned quite spontaneously, often to my benefit, and sometimes to the amusement of others.

Once, while working in Eastbourne for my medium friends Arthur and Gladys Fieldhouse, between engagements they whisked me off for a quick trip around the local beauty spots. I was delighted because I'd never been there before. We stopped near the sea and Arthur and I got out of the car to catch the ozone in our throats.

'Just follow me, Stephen, there's a smashing scenic view from up there,' he said, as we neared the dangerous cliff edge. I tentatively crept forward, craning my neck as I heard him ask, 'Well, what do you think?'

My senses instantly reeled and spun as I felt Arthur grabbing my arm while I peered down over the grass onto distant sands, some three hundred feet below. Through blurred vision I suddenly lost sight of the drop and had an overwhelming urge to throw myself from the clifftop. Arthur quickly helped me to retreat from danger.

'What is it?' he asked.

'I'm all right,' I muttered, clutching nearby shrubbery. 'But I just felt really sick, as though I could have thrown myself over the cliff. There are plenty of people who'd love me to do that,' I weakly smiled.

'Well, Stephen,' he said, 'I brought you here because this is Beachy Head and that spot is known as Suicide Point. Dozens of people have jumped to their deaths from there onto the beach below.'

I just looked at him dumbfoundedly.

'Let's get back to Gladys in the car,' I rasped, 'I need a sit down!'

Funnily enough, my soul powers brought me another startling Place-Memory while I was sitting down, but this time I was in Sunderland. It was about 3 o'clock in the morning and my good friends Adrian, Moira and Lily were entertaining me (I'll eat everything offered and stay up chattering into the early hours, I'm such a night-bird). We'd just had mugs of coffee in a last ditch effort to keep our eyes open without matchsticks, when suddenly we all felt incredibly relaxed.

'Something's up,' said perceptive Lily.

'Yes, I think we should sit for the spirit people, don't you?' I suggested innocently, as though I were ordering another teacake at a restaurant.

Moira stretched and announced, 'I thought we might; spirit people have been buzzing around this room for the last half an hour, like a swarm of bees.'

'Healing energies, I expect,' said a yawning Adrian. (Actually, it was a miracle he was still conscious – if you pegged Adrian by his nose onto the washing-line in the middle of the day he'd start snoring with no bother at all!) Anyway, after several minutes of peaceful relaxation, conducive to spiritual healing, my soul powers started working and I witnessed a remarkable scene unfolding before me. It was an ancient Place-Memory.

Appearing in the living-room, crossing it diagonally from left to right, I perceived a sad group of poor bedraggled peasants wearing ragged and dirty clothes. They were walking through the room and leaving it through the wall behind me. The ten men were shouldering muddy pick-axes and shovels and were dressed in thin soiled shirts and breeches, and they were all barefoot. The remaining women wore long dark skirts trailing in the thick mud, and their faded black shawls were tightly wrapped around their shoulders to combat icy winds.

In the centre of the pathetic procession, men were carrying a rough-hewn wooden coffin, quite small, and I sensed it contained the emaciated body of a teenage girl who'd probably died of a fever.

44

In silent wonder I watched the vision, too afraid to breathe lest I disturbed it. Experience told me I hadn't 'slipped time' and been transported into a previous century, for none of these people were aware of my presence; they couldn't see or sense me. No, this was a ghostly psychic picture of the past: a moving image recorded in the very atmosphere around us, projected upwards by the ground on which this modern house was standing, obviously built on the site of an old dirt-track road which existed many centuries ago. Gazing at the bent and weary travellers I knew they were heading for a burial place which I sensed was quite nearby.

A moment later the vision faded, and I fully described it to the others.

'There must have been an ancient burial ground in these parts,' I said, 'in that direction,' pointing over my head behind me, to where the ghostly figures had dissolved through the wall.

'That's right, Stephen,' said Lily, the eldest. 'There was such a place; just over there, where the people were going.'

I wasn't surprised, of course, for soul powers can register all kinds of things, such as premonitions. While having Sunday morning coffee with friends one day I nearly choked as dreadful psychic feelings pervaded my soul.

'Whatever's the matter?' asked my hostess.

'Something awful's going to happen,' I said.

'To my family?'

'Oh no; nothing like that, though it's really bad news, like a war.'

But what I couldn't describe at the time were my *actual* emotions; soul sensations are difficult to express, but I'll try. I felt as though a ferocious whirlwind had torn through my spirit and nothing could stop it. Then came desperate and anguished cries of the spirit, as though thousands of souls had voicelessly screamed in pain, out into the void. They pleaded as one united body for mercy, and their helplessness sickened me.

This unusual premonition remained a mystery until a few days later when the six o'clock news announced that Iraq's President, Saddam Hussein, had invaded the small country of Kuwait.

'That's it . . .' I half-whispered, 'that's the start of destruction and carnage,' which regrettably was right. To this day, no-one knows how many souls lost their lives in the short war between Iraq and practically every other peace-loving country in the world, in 1991. Nearly every nation stood against Saddam's dictatorship, and Iraq's state-controlled propaganda machine couldn't be trusted to release accurate figures.

But I'll never forget those horrifying television pictures of deadly American missiles in air-strike attacks, filmed as they were fired, and screened as they blew up targets 'live'. It was too incredibly sickening for words: people were dying inside buildings as reporters gleefully proclaimed, 'Yes! That's another direct hit! We sure are winning!'

Some of the laser-guided missiles were so accurate they could be seen smashing through specifically-targeted doors and windows, 'taking out' the interiors – and the people inside – but leaving the shell to stand; a wicked reminder of how little man's soul has progressed towards kindness and compassion.

The use of Allied bombs and air-strikes to force Iraq out of Kuwait continued unabated, night and day, fully backed by the United Nations until the Allied Forces announced a time limit for Iraq to finally withdraw its troops from Kuwait, prior to launching a ground assault to take it back by force, in compliance with a UN Resolution. Just before the limit expired at 5 p.m. Greenwich Mean Time on Saturday, 23 February 1991, I got a call from a New York journalist from *Harper's and Queen* magazine:

'What's going to happen, Stephen? The world is anxious and waiting,' she said.

'I fear he won't comply with United Nation's Resolution 660 (requiring Iraq's full and unconditional withdrawal). My soul was so disturbed by my premonition and all those soundless voices crying out in anguish, I'm afraid the ground attack will start . . .' and sadness filled my voice, for I was right: it commenced and proceeded to claim many more innocent lives before the conflict ceased.

I've always maintained that *the future casts its shadow before it* and a sensitive mind can register it.

The spirit people, of course, can also use these very same soul-energies to accomplish some other remarkable feats, like in this next case. I'd been filming for Central TV and had popped into another guest's hotel room for coffee. Tina Laurent and her husband Carl were Electronic Voice Phenomena enthusiasts who'd recorded many mysterious disembodied voices on cassettes over the years. I was oblivious to the fact that the Other Side were drawing on my psychic powers, as Tina explained the next morning:

'I hope you don't mind, Stephen, but yesterday I secretly recorded our talk because I've often wanted to conduct an experiment with the power of a good medium. Anyway, nothing unusual happened until you closed the door on the way out – '

'And?'

' – a clear, woman's spirit voice said on the tape: "Oh, he's gone now."'

Though I was thoroughly intrigued and impressed I simply had to smile back:

'You obviously missed part of her message.'

'What do you mean?'

'Well, she'd probably said, *"Thank God*, he's gone now!"' And we all laughed together.

It's a blessing my spirit people have an excellent sense of humour! Of course, they can also be quite clever too — especially when there's a powerful medium present because sensitives shed extra psychic light and energy which enables them to accomplish all kinds of unexpected things, such as moving objects supernormally. In the early 1980s when I was absolutely flat broke and hungry, my stomach rumbling like a hollow mine-shaft and with empty pockets to match my hopes, I was surprised when a spirit voice said 'move towards the kitchen sink'. After obeying, it then said 'open the old tumble-drier'. So I did.

To my great amazement, there — right in the bottom of it, staring me in the face — was a crisp, brand-spanking-new £10 note! I threw it gleefully into the air and shouted out: 'You can do *that* again, *anytime* you like!' But they never did! It was merely some temporary relief to get me through a rough patch, and they'd brought it about by drawing upon my soul power, enabling them to transport the money from one place and materialize it in my home. I've no idea where they got the £10 note, but it had probably been lost, and hopefully not stolen!

Although it takes a good deal of psychic energy to materialize such a spirit gift (known as an apport) can you imagine how much more power would be needed to physically levitate *me*? I'll never forget the night it happened; it was such a shock.

I was fast asleep but was woken about 1 a.m. with an overwhelming sensation of several pairs of hands near my legs, arms and head. I instantly 'knew' I was about to be lifted up – so I called out indignantly: *No! I'm not a balloon!'*

Suddenly everything went quiet again, so I turned over and drifted back to sleep wondering what on earth the spirit people were up to. (They'd never bothered me much during the night – it was one of our understandings: bed was for sleep.) But about half an hour later we had a repeat performance, only this time much stronger.

'Don't you dare!' I seethed, sitting bolt upright. 'What are you playing at?'

Silence . . .

Then more snoring . . .

The third time, I was rudely woken at 3 a.m. to find myself feeling as light as a feather and actually *floating* in the air! I'd been physically lifted from the bed, horizontally, as stiff as a board, and then they started sailing me off towards the bedroom door, bedclothes and all! I immediately knew they were going to unceremoniously dump me onto the bedroom floor – but I stopped it with a mighty shout!

'Quit it!' I yelled.

And suddenly I bounced back down onto the mattress, puzzled but very relieved!

I guessed there was some kind of urgent message hidden in this odd experience, as though the Other Side were trying to tell me something. It was then I remembered I hadn't seen my Dad for a while, and really ought to pay him a visit between tour dates. I began wondering how he was coping with his failing health, and then, somehow, I linked this unusual happening with him, and my feelings were soon proved correct.

I'd been supernormally levitated *three* times in

a row; and *three* days later my father was found close to death and was rushed into intensive care at the hospital. Dad almost died; his temperature was phenomenally high and the doctors treated his chest infection just in the nick of time.

So the riddle was solved: it had been a spirit warning, and an unusual way of demonstrating the power of the spirit.

This abundance of psychic power which developed mediums possess can also be projected from the body to move physical objects, even unconsciously, *without* any spirit intervention. This often happens in what's sometimes wrongly assumed to be 'poltergeist' activity. I've investigated several cases and right in the centre of the action there's usually someone (frequently a teenager) in the clutches of emotional turmoil, often in the throes of puberty when major hormonal disturbances occur in the body. Troubled emotions create and project strong soul-energies which can physically move objects in the house.

I know this happens because I've experienced it. Once while standing near large curtained windows one sunny afternoon I was feeling very angry with someone who'd deliberately spread lies about me. I felt my trust had been betrayed and the more I bubbled and boiled, the more furious I became; and that's when it happened:

All at once the long heavy drapes began swaying back and forth, as though a sudden breeze were passing through the room – but there were no windows or doors open and it was a perfectly calm, airless summer's day.

I stood perplexed, watching the weighty curtains merrily swinging away of their own accord. I wondered if the spirit people were responsible, but then I realized *my own anger was generating these forces.*

When I made conscious efforts to calm down, the drapes fell deathly still; like silent curtains in a Chapel of Rest.

Such fascinating psychic powers, because of their unusual nature, sometimes evoke unwanted reactions from people, particularly the 'medium-worshippers'. All good sensitives discourage adoration, but the compliments keep flying, I'm afraid.

I was once completely stunned when a middle-aged woman who'd gazed rapturously up into my face, glassy-eyed throughout one of my meetings, clasped my arm tightly at the end of the night, announcing with stunning conviction: 'You are my Jesus,' – and the very next instant she ran off through the crowd.

I was totally dumbstruck and shaken to the core, especially as I've always taught that mediums are just ordinary people. But I guess some folk will never learn.

What the public generally don't know is that whenever these impressive psychic energies are used, mediums burn up their vital nervous energies which must be carefully replaced by natural means: rest, pure water, and wholesome nutritious food.

Here's some wisdom from my spirit guide, friend and teacher, White Owl, about psychic power and a medium's health:

At all times seek moderation in all things. Balance is the key word. Too much work and not enough rest stresses the mind and disturbs the spirit, leaving you unfit for use by higher intelligences. Evolved spirit guides never dominate their mediums on Earth, it has to be a willing co-operation, a fine blending of minds working towards enlightening humankind.

Mediums – our priceless treasures – are carefully watched and educated to seek and maintain health, for of what use is an instrument whose personal power batteries are weak and drained? None whatsoever – which is why we counsel you to balance workloads.

Never tire yourself to the point of physical and nervous exhaustion; always be sensible. Rest the body, relax the mind, and make sure that periods of activity are properly counterbalanced by periods of rest.

Far too many sensitives overwork their abilities, and their power resources drop below the necessary levels needed by us to make reliable attunement possible.

Quality work is produced by quality instruments, and the instrument – in order to be of good quality – must be physically, emotionally and spiritually healthy.

Tranquil mental equilibrium is of the greatest aid to us when trying to contact you.

The power of soul attraction touches everyone, whether sensitive or not. Every one of us is influenced to certain degrees by people from the next world: nurses and doctors in busy hospitals naturally attract the help of spirit healers; lawyers draw keen, discerning minds to inspire fights for justice. And the reverse principle is also true: dark-minded, selfish, ignorant souls draw their own kind through the Universal Law of *Like Attracts Like*.

Each of us has a general soul vibration or, to simplify it, an average frequency of existence created by the sum of our general thoughts and feelings. Souls approximating to this frequency are naturally in attunement with us, no matter which world they live in.

In my early twenties my mediumship attracted a

famous helper from the Other Side: arguably Spiritualism's most brilliant medium, Estelle Roberts, who gave stunning survival evidence to Members of Parliament which was largely responsible for Spiritualism becoming a state-recognized religion in Britain in 1951. Up until then public mediums could be, and sometimes were, arrested by the police under the archaic Witchcraft and Vagrancy Acts, which I'll be speaking of in a later chapter.

Some mediums working in small Spiritualist churches to intimate groups of believers think they can make the giant step to addressing audiences in large public halls, like Estelle and I have done – but many can't. A great deal of skill and psychic development is required to accomplish this satisfactorily. Sympathetic Spiritualists are open-minded, patient and willing to test evidence with their intellect – even if the medium's information seems incorrect – but in public halls audience attitudes are quite different. As one wise veteran medium stated: 'They want precision, Stephen, and if they don't get it they'll get up and walk out.'

Mediums like Estelle and I served our apprenticeship *before* demonstrating survival to huge gatherings of thousands of people. We also share another link: we've both worked at the London headquarters of the Spiritualist Association of Great Britain, the largest association of its kind in the world. The SAGB, at 33 Belgrave Square, certainly puts mediums through their paces, not to mention giving them an education! Though I've made several guest appearances there, it never failed to amaze me how many sitters didn't have a clue about what a medium's proper function was, and this is where I used my soul powers, as I'll explain.

Sitters come from all over the world, many wanting

a *psychic reading*: a soul-to-soul link from psychic to sitter where the sensitive acts more or less as a 'mirror', telepathically reading facts and details from the sitters' minds and auras and then relaying them during the appointment. This doesn't involve any contact with discarnate people and has nothing to do with spirit communication. Psychics can use their own soul powers to 'read' others (or even the vibrational fields of inanimate objects which retain facts about their psychic history: a process called Psychometry), *but mediums communicate with discarnate people*. There's a world of difference and I wish more people were aware of it.

Soul powers prove most helpful in difficult consultations, like this one at the Association:

One bright morning my sitter was already ten minutes late when suddenly he burst in through the door like a cat on heat, red-faced from running, threw himself into a chair and promptly arranged his overflowing Harrods carrier bags around his feet. He was a tall blond American, about twenty-five, who was completely out of breath as he rattled out quickly:

'Oh, I'm so *glad* to get into your schedule! I've come right across London and I was afraid I wouldn't see someone today; the traffic was *dreadful!*' And without a breath he quickly continued: 'Now, what I really want to know is *this*: will I get the money to move to a New York apartment, and will I find the cash for my cosmetic surgery; *plus*, will I be happy there and when does it happen?'

I took a breather for us both!

Then for the first time he was motionless, glaring hopefully across into my eyes. I couldn't believe what I'd just heard (and was thoroughly intrigued about the cosmetic surgery: he was six feet tall, blue-eyed, classically featured with a perfectly formed V-shaped torso and looked as though he'd just stepped out of a catalogue. I wondered what pieces of himself he wanted altered! My soul powers, however, indicated it was probably a sex-change operation).

I eventually broke the pregnant pause.

'I don't think I can answer those questions today,' I said.

'*Why not?*'

'Because I don't do psychic readings here, only mediumship.'

'*Oh?* Well, the lady I normally visit tells me *everything* I want to know.'

I maintained a diplomatic silence.

'So what about my plastic surgery, my apartment and my happiness?' he asked, counting his wishes out on thin fingers.

I sensed a small spiritual lesson would be in order.

'If we examine those questions,' I gently explained, 'the common link between them all is *I*. Making those decisions is your own responsibility, not mine or that of the spirit people. We're personally responsible for what we think, say and do.'

After the shock sunk in we spent the next twenty minutes discussing this concept with true American intensity, and at the end of the day our catalogue model got more *real* spiritual help for his life than he'd bargained for when he'd dashed into his appointment. And when all's said and done, that's what it's all about – helping each other.

So many people mistakenly believe mediums can solve all their problems, but we can't. No one has all the answers, not even those on the Other Side.

Often women write: 'I'm desperate for a message from my husband. Send me his pet-name, or our childrens' names to prove he's alive.' But if only

55

more people understood the difficulties of communication between two worlds there wouldn't be so many unreasonable demands. It's not always easy for communicators to reach us, which is why a patient search within the Spiritualist movement, amongst respected mediums, should be made.

Follow those whose work has spiritual depth and truth stamped upon it.

Seek and you will find; knock and the door will be opened – but only when the time is right.

All seekers need patience, and a realization that nobody, neither in this world nor the next, can demand instant spiritual answers.

But the solutions *will* come, because there's no barrier so big that it can prevent us finding the ones we dearly love. They are not lost to us: they have survived death, and we will find them again, providing we're prepared to make a thorough and intelligent investigation.

4

Talking Animals

Animals have souls and, therefore, soul powers. They're spirits working through physical bodies just like ourselves and they also survive death.

In my first book, *Visions of Another World*, I devoted a whole chapter to stories of their spirit-returns to their beloved human friends, recording incidents of pit ponies and even elephants and giraffes successfully communicating!

To those who think animals have no intellect, let me say: you are wrong. In Sylvia Barbanell's excellent little book *When Your Animal Dies* (Psychic Press Ltd) she introduces fascinating animals who could actually *talk* through a system of paw-tapping and, in the case of dogs, barking out loud to indicate letters of the alphabet, and hence spell words. Take the story of Lola, for example, whose remarkable gifts are well worth recalling.

Extracts appear from Henny Kindermann's book *The Story of Lola*, translated into English by Agnes Blake in which Lola's bright intelligence stunned Henny with sensible answers to profound questions like:

'Lola, would you like to be a human being?'
'No.'
'Why not?'
'Because of work.'
'Lola, do you belong to me?'
'No.' (energetically)
'To whom do you belong then?'

'To myself.'

Further stunning replies were gained when the little dog, Lola, was questioned about the vital issues of life, death and the existence of the soul:

'Lola, what will become of you when you are dead? What will become of your body?'

'I will go to heaven.'

'Do you know what a soul is?'

'Yes.'

'Have I a soul?'

'Yes.'

'Has a stone one?'

'No.'

'And a horse?'

'Yes.'

'And water?'

'No.'

'Have all dogs?'

'Yes.'

But Lola's clever intellect and caring heart were most startlingly revealed when probably one of the most important powers in the universe was touched upon. Her answer profoundly shames beyond words all those who are cruel to animals.

'Lola, what do dogs feel when they look at our eyes and see the sorrows of people?'

'We feel Love ...'

These amazing replies are interwoven with intelligence and feeling, powerful forces which spring from an active thinking mind. But there are no surprises here to sensitives who have often read the trusting thoughts of our fellow brethren, the animals. Ask anyone living close to the land and they'll tell you of the bright keen minds their animals possess; animals like Kurwenal of Weimar, a clever and humorous little dachshund who belonged to Mathilde, Baroness von

Freytag-Loringhoven. She taught Kurwenal to speak in a language of barks and he expressed many surprising opinions. Several eminent minds questioned him, including a scientist who asked the little dog:

'What do you think about a dog's soul?'

'It is eternal, like the soul of man.'

And when the Baroness probed his opinions further concerning deeper religious matters, Kurwenal astonished her by replying:

'I often pray.'

'What do you pray for?' she asked.

'. . . For you,' said her beloved friend.

But such loyalty and love were not the only thoughts expressed by Kurwenal. By all accounts, the little dachshund displayed a great and active interest in all human conversations, and on more than one occasion revealed his sharp ability to fully understand speech. During one discussion, Professor Max Müller – a veterinary surgeon – stopped to ask the dog for his views on a rather morbid subject: the guests had been speaking about dogs being eaten as delicacies in some Eastern countries. Said the Professor to Kurwenal:

'Do you wish to say something about it?'

'Yes,' he replied, then stunningly said, 'the Christian religion prohibits killing.'

An incredible and mind-boggling response, I think you'll agree.

The dog has long been man's best friend, they say; and maybe they're right. Certainly Mr Wisniewski from Poland had a remarkably loving and loyal friend, a mongrel dog called Burek who would never leave his master's side. Wherever one went, the other ambled along, following behind; they were an inseparable pair like father and son. But sadly, after a short illness, Mr Wisniewski died and for a fortnight his faithful

59

dog went missing. Friends and neighbours hunted high and low, searching the countryside for Burek but they couldn't find him anywhere.

Worried because he might be freezing, hungry, cold and grieving, someone was inspired to set off in another direction . . . and there in the cemetery, lying across his master's grave, poor Burek was found, close to death. Emaciated, starving, ill and on the point of collapse he refused to leave his master's side. 'Come on, boy,' they said gently, 'your master's gone away and won't be coming back now . . . ' – and only then did the loyal Burek allow himself to be tenderly lifted and gently carried home to be fed, washed and cared for.

Who could ever forget such wonderful love and devotion? In a strange kind of way perhaps Burek's great reward was forthcoming, for the next day the old dog 'died' peacefully and went to join his beloved friend and constant companion in the Beyond.

What a remarkable creature. But perhaps no more so than an ordinary chatty budgerigar named Twink (!) who shared her life with a Mrs Passmore. Twink was loved by everyone because of her endearing characteristics, especially when she did her popular, clever party-piece which usually proved to be quite a show-stopper! When requested (politely) she'd recite the entire *Lord's Prayer*, often at such great speed that sometimes little Twink would stumble over a difficult phrase, calling for some human prompting. Then she'd carry right on to the very last sentence, even remembering to say 'Amen'!

Twink also fully recognized humans as they approached, suddenly exclaiming things like 'The rent-man's coming!' (when he was!); or 'Georgie's here!' (as Mrs Passmore's son paid an unexpected visit!).

Such wonderful examples of our brethren's bright

and happy ways make it so hurtful to contemplate the cruelty dealt by uncaring man to dear little souls like Twink, Kurwenal and Lola – but I'm afraid we humans are a long way from giving our friends the kindness and respect they truly deserve, as was clearly highlighted by one of my friends recently.

'It happened in a busy Hong Kong marketplace, and sickened me beyond words.'

'What did?'

'Well, a British soldier and his young eight-year-old son were walking past the market stalls when the little boy spied a small puppy and instantly fell in love with his big sad eyes. He pleaded with his dad, "Please, Daddy, can I have the little dog? Can I have him?"

'Eventually his dad gave in and the boy smiled into one of the cages, pointing out his puppy to the stall-holder who – in a trice – grabbed it by the scruff of the neck, squealing, then threw it onto a wooden board and chopped off its head in front of the horrified child.'

My heart skipped a beat. I couldn't believe what I was hearing.

'And as if this wasn't barbaric enough, he then took a sharp machete and skinned the puppy. The shocked boy was inconsolable, racked with heart-rending tears and his father was so stunned he simply led him away.'

I was equally appalled, loving animals as I do. How could the soldier justify this cruel act to his sensitive son without admitting man's wicked disregard for Animal Rights? He could not. No-one with the slightest degree of sensitivity could. There's no excuse for such cruelty yet it continues all over the world each and every day.

Another similar degrading incident reached my

ears the other day. It caused a woman I know to be physically sick in a Bangkok marketplace where she watched a man ordering some of the crudely advertised 'Hot Crispy Snacks for Sale'. Filling the order, the merchant scooped up a handful of day-old, chirping, naked baby chicks and automatically tossed them alive into a wok full of burning oil.

I make no apologies for recording such disgusting acts so graphically. The only way to make people sit up, take notice and then do something to stop these travesties is to present the shocking facts. Hopefully, soul-revulsion may birth a new saviour for our brethren; perhaps caring people will form or join pressure groups, canvass and sign petitions as well as write to these barbaric governments, doing everything possible to stop the mass murder of the innocents.

Some insensitives still say animals operate with instinct alone. What absolute nonsense this is: they have individual personalities. When Mr Bryson died (he founded the animal sanctuary where my cheeky but lovable, and now-famed cat, Sooty, came from), many helpless creatures he'd saved from degradation, death and slaughter paid their last respects to him on his funeral journey. They owed him the greatest debt of all, the gift of their lives, and wouldn't let it go unheeded because they knew he was their friend. (Once, he'd travelled from England to France just to rescue one horse from being slaughtered.)

A pall of sadness fell over the sanctuary on the day of his final procession, the many animals he'd helped becoming quiet: Percy the pig, on whose back children used to ride, some ponies, a goat, and the huge cattery as well as all the dogs. As Mr Bryson's cortege moved along the streets lined with grateful people and their beloved pets, the hearse went past some fields when something wonderful happened: horses and ponies, whose lives he'd saved, trotted to the edge of the fencing and stood silently watching, as if to say 'Goodbye' to the man who'd shown them so much love and kindness.

What greater tribute could any man wish?

Somewhere in a book it's written that God marks even the smallest sparrow's fall, something I accept because I've had evidence of it. Once when driving down the motorway at breakneck speed late on a cloudy moonless night, all at once a spirit voice urgently told me to 'Swerve to the right!' My body instantly reacted – just in time to see the moon break cover and pick out three starlings grouped in close formation zooming past my windscreen within inches of sudden death. If I hadn't obeyed the voice I'd have killed them outright.

How much more then will God, I wonder, through His ministering angels in Spirit care for us, His children, when such tender concern is shown for our animal brethren?

It's through the exercise of our compassion that we forge closer relationships with all life-forms, but how I wish more of us were as kind to animals as my medium friend Clare is. She actually took the trouble to set a wild brown rat's broken leg in a splint (made from two matchsticks and some sellotape) then fed and nursed it until it healed, after which she released the creature back onto the waste-ground where it had been found in obvious distress a month earlier.

Can you imagine how grateful that tiny animal must have been to her human friend after such tender loving care? If only everyone was this kind to our brethren they'd spiritually evolve much faster, advancing in leaps and bounds – and so would we.

I'm no angel but I've always stood up for the underdog and Digger was no exception. I named the stray dog 'Digger' because he'd suddenly appeared outside the flats where I live and had dug out a little dirt-filled hole amongst some shrubbery for warmth. He was a black-and-white (but mostly black because of the dirt) Jack Russell terrier, ever so timid, pathetic-looking and sad when I found him.

'What's the matter, boy?' I said calmly, trying not to frighten him. 'Haven't you a home to go to, my handsome?'

But he backed off warily, very fearful and not knowing what to make of me.

'Come on,' I said. 'Here, sniff my hand first and then let me smooth you. I won't hurt you, boy,' I cooed sympathetically, reaching out my open palms to him. But as soon as I moved forward he belted away as fast as his little legs could carry him, eventually stopping over the road to glance back, half wanting affection but terrified of human contact. It was then I knew he'd been badly mistreated; my soul powers sensed his aura and discovered he'd been cruelly thrown from a fast car on the busy road nearby.

Poor little chap. But try as I might I couldn't coax him inside, so I decided on another course of action. Though he didn't return to his dug-out in the bushes until late that night, by the time he appeared I'd put a saucer of milk and a huge plateful of cat food out for him. Sooty glowered wilfully into my face and started growling in a low-pitched menacing way, because I'd defiled the holiest of holies – her food dish. She immediately prowled around mewing and protesting loudly, but I leaned over and stared right back into her bewilderment:

'Now, that's enough of that, *Madam*! We've got to be kind to Digger,' I explained. 'Some little boys have nowhere to sleep tonight and no-one to love them –

not like you: you've got the life of Riley in this house *and* the pillows on my bed!'

Grudgingly, she understood; at least I think she did, though two green beady eyes clamped themselves onto her food bowl, and followed it right down the steps and out into the cold winter night.

I was quite worried about Digger because when I retired he was nowhere to be seen and I just couldn't sleep, all I could think of was his dear little person, cold and lonely in the frosty night air. So I dozily got up in the early hours and went out to search for him again. Quickly yanking on my trousers and hopping down the stairs grappling with a coat and flipping my slippers on, I scuttled into the wet grass only to find his food bowl empty and the milk had all been wolfed. The poor dog must have been starving; not one morsel had been left.

Suddenly, in the moonlight, I caught sight of him in his little dug-out: it was only then I had a good chance to get a close-up view, and his little ribs were sticking out through his muddy coat – he was so painfully thin.

I was moved to tears, but he wouldn't let me touch him, quickly dashing off again into the night and standing firm across the road, glaring, waiting, hoping ...

The weatherman on TV had predicted a bitter icy night with frost and temperatures at least three degrees below zero; so I grabbed a couple of old thick blankets and a cardboard box, put them on the landing outside my flat (which is quite warm and comfortable), then coaxed the stray dog in through the front doors with promises of food and warmth, delivered in sympathetic tones. There, he gratefully enthroned himself in his cosy woolly bed looking up at me with such grateful, pathetic eyes.

On wishing him 'Goodnight', for the first time he

allowed me to smooth his little frame and as I did he licked my fingers as good as to say, 'Thank you for caring.'

'God bless you boy,' I said. 'Sleep well, and we'll see what we can do for you in the morning.'

Before I closed my eyes that night I sought further help, turning to the Greater Power.

I also asked the spirit people to help me find Digger a good home. (Sooty has a black-belt in judo and would have wrestled the poor chap to death!)

'Please don't let the authorities put him to sleep. Thank you, my friends.' And these were my final requests to the Other World.

But the next morning I got a shock: Digger was gone, along with his cardboard bed and blankets. The wicked old witch from the landing beneath me had thrown him and his belongings out into the freezing night; and the little dog – already so badly frightened and mistreated – was now nowhere to be seen.

I couldn't believe how cruel and selfish people could be.

When I confronted the wicked witch of the west, I'm afraid I let my feelings rip about her flint-like, insensitive heart, to which she spat back, 'We don't want stray dogs untidying these landings. I'm not having that sort of nonsense round here.'

And there speaks the collective voice of the Children of Darkness.

Outside, the morning mist of dawn was tunefully pierced by the high-pitched whistling of the milkwoman arriving at our block: I greeted her with: 'Have you seen the little Jack Russell? I've been calling him Digger.' And I told her why.

'Oh, I wondered whose he was,' she said. 'He's awfully dirty and nobody's come to get him these past few days; poor little thing. He must be lost or homeless.'

'Can you help him?' I pleaded. 'I don't want someone destroying him, and I've knocked on all the doors and no-one knows him.' Obviously an animal lover, I saw her eyes blurring.

'I'll see what I can do,' she said, kindly, making me feel much happier about his fate.

And I wondered if my prayer was going to bear fruit . . .

Two hours later she was back with a car full of children clutching warm blankets and dog food. There was also another puppy in the back, too, barking away as happy as Lassie.

'I've found him a good home,' she triumphantly announced, stepping onto the pavement and smiling. I was so overjoyed and pleased, for when she approached Digger, this time, he seemed to strangely know salvation was at hand, and instead of legging it, he didn't move a muscle – his little body stood firm. He just looked at me, then at her, then at the children and his new pal in the back of the car, as if to say, incredulously:

'For me? Have they come for *me*?'

I glanced back at him, smiling and nodding my approval – as whistling Annie lovingly scooped him up in a warm embrace. He wagged his tail so much we thought it was going to come off. I never thought I would ever see a dog smile – but I did on that day.

'Come on, my old son; you come along with me and we'll take care of you properly,' she cooed, folding him in a fluffy woolly blanket. (His grin was immense.) Then she smoothed him, kissed him, cuddled him, put him in the car with his new playmate and whisked him away to a nice warm spot by a blazing fire, beside which sat a huge plate of proper dog food and doggy-biscuits, plus a new life of friendship.

And from that day onwards the milk-lady and her

family cared for little Digger, lavished love upon him, and called him their very own.

For months afterwards, whenever I saw her I'd say, 'How's the dog, then?' and she'd tell me how he was keeping. By all accounts he was leading the 'life of Riley' – just like my cat Sooty!

But each day I remember the day Digger left, all I can see are his big brown eyes seeking me out and staring directly at mine as her car pulled away and turned the corner on that frosty morning.

His stubby tail was happily wagging away for the joy of his new friends, mightily strong for all he was worth. His heart belonged to them – but his eyes were mine, and saying:

'Thank you for caring, my friend.'

God bless you, little Digger, wherever you are . . .

5

The Terry Wogan Show
(Or: The Night I 'died' on Network TV!)

When the telephone rang, Britain's primetime television chat show, hosted by Terry Wogan, booked me for an appearance. It was to be an interview followed by a 'live' spirit message – a national 'first' for the BBC who'd never done this before, and it immediately provoked excitement.

Though I grumbled at its possible failure, I agreed to do it, but with reservations. I'd demonstrated on TV several times before with quite successful results, but none which could be regarded as first-class mediumship owing to the difficult conditions under which they took place. When the clock's against you and 'instant' results are demanded by millions, this creates an immense amount of stress in any sensitive, which adversely affects spirit contact.

Asking mediums to deliver immediate results on an entertainment show is stressful enough, but to do so 'live' would have been like asking Beethoven to compose the opening strains of a new symphony in four minutes flat (or sharp!). I doubt he could have done it, but because the researcher at the *Wogan* office had treated me so kindly, had seen clips of my other TV work and was 'confident' I could manage it, I reluctantly agreed.

I was delighted, however, when they said: 'Considering your reservations, we've decided your item will be *recorded* "live" on a Tuesday night in

London, then edited and broadcast as part of a future Friday night *Wogan*; Friday shows are usually taped earlier in the week.'

With a grateful sigh, I began to feel much more relaxed about the whole thing, but then arrangements were suddenly changed. Just days before filming the phone rang: 'Stephen, one of our guests has cancelled for Wednesday night. Can you make it?'

'Well, I'm available,' I replied.

'But it'll be *live*: there'll be an interview with Terry and then about four minutes to give a message to someone in the theatre audience. What do you say?'

Uneasily, I recounted the difficulties again, especially when trying to successfully place a link with the correct recipient in such a short time. But, with implicit trust in my spirit friends I fearlessly assented, reasoning they'd rise to the challenge as they'd done before.

Replacing the receiver, I had grave misgivings about the clock beating me. But before long I was trundling off to the BBC Television Theatre in London and being ensconced in the plush and spacious Copthorne Tara Hotel, courtesy of 'Auntie Beeb'. After a sumptuous dinner I was chauffeured to the theatre where the first thing I did was sign a charity autograph book – to be auctioned for the famed annual *Children In Need* television appeal, something I'd done a few times before. Then I was greeted by Jane, the charming researcher in charge of my item, and we went upstairs into the green-room.

My publisher's representative, Sue, was already quite excited and really looking forward to the event. I wasn't nervous, though I was covered with a grey cloud of apprehension, but I kept telling myself, 'Stephen, don't worry. You've done it before, very successfully. Trust in God; the spirit people have never let you down.'

Soon I was on the studio floor where everything was chaotic hustle and bustle. Before transmission I was allowed a very quick chat with the audience to prepare them for what would follow, simply because they'd come for entertainment and not to hear messages from another world.

Everything happened so quickly, it was like a lightning-fast dream: I explained how vitally important it was for recipients to speak up – or else the line of communication goes 'dead', breaks down and fails – then the floor-manager shuffled me off to be hastily wired for sound.

I was supposed to get fifteen minutes peace and quiet, alone in my dressing-room, to relax and tune in to my spirit voices, but time was so pressing that this never materialized: everything whizzed past. (Such is live TV!) And the next thing I knew there was frenzied activity and we were counted down to 7 p.m. when live transmission was to begin and millions would see the show.

I was now seated on the famous plush set and I hadn't yet been introduced to Terry Wogan who, like a true professional, cool, calm and collected, was wandering around the audience, entertaining them while sipping a cup of tea. Then the floor-manager urgently shouted:

'Come on, Terry, thirty seconds! The titles are running!'

'All right, all right,' he replied suavely, then turned to the audience and said, 'Please excuse me but I have to go. We've got a show to do, you know!' Not one bit ruffled by all the fuss around him he called out, 'Don't panic, I'm coming!' And he just about managed to sail behind the scenery as the titles finished and the programme started, when he emerged to thunderous

71

applause, giving me a gracious nod as he did so.

I was what they call a 'top of the show' guest: first on; and after Terry's witty topical jokes about the British Budget and the Poll Tax, he introduced me with a smile as 'Britain's Top Medium' which brought more welcoming applause and we shook hands warmly as he joined me on the set.

There then followed quite a long, informative interview about my work and beliefs. But, as smooth and professional as Terry was, I was disconcerted by something he did: after asking a question, and while I was answering, his eyes weren't looking at me at all but were focused somewhere over my shoulder, darting quickly from side to side.

In a flash of a second – when my face wasn't on camera – I saw why: he was reading the script from large cue cards (known as idiot boards) so what seemed like a serene medium was actually quite a surprised one! I've been on TV so many times I'm well used to presenters gazing into auto-cues (glass screens covering the camera lens on which a reflected 'invisible' text appears, allowing them to gaze at the public while also reading their lines) but this was the first time I'd encountered cue cards. Well, we live and learn!

For the first time on British TV a colour picture of my spirit guide, White Owl, was shown and we discussed him and his role in my work. Then, after what seemed like only a few moments, all of a sudden Terry said (as I knew he was going to):

'Would you please give us a demonstration? Do you feel you could here?' And I was up on my feet replying:

'Well, I'll try, Terry . . . ' and down to the floor I went, having been told to stand on a mark for the cameras to focus on me. The lights on the set

dimmed and a bright follow-spot came up, directly
obliterating my view of the back rows of the audience
(something I'm always careful to avoid in my theatre
meetings) and then the crowd was lit for viewers to
see my recipient. As I rose, I'd heard a man's voice
from the Other Side faintly calling 'Doris . . . Doris,'
and – though that's all he said – I immediately *knew*
he was the father of someone in the audience. So I
launched into my connection, only to be greeted by
two hundred utterly silent faces . . .

My worst fears were realized: not a living soul
claimed the link. Then I remembered a small golden
spirit light, about the size of a golf ball, which I'd
seen a moment previously, bobbing around above
a woman's head in the gallery, accompanied by a
voice telling me the person was 'in the front row'.
Wrongly thinking this was where the link should
go, I pinpointed her and asked for a reply. What
then followed can only be described as a seeming
disaster: I had the *right* message, but the *wrong*
recipient! (My true recipient turned out later to be
sitting *in the front row of the stalls*, and the light
I'd seen was just a manifestation of psychic energy.)

I knew exactly what I was hearing from my communicator but the poor woman I'd selected refused
every single fact with a more than positive '*No!*'

I soon realized many of the audience were amused
by her responses and therefore they began to laugh.
When I knew this could be because I was with the
wrong recipient, I asked:

'Does anybody around that area understand any
of that?'

But no hands rose, none that I could see, and no
voice spoke up. But because I was positive that my
message, at least, was correct, I valiantly persevered,
well aware that it isn't always easy to place what

amounts to a 'telephone-call' from the Other Side; sometimes when indicating a specific area we can miss the recipient by just a few seats or rows. Plus, adding to my difficulties, the follow-spot was strong in my eyes and I couldn't make out all sections of the crowd.

As no-one seemed willing to claim the connection, I thought, 'Soldier on! The clock's against you and the most important thing is to get this man's message across; someone here fully understands it.'

So that's exactly what I did.

I delivered the spirit Dad's link through increasing audience amusement, worsened by my recipient's terse refusals. But dignity carried me through, though it certainly wasn't easy, especially while being humiliated before ten million people. Nevertheless, I obeyed the spirit Dad's faint voice to the letter. 'At least he'll be grateful I did my best,' I thought.

Eventually I even managed a few wry smiles myself at the lady's replies, something clearly seen on the video recording. It's just as well I have an excellent sense of humour, for at one point I announced to the woman that Dad in the spirit world mentioned another family member:

'He speaks of a brother,' I said.

'What? You mean his own brother?'

'Yes, I *think* his brother.'

'*He never had one!*' she snapped back loudly.

This caused further belly-laughter in the crowd – at least in *some* sections; others felt genuine sympathy for me, as I was later to hear in many letters. At this point I expect many mediums would have just keeled over and died purple with their legs in the air, but I didn't – I retained my composure and carried on, asking seriously:

'Are you sure?'

'Yes,' she replied curtly. So I added a piece of my own advice and suggested she research to see if a child had been lost or miscarried, because I was so certain of what I was receiving: I was *sure* he'd had a brother; I knew it was right.

And all this time the inexorable ticking clock brought the end nearer and nearer while I 'died' a little more with each passing second. This highlights some of the difficult problems when working for the media: audiences seek enjoyment, not communication, and their attitude is therefore not as reverent as it should be when contacting loved ones from another world.

If I'd given this message in a Spiritualist church or at one of my own theatre meetings the recipient would probably have replied, 'I'm sorry, but I don't understand', and no one would have laughed.

Towards the end I sensed Terry Wogan approaching from behind me, and saw the floor-manager in front waving his arms to indicate my time was spent. So I did my best to conclude with dignity, but naturally I was very disappointed it hadn't been the success we'd all hoped for, even though I was certain my message was correct. Terry put his arm around my shoulder and said:

'Stephen, that wasn't very successful, was it? You missed everything there.' And the next thing I registered was applause and I was being steered away towards Jane, the friendly researcher who'd engaged my item for the show. I looked at her pathetically and said, 'Oh, my God – dig a hole and bury me in it.' I wouldn't have been one bit surprised if they'd whisked me off in a wheelbarrow shouting 'Open the trash-can, boys, here he comes!'

Offering comfort, Sue from my publishers said:

'Don't be too concerned, Stephen, it's just bad

luck you didn't get the link accepted.'

Jane reassuringly added: 'I've seen video tapes of your previous successes on TV, on Central and Ulster, that's why we invited you on. Don't worry; it was OK.'

That evening's producer also chipped in: 'Cheer up, Stephen, it was an excellent interview.'

Though comforted, I was naturally downhearted and wondered how the public would react. I already knew the anti-paranormalist brigade would by now be frothing at the mouth, eyes bulging out on stalks as they rubbed their hands with glee and saying: 'So Britain's renowned medium is a flop!'

Terry had previously mentioned my forthcoming UK tour which followed this appearance so Sue asked: 'This isn't going to alter anything, is it, Stephen?'

'Good God, no. I've done this work for years. It'll take more than laughter to stop me.' Then I apologized profusely to Jane: 'I hope I haven't lost you your job,' I said quietly. 'You placed your trust in me; and I did do my best.'

'Don't be silly, Stephen,' she replied sympathetically, 'it's been hailed as a good item. It's just unfortunate we didn't get the results we'd have liked.'

And then something very pleasant happened. Terry Wogan walked across to my corner while I made an effort to rise.

'Oh no, no, no, Stephen. Please don't get up. Give me your hand.' And we shook hands. 'I found your book very interesting, pity you had a bit of bad luck there tonight,' he said. 'But thank you very much for coming on the show.'

'Terry,' I lamented, 'the press will have a field day.'

'Oh no, I don't think so. You did your best, but there's one thing I want to tell you. The floor staff said there was another woman in the crowd waving her arms when you asked if someone else could understand what you were saying. Perhaps your message was for her?'

'Why didn't she speak up?'

'I don't know; but I thought you handled it very well,' Terry replied kindly. 'Would you like to come back and try again sometime?'

'What? After *that*?!'

'Yes: why not?'

I was so numbed, all I could manage was:

'Well, Terry, that's very kind of you and thanks for having me on the show.'

'My pleasure,' and we warmly shook hands once again as we parted, my final comments being:

'Well, there might be a glimmer of light yet. I hope the recipient will let us know.'

Jane said, 'Don't worry, Stephen, something positive may yet come out of this.'

'Yes,' I said, 'a phoenix might rise from the ashes!'

As I left to go to my hotel another producer stopped me in the doorway to shake hands, saying, 'I was very sceptical about you and your work, but I was impressed tonight. I'm much less sceptical now.'

'Why on earth is that?' I asked.

'Because you persisted, despite the refusals, and stayed with it without changing one fact – right to the end. A charlatan wouldn't do that; he'd have moved on quickly and found someone else. So you struck me as being genuine.'

I was comforted.

'Thank you very much,' I replied quietly.

'Besides,' he went on, 'if you'd got a too-positive

response some would only say we'd fixed it up.'

And I must say, I could see his point.

But isn't life (and mediumship) strange? – for later at the hotel I gave an interview to the *Sunday People* during which the reporter's 'dead' father made a spontaneous appearance and brought 'excellent' evidence, with startling accuracy. He knew all about her mother's varicose veins and bad legs, plus the journalist's eyesight, saying quite succinctly, 'Tell her she will never go blind'. This calmed the fears only she knew she had: she and her father in spirit, that is.

He also correctly relayed memories of his 'sudden passing through a coronary'. Quite impressed, this reporter's article rated my accuracy 'On the day' as '7 out of 10'; and for 'Reassurance: 9 out of 10'!

Life certainly is peculiar and seems to swing from the sublime to the ridiculous so quickly! Proof of this came quickly in the form of a few scathing press reports following my appearance, the *Daily Express* and the *News of the World* – two very different newspapers – being the worst. Their TV columnists described me with such phrases as 'A young man with piercing eyes and neat moustache who looked like a Mazda salesman', and also 'Medium – not very well done, I'd say'. That last 'witty' quip came from Charles Catchpole of the *News of the World* who also referred to my unfortunate female recipient as 'A lady who was about as friendly as a shark with a toothache'.

But Peter Tory in the *Express* treated me cruelly which resulted in my complaining to the newspaper. He used the sub-heading 'Wogan's guest hasn't a ghost of a chance as a crowd-pleaser', and claimed my appearance offered 'a genuinely hilarious, unintended comedy'. But I wonder if he would have found it so funny if *he* had been the spirit father trying to reach his loved one? I doubt it.

After a three-month wait I gave up all hope of an apology. I still hadn't received the courtesy of a reply; the 'gentlemen' of the press were silent.

Meanwhile, back at the ranch (the *Wogan* office), dozens of letters poured in from undiscerning viewers around Britain claiming my spirit message was actually for *them*! But, with the greatest of respect, they'd nearly all misinterpreted and twisted the facts beyond recognition: misquoting the details, adding their own ideas and names to them, or taking them entirely out of context.

People wrote saying really odd things like, 'I sat on the edge of my seat and peered into my television and willed you to give me a message from my husband, and you did!' But my link was from a father to his daughter!

One young viewer, who hadn't even seen the show yet, wrote to tell me I'd got it wrong. It wasn't his dad communicating but his uncle and he finished up by asking: 'But who was Henry?' Who indeed? That name wasn't even mentioned!

The spirit message wasn't intended for anyone out there in TV land, but was a positive connection for someone *inside* the television theatre on that night, which was later verified.

Events took an unusual turn when the BBC received a letter from a woman in Huntingdon, Cambridgeshire, who was a lecturer in a College of Higher Education. *She'd actually been in the theatre as the message was delivered and everything that was said applied to her and was correct. It was her father communicating.* Her letter, which she simultaneously sent addressed personally to Terry

Wogan (and a copy to myself) is signed: Mrs Judy Brewer.

She had attended with her son-in-law, who had brought her daughter as a birthday treat, and wrote: 'It was quite an uncanny experience and I just thought you might be interested to know (about it). It does seem strange that I matched on all the points ... I will also send a copy to poor Stephen – it might make him feel better.'

It certainly did! I can't tell you how relieved I was, for I'd known all along the details of my link had been right. Imagine my joy as I scanned the following words, which I've now placed side-by-side with the verbatim televised evidence:

Stephen	Mrs Brewer
Doris: and there's a man saying he is Dad (communicating). He's here, with Doris.	Dad had died; Doris was my aunt, Dad's sister-in-law.
Tell her to watch her lower back.	The lower back pain (mine) was treated for six months last year by a chiropracter.
They are mentioning Tom and Arthur; these are friends or relatives of his that have gone Over.	(By phone) He knew a lot of people. They could possibly be friends, we'll try and trace them.

Here the video shows me asking if there's anyone else who can accept this connection, as I'm obviously unhappy with the response from the wrong recipient; but I also state I feel 'so strongly that I'm right.'

He's talking about his *chest*, and how he passed over. He was tired before he went	(By phone) Dad had cancer of the lungs.

over to the world of spirit. He says the days were not always easy for him before he went.

He's close because there's going to be a birth – the child is already here, being carried by someone. And within a period of about eight months or so, you will have news of that. He's wanting to tell you that quite clearly.

On recounting this story to my mother-in-law and reaching the pregnancy bit, I have now learned that my ex sister-in-law is pregnant.

He's talking of George and Mrs Walker, these are people who link with him on the Other Side.

Yes. George is his brother and Mrs Walker: when I was small I literally lived at this person's house which was just across the road, and, to this day, I still call this eighty-five-year-old 'Mrs Walker', rather than her Christian name, Florrie.

Did you change your coat before you came out? Why is he talking about a choice between two coats here?

I didn't change my coat, but I had asked my partner if my Mac was OK and whether my skirt was hanging below: something I do not usually do.

He's talking about sifting through a jewellery box here; somebody's been going through a jewellery box he said. And they couldn't find an earring: they had one but they couldn't find another one.

On the way to work in the morning I had forgotten to wear any earrings and so, en route, at my swimming club, I asked the attendant if they had a lost property earring box? He produced a *jewellery box* and in looking through this box for a pair to borrow, I found a lost earring of mine anyway. *It*

81

was still in my pocket at the show.

He talks of a brother: I think his brother.	Yes: George (name already given, married to Doris).
Also he's mentioning: 'Take care of your eyesight'.	One of my eyes was bloodshot in the corner in the morning, and I had bought some Optrex. The next day, the other eye played up.
Mrs Walker lived close by and would have been known to your Dad.	Yes: She lived across the road.
He's been in somebody's home, close to you, and they've been talking about a move, to do with a house.	(By phone) Yes: my daughter (his grand-daughter) is moving into a cottage next week.
He is with his father tonight, either him or his Dad had a very bad leg.	(By phone) His Dad had passed. He was always complaining about his legs.

He had a very difficult job to get through actually, it's a very faint link – but I'm not going to turn him away . . . He's sending you all of his love, Will you research and write to me and tell me if those things were right? Because sometimes that (information) is more evidential, because it can't be telepathy between us . . .

Mrs Brewer's letter cheered me up and thrilled me: the link had been quite precise and all correct. But can you imagine the effect it would have had on ten million viewers if she had produced from her pocket the very earring her father had mentioned and held it up on camera? It would have been electric, which is no doubt what the spirit world had hoped for.

My manager immediately wrote asking the BBC 'to do the honourable thing' and offer a further opportunity to tell millions the outcome. But this, they said, wouldn't fit into their schedules, even though Mrs Brewer indicated her willingness to be interviewed as a guest.

'Well, at least I was proven right!' I philosophically mused, and on two counts, too: not only the message but also about that pheonix spreading its wings and sailing upwards from the ashes of disappointment. And I don't mind confessing – had I been able to get hold of that bird I'd have smothered it in kisses, during a rare short bout of hysterical passion!

6

Seance Secrets

So many delicate mental processes are at work when two worlds are tuning in to each other, little wonder messages can sometimes go 'wrong'.

These seeming 'failures' have prompted me over the years to interrogate the spirit world about the art of communication, particularly about what goes on behind the scenes at seances.

Here, for the first time, is my spirit teacher, White Owl, with some fascinating insights which throw light upon, and answer many of, the intriguing problems involved when Two Worlds are blending as one.

White Owl

This is how we in the spirit world perceive the events which happen 'backstage' at public and private seances.

Though audiences are aware of the calendar dates and times of my medium's work, we are not in this world, for there is no chronological (clock) time in eternity; but I pick up Stephen's thoughts of when a meeting is approaching.

We work with the language of Thought; telepathic messages are instantaneously flashed from mind to mind in my world, and some guides are able to transmit thoughts from one world to another which exists at a higher rate of vibration.

When I am aware of service to perform on Earth, after my calls to a specialized band of helpers have been transmitted, I then delegate my current activities to other people and make my way down to Mother

Earth, homing-in on the frequency of Stephen's mind (for every soul has its own unique wavelength within which its mind vibrates).

Sometimes we find our medium driving along a motorway or just waking up in some strange hotel after having had a long conversation with me in my world while his spirit had been travelling out of the physical body, at night.

Occasionally I find it necessary to remain beside my medium for the whole day on which a demonstration of psychic power is to take place, from the moment he wakes on Earth until the conclusion of our work together. It is not my function to protect him but rather to carefully monitor his mind and emotions so that when our time of joining comes I know what has affected him that day; how much stress, relaxation, tension, laughter, etc. All these expended energies can help or hinder our at-one-ment, and I like to be fully informed of his activities in order that I may provide the closest possible blending of our two minds at the point of contact.

Mediums activate their own auric-protection, their general character and inner motivation drawing unto them persons from my world who are in attunement with these forces. The only fear mediums need have of attracting any undesirable influences stems from themselves: their own lifestyles, thoughts, feelings and true reasons for contact.

Motivation is the keystone upon which co-operation from my world is built; and *Like Attracts Like* is the Universal Law in operation at all times.

We can do nothing to alter or meddle with this power of attraction; the Law cannot be cheated.

We wait for attunement to take place at the meeting-point, but if our medium does not desire our closeness and refuses it, or is unable to raise his mind-vibrations to approximate to our frequencies, then we are powerless – and our influence will be unregistered.

In all the time I have worked with Stephen there have only been two occasions when an appointed

85

meeting was cancelled. He was not at fault: once, his driver did not arrive, and the other time he tried to reach a venue through four feet of drifting snow but failed to make his destination. On both occasions I knew *before* he did that the demonstration would not take place; I foresaw the weather conditions and also saw his driver was fast asleep. I then immediately sent out thoughts to the spirit people who co-operated with the organizers in your world, and alternative arrangements were quickly made for different mediums to step into the breach: other sensitives were inspired by their own spirit-friends to attend and serve.

Through a strong sense of duty and loyalty to us over our years of service together, Stephen has earned our unstinting co-operation and trust. We are always there to serve, because he always is. *Like Attracts Like*: souls draw around them others similar in nature to themselves; if only all on Earth understood this.

When one sincere servant of the spirit steps forward to meet the needs of others, a thousand souls from my world step behind him, ready and willing to help. That is the Divine Plan: those who serve are served, and we will never fail our instruments, providing they return our love and keep it burning bright by pure motivation based on the desire to spread knowledge and healing to mankind.

Now a few words about what occurs on Our Side during a public meeting.

Firstly, it is known to us beforehand who will be in attendance. We have access to a complicated network of interlinked thoughts and information which can be tapped to discover who is likely to be present at the event. Though not an infallible system, it is very reliable, for everyone intending to come will have carried these thoughts in their minds for some time, and they are registered by trained people on Our Side. If, however, one of our projected recipients is *not* going to attend, then other spirit communicators are chosen and their relatives and friends on Earth are checked to see if they will be present. So one link replaces the other.

Ours is a very organized world: the power of thought is the quickest means of communication and, because of this, everything can be monitored faster than lightning speed. We do not just gather on Earth and hope for the best, there is a great deal of unseen order and activity behind working mediums. There are many souls on our side who lend their valuable services towards the success of a demonstration. It is not a haphazard spur-of-the-moment happening, but usually a well-planned and precisely actioned event, even though it can seem to be 'chaotic'!

Now a little about the spirit power and energies we require when joining the two worlds as one, for this is an often misunderstood aspect of our work.

Everyone who attends possesses an electromagnetic field of energy – the aura – which is either vibrant with electrical impulses or sometimes (more often than not) it can be rather depleted. This accounts for the differences in energy between souls who are healthy, cheerful and optimistic, and others who are depressed and miserable.

So, to us – as far as our work is concerned – each person is a unit of fluctuating energy, a battery of power, each contributing to, or drawing from, the electrical atmosphere in the auditorium and surrounding areas.

When we are confronted with a thousand miserable and depressed people then the auric power available to us is considerably diminished. This can make our task much harder because we need to blend with human electromagnetic impulses to aid our work. Black and turbulent thoughts (negative influences) impede our efforts.

What audiences contribute to public meetings is of vital importance to their success or failure. However, the medium is by far the greatest stumbling-block to our organized transmissions, as I shall soon explain.

If crowds do not emanate feelings of sympathy, kindness and attention towards Stephen then a great deal of their energies cause electrical disturbances in the auditorium which are unhelpful, and their auric power often becomes unavailable to us. If they are in grief, introverted, disinterested – or even bored and tired – their vital energies flow *inwards*, making them more difficult for us to tap. This can drastically affect the quality of demonstrations in much the same way as a transistor radio does not operate properly if its batteries are low. So it is with mediumship.

Audiences create – by the blending and mixing of their auric fields – a huge photosphere of electromagnetic power (with other 'whirlpools of energy' moving within it) which is inside and often surrounding the meeting-place. When souls give their undivided attention or focus their minds on something *outside* of themselves, their energies flow *outwards*. Depending on the quality of this power our work is aided or hindered.

We sometimes convey this general 'power report' to our medium in his dressing-room, before he takes the platform, particularly if conditions for contact are going to be poor. Along with his own sensitivity Stephen then obtains a reasonably accurate overall 'picture' of audience conditions, and whether or not the people will be co-operative or reticent to join in the spontaneous three-way spirit communication link, which, of course, is vital for the evening's success.

Stephen's own expansive aura can also be full of energy or adversely depleted, depending on his physical health and the peacefulness, or lack of it, within his mind. When he makes contact with the public his sympathy and compassion (soul-energies) go out to them. If the people are relaxed and comfortable with him then they are particularly receptive to his power and they quickly warm to his personality. This means that some who may have entered as cold and unresponsive beings will now – almost unconsciously – find themselves more at ease (because of interest in the medium) and hence they will automatically project and contribute more energies to the proceedings. They are now adding their personal power to his, and very often in his opening remarks we have heard Stephen say, quite correctly: 'According to what you give, so shall you receive.' This sums up the process quite well.

Without doubt, the greatest obstacle in any two-world communication is the medium. Physical tiredness impedes our thought-flows reaching him. If the body is nervously exhausted then it cannot function properly: the body only responds clearly to mental orders when it is fit and well.

But by far the most hindering of all is the medium's mind. If a sensitive is emotionally upset or clouded by psychological concerns, this sets up swirling energy-fields which can sweep away any of our subtle thought-forces and diminish contact with us. Instead of a peaceful, calm countryside scene where silence and harmony reign and everything is in a state of equilibrium and balance – this is the ideal mind – we now have to work through a mighty cyclone which is ripping through that tranquillity, causing untold havoc and destruction: this is the mind of a psychologically disturbed, mentally disquietened being.

The most difficult sensitives to reach are those who are just starting out on their development, for they haven't yet learned the ideal mental and emotional states of peace and balance we require to obtain and hold a close rapport with them. These mental conditions are essential for successful attunement to occur. That is what psychic and spiritual development circles are for: to learn self-control and the stilling of turbulent forces which so badly affect our links with you on Earth.

Mediumship means attunement.

When successful attunement takes place, communication flows. When attunement is out-of-focus the receiver does not register us clearly. It is easier for us to reach mediums when they are cheerful, bright, optimistic, calm and mentally tranquil, and also positively expecting success. But any fears or worries, anxieties and doubts – all of which create mentally paralysing, negative forces – and our clear links with them are seriously hindered. This is why sittings are unsuccessful in the presence of hostile minds. Those who wish to scientifically test the existence of us in Spirit must first look to their hearts before their intellect, textbooks or their own stony beliefs. Open-mindedness and sincere kindness are essential ingredients for successful communication to occur.

But let us now move on.

Seen by us, the meeting-place is of little importance and its walls do not entomb us as they do you; we can pass through them because we vibrate at a much higher rate than the physical atoms of the bricks. What we are conscious of is a vibrant pulsating electromagnetic light, a vast battery of life-power upon which we may draw and with which we must successfully blend in order to gain good attunement.

Around the immediate area of contact a large band of helpers in my world is carefully gathering and assessing all the electrical, mental and emotional conditions, and is also speaking to people who will try and communicate later. But, although eager to relay their messages, communicators are not allowed to storm the medium: everyone is directed and organized, and chaos is not permitted within the photosphere of sensitivity.

Through the generated power of our minds and auric fields – which we closely blend with Stephen's – communicators then step near the medium and try to be heard, seen or sensed. If their attunement with his mind-frequencies is good, then they are successful (usually in varying degrees). To aid this, around Stephen himself there is another sizeable group of spirit operators charging his electrical fields so that he sits within a highly sensitized sphere of energy. Communicators are then shepherded forward, one or two at a time. It is a very controlled process.

Neither are their messages 'off-the-cuff' haphazard affairs, but they are usually quite well prepared. Communicators have been thoroughly counselled and reminded: 'Your loved ones in the audience cannot see, sense or hear you, but you must try and prove your survival. What can you say; what memories can you bring; what evidence could you give, or facts could you convey which would undoubtedly establish your presence?' They are also carefully advised to *concentrate* at the time of their transmissions and not to mentally 'wander away' or stutter incoherently – though some do just that, being emotionally overwhelmed at the moment of contact.

In the early days of our association I stood very close to my medium and acted as what we term a Control. It was my function to tune my mind so precisely with his that we almost became one individual; communicators then expressed their thoughts to me which were instantly registered by him. In the initial stages of a medium's development, while he is still learning to build his own sensitivity, very often he does not work directly with communicators, but rather with spirit controls. These are highly trained experts in communication who take overall charge of the medium and his work.

There are also others present who monitor his health and vital physical systems while the mediumship is functioning. But once a medium's abilities are strengthened and well-established the controls step aside and the sensitive then works directly with the communicators on a positive mind-to-mind link. That is why people have sometimes remarked about Stephen's messages, 'It's just as though the spirit people are standing beside you. You make them very real.' To which he has often replied, 'They *are* very real.'

Because we are human beings and not automatons or machines, communication sometimes falters, breaks down or appears to fail. It is then my task to direct Stephen back on the right track. I will often 'step in' mentally and say: 'You have made a mistake,' or 'Go back over it.' I have even had to tell him: 'Your recipient is lying,' when one man constantly refused evidence we knew to be true.

My medium hears far more from us than ever he

expresses and that is because thought is lightning-fast, many thoughts conveyed in the time it takes to physically vocalize one word.

Our mental links are sometimes so subtle and tenuous that it comes as no surprise when our connections to the medium suddenly break. There is then hurried activity here to do all in our power to re-establish solid contact as quickly as possible.

With so many varying conditions which can adversely affect our success we are always delighted when the meetings go well, for this indicates a good job of work has been accomplished. After all, mediums and guides have difficult tasks, delicate operations: rather like the fine tuning of a radio set into a transmitted station, the wavelength has to be just right. We can, and do, frequently miss our channels.

Because Stephen's abilities are now reasonably established (there is always greater development ahead, and no medium for the spirit world is ever fully developed), he works directly with communicators and often hears their voices as they were on Earth. Sometimes their language is none too polite! This, we believe, adds to the authenticity of the messages because he is often amused by what he hears and therefore spontaneously laughs. He is also sometimes emotionally moved by the deep poignant sadness as certain communicators remember their last moments on Earth, and this often makes audiences realize that what is taking place is indeed a very real process.

Stephen has always had a certain soul-empathy with others, even in childhood. This is a function of his Psychic Being in operation. His soul tunes in to the person speaking to him and he becomes aware of a portion of *their* soul. If someone was in emotional pain he would feel empathy with, and sympathy for, them.

All good mediums are sensitive beings: it has to be so, or they could not be channels for the subtle and refined forces of the Spirit.

Those who don the mantle of service as prophets,

seers, visionaries and mediums must expect their emotions and thoughts to become far more acutely heightened than the average person. It has to be so; a human receiving and transmitting station – or medium – can only be in touch with eternity when the psychic faculties are sharply, finely tuned. And once our co-operators have discovered and unfolded their innate soul sensitivities they cannot ever lose them: they remain operational for ever. This is why we advise all mediums to cultivate tremendous self-discipline and a willpower of iron, and to master control of the self: a medium should always be in full charge of his abilities, and not vice-versa.

It is the medium who 'tunes in' to our world (where we are waiting) – and the medium who 'tunes out' of our wavelengths.

We are not dictators and you are not puppets dancing on our strings. It is always a conscious and willing co-operation between us, for our work is founded upon a mutual link of love, trust and service – not domination.

Behind Stephen, as he works, there can be upwards of eighty spirit helpers surrounding him at large public meetings. But there are also countless other spirits who come to witness demonstrations, too. They know they are not going to get a chance to communicate but nevertheless they remain in the vicinity to observe the powers at work, or occasionally they move unseen amongst audiences and perhaps stand by their special loved ones, trying to convey the thought of their presence and continued care and concern. This has prompted some of the public to say, 'Although I didn't get a message from the medium, I felt my people were there.'

The joining of Two Worlds can be an emotional, soul-stirring experience and it is not uncommon for people in both planes to weep when messages are being relayed. Their souls are touched. But of course there is also much laughter, too, especially when comical memories are transmitted, or when things go wrong.

Sometimes when two or three communicators are waiting near the sphere of sensitivity and one of them is unsuccessful – or recipients are unwelcoming – a new communicator will jump his turn and transmit a brand new link and, of course, Stephen receives it! This is a 'crossed-line' effect, when two messages are coming in at once. Not all spirit people are well-mannered. After all, they are human beings under emotional pressure and we have to make allowances. But through all this confusion Stephen must remain calm at its centre and try to sort it out; sometimes having to start the link again until the lines are 'cleared'.

There have been times when we fully know, before we even try, that messages will go unclaimed by audience members. There are many different reasons for this which I believe Stephen has written of, but the main one is *fear*. Thoughts of public humiliation or embarrassment also make recipients unwilling to participate. In Stephen's case all these fears are groundless, for he conducts himself with dignity in public. But audience fears make our work so very much harder than it already is.

After transmission, communicators often weep at the realization of their success in getting, perhaps, only a few words through to those who love them; or if their links have been refused; or if they have not quite been accurately attuned and Stephen has not heard or sensed them properly. It is regarded as an experiment by my world too; but communicators are not left comfortless. We take them aside, congratulate them, console them and speak about the joy they have added to the evening's events and to their loved ones' lives.

When Stephen is inspired to conclude the meeting, which often lasts two and a half hours, applause rings out in the theatre and we know our service has been appreciated.

But we are not always certain at this time just how much of what we have transmitted has actually been received by him and delivered to the audience. This is because we are concentrating on our medium as well as focusing on communicators and energy-levels. (There are even doctors monitoring Stephen's heart-beat to ensure he is not overstrained or anxious. If he is, then they step closer and calm him by the power of their thoughts and inspire him to slow down and not to rush. There is a great deal of hidden activity out of physical sight.)

Afterwards there is usually a celebration on our side, a raising of joyous voices which makes every effort worthwhile, during which we have the inevitable dissection of the evening: not only by the communicators but also by our experts here. We are learning all the time.

We then leave Stephen's orbit and go our separate ways. We are not always beside him: spirit controls gather to perform specific functions and then depart until the next call to service.

No one in my world is at the beck-and-call of anyone in your world.

No one with you has the power to demand or command us to do their bidding; and we are governed by the same laws here. We cannot make anyone on Earth accept our teachings or inspiration.

Free will is a Universal Law.

After service, mediums often notice their personal power reserves have been drawn upon; and this is so. All mediums utilize their own energies when working with us. The physicist's definition of work is anything which burns or expends energy. That is correct. In a medium's case the main loss of energy dissipates through the physical nervous system.

But the more power the audience gives the less of the medium's own energies are utilized. All public demonstrators feel slightly tired after services simply because a great deal of power is burned up in their trying to convey meanings succinctly, as well as to physically conduct the meeting. It is very stressful to stand before a thousand people with nothing in your head except utter trust in the voice of the spirit, and a prayer that we will maintain our mental connections with you and prove our presence to the listeners.

The communications are 'live'; there is no script or rehearsal, it is all spontaneous; and it either spontaneously succeeds or fails. But *we* will not fail you.

It is my custom to remain close to Stephen for a short while after working, to inspire him to rest and get plenty of sound sleep, pure water, good food and clean air, for these are the constituents which build up the physical body and replenish the nervous system. I also impart some of my own power reserves to help him in these processes. His spirit will never tire, for the spirit is forever linked to the eternal source of life, the Great Spirit – God – though the mind can sometimes become quite weary and in need of a change of surroundings and tranquillity.

The great tasks upon which we in the Spirit are engaged, this work of spreading knowledge of an eternal life and all the deeper implications it brings in its wake, calls upon all the physical, mental, emotional and spirit resources of the human instrument; and we feel extremely grateful and privileged whenever we link with mediums who have dedicated their lives to helping us preach the good news: *There is no death. You cannot die. You are as immortal as Consciousness Itself.*

To all Servants of the Spirit I say: never be downhearted or allow doubts to assail you about your magnificent efforts to spiritualize and enlighten mankind. You are representatives of the greatest power in the Universe – the Great Spirit of Life. You are His Ambassadors, carriers of the Living Light of the Spirit, a light which will ever guide you and never falter. Neither will it ever be extinguished.

We are here in your world to stay.

We need no church, no special creeds, no certain race or person – but we will work with all those whose hearts are pure and whose minds are fixed upon helping mankind towards the discovery of eternal spirit truths.

Go forward then with love in your hearts and the desire to help all those who stand in spiritual darkness and ignorance of the truth, and we will step with you.

We will not forsake you, or leave you comfortless.

We are your friends and we love you.

We are attracted to you by the goodness and compassion in your hearts.

There is still much work for us to do: the harvest is plenty but the labourers are few. But if you will only co-operate with us, together we can change the world.

7

'O Great White Spirit . . .'

(White Owl delivers an invocation prior to rendering
public service.)

Oh Great White Spirit,
Thou who art omnipresent and omnipotent,
the Great Mind interpenetrating all forms of life
and consciousness,
we raise thanks from our hearts and minds
for all Thy blessings which have surrounded us
this past week,
and right throughout our lives.

Gathering together in Thy name,
we wait within these sacred walls
to hold a service of holy communion between souls
on Earth
and those in Higher Realms of Light,
this ground having been hallowed by the Power of Love
generated by these, Thy Children.

Grace us now with a mighty blessing upon our efforts
to bridge Two States of Being
with a clear and flowing link of Thought,
so that the Great Message of
Eternal Life
and
Eternal Love
may be proclaimed once more
by Thy Messengers of Light.

Silently have we come from realms of higher
consciousness,
patiently we seek Thy Spirit of Truth
that it may permeate our Thoughts,
Words and Deeds.

Most Gracious Spirit,
Mother/Father Principle,
we cannot help but be mindful at this time
of all Thy Children,
in all Thy Kingdoms,
who feel so bereft of compassion in their lives;
those who feel neglected,
lonely, comfortless and afraid,
believing that the very light of their days
has been extinguished by the darkness of grief,
personal loss,
or the stifling powers of hate and ignorance.
Grant us, we pray,
further strength that we might hold aloft a
Torch of Truth,
to light a new way for them;
so that they may know they are
openly Loved,
secretly Guided,
and ever Supported
by the strong hands of Ministering Angels,
both seen
and unseen.

O Great White Spirit,
just as You have never forsaken
any of your Earth Children
(not one)
especially at their times of greatest need;
so shall we stand always in readiness
to render Service to them
through You.

All we ask in this Great Work
which we have undertaken to help

spiritualize the Universal Family
is that the Inspiration,
Guidance and Courage
will flow unabated
from the Wellspring of Eternal Light,
until the glorious day dawns when
Peace reigns in the Souls of all Your People,
in every World of Consciousness.

We also now transmit
a special Stream of Thought
for the Animal Kingdoms on Earth:
that Man may come to Love them
as he ought to Love himself,
and give them the respect he should
show to his Brothers and Sisters.
May the time come soon when these,
Thy Gentle Creatures,
are set free from oppression
and the cutting chains of cruelty
which have been locked and fettered
on them by Mankind.
May their innocent blood be spared.

Universal Father
and Mother,
Unfailing Guiding Light,
bathe us all now
in the Radiance of Your Wisdom.

And accept from me,
One of Thy many humble servants,
my heartfelt thanks;
and those of this man through whom I speak
(my Earthly friend) –
and also the sincere gratitude of these,
Thy People, who have gathered here tonight
in the name of Eternal Love.

May Peace be ever with us:
Surely, so let it be ...

8

Home-Boy

Spirit guidance from White Owl, and many other
friends in the next world, has dramatically influenced
the direction of my life several times; not the least
of which was a spirit-predicted move away from my
native Wales to live in the North-East of England, in
1985.

As readers of my previous books will already know,
I spent two dreadfully soul-searching, long hard years
living in the freezing-cold town of Gateshead, Tyne
and Wear, and I was more than glad to return down-
country, in 1987, to once more plant myself back in
rain-soaked Welsh soil.

It was lovely to be home again and to pick up old
friendships. Being back, however, inevitably meant
missing the North and its warm-hearted people. Such
is life! But what I certainly *didn't* miss was the dis-
gustingly dirty catchment area I'd felt trapped inside
up in Gateshead: like a twittering frantic bird in a
stinking cage I prayed many nights to be released
into freedom. No tears were shed over leaving that
awful council estate, I can tell you! Yet, little did I
know, returning to Wales meant I'd be jumping out
of the fire and right into the frying-pan!

But the funniest part of the wrench, which friends
and I undertook without professional removers because I had no money (we never learn, do we?), was
getting my battered 1940s piano into the rented truck.
The upright honky-tonk joanna had only cost £40 in

a clearance junk shop (the piano-tuner said I'd been robbed!) but it had a nice deep tone right up to the day of moving, even though it was way off-key.

I stood aghast and full of admiration for my friends Adrian, Graeme and Jim, who threw it up onto the truck as though it weighed just a few ounces instead of a dead-weight ton! But the story at the other end of the journey was quite different as another three of us (and three weaklings at that) staggered to shift it up the fifty-five stone steps into my new flat in Swansea. We could hardly budge it without wrenching our backs or getting a few spontaneous bars of 'Land of Hope and Glory' out of it! The air was positively blue and so were we!

Three buckets of sweat later, we'd finally got it up the first flight – one step at a time, amid cries of 'Allez-Hoop!' as it clanked and zinged on the concrete stairs. And as if the backbreaking agony wasn't enough, they nearly dropped the bloody thing on my foot – *twice*!

But to be back in Wales was marvellous and, except for the exasperating strain of moving, the spirit world had been very kind, for my new flat was right next door to my old friend Jeff. The Other Side had 'engineered' it so precisely that I returned to the *same* block of flats and *exactly the same* landing I'd moved away from two years earlier. In fact, my new place was right *next door* to my original flat.

It was just as though I'd never been away, but it was only after these events had taken place that both Jeff and I realized the Spirit World had meticulously planned it all years previously, with some greater purpose in mind (to be shortly revealed).

Looking back, we could clearly see the paranormal signs our spirit friends had given, making it a quite remarkable achievement.

It had all started when I first left my Dad's home in 1981 and discovered that flat 19 was free in a nearby maisonette block, so I knocked at the door. It was empty, but out trotted an old lady from number 20, next door. This was chatty old Muriel, the singing drunk who could give the best lubricated rendition of 'Oh, We Ain't Gotta Barrel o' Money' I'd ever heard.

'Come on in, love, and have a gander about,' she beckoned, 'my place is the same as number 19's.' And, being a born nosey-parker, I did.

So the first flat I had seen in that block was Muriel's, and shortly afterwards I became her neighbour – the proud tenant of number 19, where I lived for five years.

The next piece of the spirit jigsaw fell into place just before I moved away from Swansea, to live in Gateshead. I told Jeff, whose family had often been so kind to me when my larder was empty:

'Look, your grandmother's dying of cancer and you're living too far away from her to offer daily help. Why don't you ask the council for my flat (number 19) *before* I give the keys in? You might get it.' And he did, which also fulfilled a really strange spirit prediction delivered to us years previously.

Five years earlier, we'd been drinking coffee at 19 when quite out of the blue – about six inches above Jeff's head – there had come a physical sound manifested by the Spirit World. Both of us gawped at each other as the distinct tones of tinkling wind-chimes sang out in the empty air. Furthermore, they were *my* door-chimes which were then currently hanging behind my front door at 19.

I dashed out into the hallway to examine them, but they weren't moving: the door was firm closed and there wasn't a breath of air about. Anyway, the ghostly wind-chimes we had heard had emanated from above Jeff's head in my living-room, not in the hall.

'Jeff,' I announced spookily, 'It's a message for you. You're going to move out of your parents' home into a place of your own – in about four months time, just after Christmas.'

'How on earth can you say that?'

'Because a spirit voice is telling me so.'

And it was right. He got his flat on the outskirts of the city.

But years later, when I'd just left number 19 to move to England, those ghostly chimes proved even more accurate, for the council agreed he should live closer to his ailing grandmother and they agreed to his request – and he was granted tenancy of number 19, the very place in which we'd both heard those mysterious spirit bells . . .

Quite clever of the Other Side really and, of course, on my return to Wales two years later I became his new neighbour when the authorities gave me the keys to number 20 – old Muriel's home, which was the very first flat I'd seen in that maisonette block!

(I don't believe in coincidence.)

Anyway, I soon settled in, but only after recovering from a bout of nervous exhaustion which so completely shattered me at the time that I thought the TV newscaster was speaking Martian – the strange soul's words kept fading in and out as though her microphone was faulty. But nastier experiences were to follow.

I soon learned Swansea had drastically changed while I'd been away. The state of the maisonette block was now much worse and some odd tenants had moved in.

In one of the flats lived an old dear we'd nicknamed 'Slack': she was very short, very round, very fat and very dirty. Her long greasy yellowy-grey hair was always plastered to her head and hanging like rats' tails down to her shoulders. On several occasions I'd lamented to Jeff, 'If you rolled frozen chips up in it, they'd probably cook themselves in five minutes.' Even though quite old, she could walk, talk, move and had most of her faculties, poor soul, so I felt there was no excuse for her uncleanliness.

Said one of Slack's disgruntled neighbours: 'Do you know, she's been here thirteen years and she's never once washed her bed sheets?'

And if she opened her door as you passed, you were knocked sideways off your feet by the most disgusting smell wafting out: sweat, dirt, stale body odour, heavy fried fat particles hanging in the air and sticking to your clothes and face, and even – yes, I'm sorry, readers – but a *down-beneath's* smell. It was so revolting that in the end I learnt to hold my breath until my face was bright blue, while galloping outside into the fresh air.

When the poor dear did eventually move, being carried away owing to sickness, the council immediately arrived before the flat had a chance to go cold and *completely* emptied it, chucking her tawdry belongings onto an open-backed lorry. Then my jaw hit my chest as I watched the three men donning white plastic spacesuits, sealed hoods, gloves and shoes, then special face-masks and eye-goggles until they looked like something out of *Star Wars*. No germs would have dared to approach them, but even through all that protection they were pulling wrinkly faces and scrunching up their noses as they moved in with back packs and high-powered spray-guns to fumigate the whole dwelling.

Amazed, I stood up on the balcony as the fascinating scene unrolled, when a female neighbour (often prone to appearing in public with an old pair of elastic knickers on her head, covering freshly washed hair) joined me to witness the sad spectacle.

'Poor Slack,' I murmured.

'Dirty old cow,' she said, then scuttled back indoors.

Saying goodbye to Slack wasn't the only farewell I had to make in Swansea; the peaceful home city I'd known had radically changed in the two years I'd been away. Its crime rate had soared beyond all recognition and many people just didn't feel safe on the streets any more. The newspaper regularly splashed horrific stories across its front pages: terrifying accounts of murder, arson, rape, child abuse, theft and senseless violence.

About a mile from my flat one young man was murdered in his own front garden, the slaughter being executed by machete. His assailants almost severed his head from his body. In the same area, a frail pensioner suddenly woke at 4 a.m. to find a masked raider leaning over her bed with a carving-knife glinting in his hands. And one deaf, and partially blind, old lady awoke one morning to discover her bedsit had been ransacked and turned upside-down during the night. She had been asleep in it at the time, and the vandals had urinated all over her bed, and then smeared their excreta on the walls.

Another newspaper headline reading 'Our Mean and Cruel City' told of a wrecked home where the thugs, before they left, had cut off a pet bird's head.

(What on earth is happening to the people in our world?)

Immigrant Asian families were also being harassed by delinquent teenagers who chased their children through the streets with cricket bats spiked by six-inch nails, and the whole feeling in the city was coarse and aggressive and smacked of hell, some of which I was about to experience for myself . . .

Into the flats came two young lads whose parents couldn't cope with them, and we soon learned why. In their first week of residence they'd smashed every window in their home and there were continuous rounds of screaming fights during one of which a shot-gun was fired four times.

The days were noisy and unpredictable and the nights were impossible, too. There wouldn't be a book long enough to catalogue the times I rang the police in the early hours, begging them to silence the youngsters' blasting pop music and fighting. But after each visit, as the police car drove away, the volume dramatically increased in defiance of complaint, and then stayed louder until dawn.

Decent people can't live with others who have no respect for law and order, and for the next three years I was plagued to death by tenants' noise, suffering constant sleep deprivation. I've always been a light sleeper (I can hear a fly snore at thirty paces) but now I couldn't fall into REM sleep (rapid eye-movement sleep, where the body drinks in its deepest refreshment).

Within weeks, my eyes were red, sore and as dry as sandpaper, and I was thoroughly irritable, short-tempered, nervous and dead-beat tired. I felt like a walking zombie from the film *Night of the Living Dead*. But worse than all this, since the arrival of those lads an array of other dubious characters began gathering at all hours of the day and night in the dark grounds outside. Subsequently, crime took an immediate upsurge but we tenants failed to evict our problem-makers, even though we'd signed official petitions and letters of complaint.

It didn't take long to realize that I was once again living in hell. But what could I do?

Fear of feeling trapped by my circumstances forced

107

me to use some cash my Dad had given me to buy a small car and quickly learn to drive. There's nothing like necessity to get you moving and, at least when mobile, I reasoned I'd be able to escape trouble when necessary. Friends, however, immediately fell into apoplectic fits and howled with derision at the thought of me behind a 'heavy steel killing-machine'! And Jeff, ever amusing, drily announced: 'I wouldn't like to be in a car with *you* on the motorway – you'll be doing fifteen miles an hour, like *Clara Cluck*! (whomsoever she is?) God help the other drivers!'

But, with characteristic determination, I got my little Ford and off I went. Mind you, I did wonder if each time I took the wheel, the police should be warned to clear the roads! Witty friends, of course, reckoned, 'It isn't the roads that need clearing, Stephen – it's the pavements!'

'You wait! I'll shock you all!' I admonished. And indeed I did! With less than eleven lessons the big Test Day arrived and I sat in the Ministry of Transport building with several nervous candidates, but I was as cool as a cucumber while everyone else sweated golf-balls, desperately keeping up a pretence of being calm. I soon realized why.

Suddenly a door flew open and, one by one, in slithered some grey-faced, blue-lipped zombies in trilby hats: the dreaded examiners! 'What a motley crew,' said the plump girl chewing bubble gum next to me. 'You watch now,' she continued, 'and six coffin-bearers with a full box will be in.' I must say they did look miserable. '*C'est la vie*,' I said, gulping with a dry throat and inwardly praying, 'Please God, give me a human being.' Then they sharply shouted out their victims' names and marched them out into the sunshine.

I was the only one left. 'They've forgotten me,' I

grinned at my driving instructor seated beside me, when all at once a tall smart man walked through the door. He looked quite normal.

'Mr O'Brien?'

(Thank you, God.)

My faith in the deity restored, I couldn't understand why my teacher looked aghast, until I later discovered that Mr Normal was the boss of the entire complex! However, from the moment I sat in the car, did the test, came back and answered the questions, I hadn't been out twenty minutes and had completed a perfect drive – not one mistake. My examiner didn't mark his paper once.

'You've passed.'

'Oh, I'm chuffed!' I said as I flung my L-plates twenty feet up into the air. *Now I had my wheels and my freedom*, which shocked my driving instructor because in my mock test just an hour earlier I'd nearly killed us both on a box-junction!

So off I went, racing about everywhere, never even walking to the corner shop for a loaf of bread – and within a month I was overweight. But how I loved to speed! Like a fighter pilot on his first mission I zoomed up open country roads and motorways faster than a bat out of hell.

So much for *Clara Cluck*!

On one fast stretch, all of a sudden I had a tremendous sensation that 'someone' was sitting in the back of the car; I'd actually heard the rustling of long silk taffeta skirts and was positive I had a ghostly back-seat driver. Jerking my head around, the car swerved slightly out of control – so I had to stop, switch off the engine and have a proper good look. But there was nobody there.

'Stephen,' I muttered, 'you're right off your toot.' (Loopy.) But those Edwardian skirts had been such a real sound that I got out of the car and even opened the boot to check if anything was loose. Later when I told some psychic friends they just laughed.

'Well, you're bound to have ghostly company, aren't you? We who value our lives have been praying like mad for you since the day you got behind that wheel!'

But no matter where I went, I had to eventually drive home.

The two troublesome teenagers and their 'partners-in-crime' were still causing our block a great deal of bother. Following each police call, another wicked act usually took place: my car windows were smashed in three times, the doors were kicked and dented, then the steering wheel and ignition were broken; and one night two boys bodily lifted one side of my car up off the road while a third removed the wheels. Every evening after this, before retiring, I'd waddle out onto the communal landings and glance down at the car to see all was well – until one night I got a shock: across the road I spied a dirty-looking youth in jeans and a leather jacket who, once his eyes met mine, ran like fury towards our flats.

I immediately panicked, and to this day I don't know what made me do it but I quickly grabbed Sooty, my cat, locked my door and hammered on Jeff's until he answered it, bewildered.

'Let us in!' I gabbled. 'Trouble's coming!' And I was right: I must have been inspired because as we fastened Jeff's door the youth smashed all the entrance hall glass with half a building-brick and then ran up to our landing. But the strange thing was, he battered furiously with the brick on Jeff's door, behind which we both stood – not mine.

Opening it, together we faced the heavily drugged twenty year-old: his eyelids were dazed but still flickering, he wasn't drunk for there was no smell of it on his breath. Swaying deliriously and drooling at the mouth, with blood pouring from cuts and bruises all over a recently beaten up face, he stood defiantly, clasping the brick fast, lifting it up and demanding to know:

'Where's the drugs?'

'You've got the wrong place,' I said, loud and boldly. 'Try downstairs.' And, stunned by my strength, off he went to hammer on another door.

'It's a good job you knocked,' said Jeff.

'Two are stronger than one,' I replied.

But how I wish I'd had company when I was later attacked by some of our new tenants' other 'friends'. It happened in the dead of mid-winter, one night when the snow lay thick and hard on the ground; the kind of freezing weather which prevents getting a good foothold no matter how hard you try. As I stepped warily out of my car and slid in the darkness towards the entrance hall, quickly – without warning – I suddenly felt the sting of compacted ice hitting my face. Underneath the windows where the troublemakers lived stood twenty-five angry delinquent yobbos, screaming abuse at passers-by.

They were out for trouble.

As I confronted one of my assailants from the front, another came up unseen from behind and pulled me backwards: I slipped on the ice and crashed to the floor, face-down. The next thing I heard was a rough voice shouting, 'Get him, boys!' as more compacted ice was ground into my neck and my head was pinned down by two pairs of hands and someone's foot. I couldn't move a muscle, they'd locked me into the snow and all I could see out of the corner of one eye was a large booted foot in front of me. Then I panicked because I could hear more crunching footsteps approaching, and I can only remember one flashing thought: 'Oh my God, this is it. One kick in the face and I'm blind.' It all happened so quickly and I was helpless – completely overpowered and frightened. Unable to defend myself against so many, I was paralysed – and even if I could have moved I wouldn't have been able to get a foothold on the glassy pavements.

Though three of them were kicking me, somehow, don't ask me how, I managed to knock their legs and scrabble upright and hit them away as I quickly dashed through the door, sliding and falling, then slamming it tight shut behind me.

Shaking from head to foot, and breathless, I ran up to my flat, panting, as fast as my wobbling legs could carry me. It seemed an eternity before I could get that quivering key into the lock, I just fumbled and shook until it eventually clicked. Then once inside I slammed the door and instantly fell into an armchair, and also into shock with the realization that I'd been mugged.

After several minutes trying to regain my strength, trembling towards the telephone, I rang the police – but they didn't want to know. The bored officer said, 'Well, it's very bad weather tonight and we don't have many cars on the road.'

'But I've been attacked. Can't you disperse them before they injure someone else, someone elderly?'

'Thank you,' he said disinterestedly, as the phone clicked and the line went dead . . .

He was my only hope of support, for Jeff had gone out for the night and no-one else in the block gave a damn whether other tenants lived or died.

All I could do was patiently wait for the police, but no-one came; and the noisy rabble only melted away two rowdy hours later, after hassling other innocent folk.

By then, as well as being thoroughly shaken I was also furious because they'd not only got away with blue-murder again, but also thought they were beyond reproach and totally unaccountable for their actions. *I was livid*. 'Everyone should be answerable for their actions,' I seethed; but there was no-one listening, only Sooty, who came purring to my side to give soothing comfort to her friend.

Still disturbed and quaking, I retired early after making sure the door was securely fastened: I bolted it, latched the Yale lock, then turned the cheap mortice deadlock three times and left the key still in it on the inside. There was absolutely no way they were going to break in and finish off the job, not without a struggle anyway.

But try as I might I couldn't relax. I was tossing, turning and sweating until way past three in the morning before I eventually drifted into a very light sleep.

The nightmares keeping me awake were 'What if they'd decided to get me in the house? Who would care? They'd only have to cut the phone wires – as they'd done before – smash the door through, and the end would come quickly.'

My vivid imagination knew that had I been killed outside on the icy pavement the police might have eventually arrived saying, 'Oh, so he's dead, is he? Yes, well, we'll just have a potter around and see if we can find out who did it.' Justice in Britain just doesn't seem to exist any more – not for the Just anyway.

Several days passed and I was still very sore and bruised when concerned friends advised: 'Stephen, you *must* get out. There's no way the council will move those trouble-makers.' But every official claimed it was 'extremely difficult to evict tenants. Even with

113

a Court Order it could take six months to a year, and even then there's no guarantee they'll be out: courts don't like depriving people of shelter.'

'Well, what the hell is the law *for*?' I demanded, 'to support the victims or the criminals?'

Their silence infuriated me all the more.

'The law, sir, is an *ass*!' I quoted vehemently. 'If tenants have more than ten complaints against them, the police should have the power to investigate.' But the only reply I heard was my own voice muttering: 'Stephen, you don't belong in this world; there ain't no justice here and neither is there peace of mind.'

Inside I was bubbling with anger. But what can you do when you're caught in a poverty-trap? Only money can break the chains, and I was broke. Wealth buys freedom in the Western world, but if you haven't got any you just have to suffer the consequences . . .

However, I was grateful for one thing: despite getting on each other's nerves, as friends often do, living next door to Jeff turned out to be a godsend. For the first time in my life I had at least *one* decent neighbour; an increasingly rare commodity these days, and one which the spirit world had definitely prearranged because this aided the formation of Voices Management.

Voices (its name was given to me by the spirit world) is the professional organization Jeff and I set up to co-ordinate my national tours and public appearances after my first book, *Visions of Another World*, was released in September 1989 and became a bestseller. Jeff became my manager, rather reluctantly at first, ('because you're such a bloody perfectionist'). But what better arrangement than medium and manager living next door to each other? Besides working together, when times were rough and I was out of food all I had to do was knock on his door and cadge some chips, and several suppers were made by combining our last ingredients and sharing a meal in this way.

I was really glad when Voices was born; to have good management at last was a pure delight, for I felt that I had suffered so badly at the hands of several societies and promoters who'd been far from professional, or honest with me. If you'd said to some of them: 'Right, there's an empty hall – put a thousand people in it and organize some chaos' – they couldn't have done it.

By November 1989, after an exhausting and trouble-stricken tour, I'd had 'a gut's full' (as we say in Wales) and Voices quickly assumed all responsibility for my venues, press and media engagements, plus other aspects of promotion work such as the merchandising of inspirational greeting cards, educational audio-cassettes and colour souvenir picture-programmes, and other items, which were made available to the public by mail order, and at meetings. (See page 303 for details.)

Before Voices, I felt that I had suffered terrible mismanagement, and Spiritualists were by far the worst administrators. They'd book halls and either not advertise properly (which meant poor attendances) or else there weren't adequate lights or – worst of all the sins in a large venue – no microphone system. At one 400-strong meeting I specifically informed the organizing committee that my voice wouldn't carry in their leisure centre so I'd need powerful microphones. 'OK,' they said, but when I arrived at the packed out hall (and physical bodies swallow up acoustics), you guessed it – not a microphone was in sight. Furthermore, my protests were promptly squashed with:

'Other mediums have worked here, and *they* didn't need them.'

'Maybe not, but I *do*.'

'Well, it's too late now – you'll have to manage without,' said the pompous secretary. At the time I had a sore throat and then spent the next few hours using all my energies screaming my lungs out to be heard when, had some forethought been forthcoming, I could have better used them in linking with the Other Side.

This kind of selfish thoughtlessness cripples my work and morale, for, as you can probably guess, most of the hard-of-hearing often sit right at the back, even when there are empty seats in the front! Funnily enough, I once heard a medium say to such an old dear in the back row:

'Can you hear me, my dear?'

'Pardon?'

'I said "*Can you hear me?*"'

'Not very well, I'm a bit deaf.' To which the irate medium returned:

'Well, there are plenty of empty seats in the front. It's your own fault for sitting at the back, you silly old duck!'

Seating arrangements used to be another huge bugbear: people would bob their heads about all night, unable to see me clearly. Chairs were hard and uncomfortable and in the intervals people were often overheard complaining of 'a numb bum'!

Adding insult to injury, many venues were also freezing cold in the winter. Now, who wants to exchange a comfortable warm home for a miserable, damp hall with rock-hard seats?

And on the other side of the fence, in all my years of travelling I know for a fact that nearly all mediums are unpaid, or desperately underpaid workers, many being left way out of pocket after their services. Contrary to media belief, Spiritualist churches are generally very poor indeed; as registered charities they struggle to survive on meagre coppers tossed into the collection plate.

Once, years back, I remember leaving an electricity bill and a few weeks rent to buy a smart suit, shirt and tie – for shame's sake, because I was to share a theatre meeting with veteran medium and author, Doris Collins. I eventually purchased the whole outfit for less than £72, which was the best bargain I could find.

I tried my new clothes out at a church service in the Welsh valleys at which two hundred people attended, and the president praised my appearance. I explained about the debt and was told confidentially, 'Don't you worry, Stephen, we'll help you out with it. We'll make sure you're all right.' I was very grateful and after the service – which grossed about £350 for repairs to their damaged roof – some crumpled banknotes were folded into my hand which went straight into my pocket.

Outside, in the drizzling rain, I opened them and was absolutely stunned, shocked beyond belief. I'd been given the princely sum of £2, which didn't even cover the petrol.

Ridiculous media claims of mediums being millionaires are absolute nonsense. I personally know, and have been privileged to have shared the platform with, very many sensitives in Britain and they work extremely hard for very little – if any – financial reward. It's only the few who make a decent living. And jolly good luck to them: 'The labourer is worthy of his hire'.

Most mediums must be content to just dream of the kind of wealth that many of their critics possess. But then, it's good to have a dream.

Since my earliest years I've always been a day-dreamer: an idealist, a follower of causes; something

117

which made me feel as though I was lost on Earth.

I was a stranger here, a sensitive changeling whose mind and spirit floated high in mental clouds but whose feet were firmly rooted in clay.

There's no doubt that my childhood dreams were responsible for what I am today, for yesterday's dreams are tomorrow's realities.

Little Dreamer

dream your dreams
    little dreamer
wrapped around in velvet sleep
breathing deeply through repose,
an angel crowned with golden curls
    playtime's over
    and night unfurls
    her dark blue robe of starpoint lights
dream on
    little dreamer
snug beneath pink-quilted sheets
so warm and soft and tight
then float away into blissful sleep
and leave the blackened night
far behind you –

        to sail the tides of time and space
        in a sailboat made of paper lace
        entwined with silver threads of light:
        onward through cloud-mountained night
        into the land of peppermint dreams
        past flights of dragons
        your dreamboat gleams,
        manned by a soul
        who dreams and schemes

and way up there on the cloudbank's height
floating free and rushing like the wind
you'll plan your little plans
and set tomorrow's course with your rudder in your hand

and then fly high
  little dreamer
over the milky seas so white
through rising waves of uncertainty and doubt,
flapping the flag of masterplan
and shining brilliant hope-lamps (that'll never go out)
as your paper-lace dreamboat rocks and sails
through all the pictures of your ancient past,
and all the future roads your life entails

then go skim the verdant trees
becoming the spirit of the breeze
that beats the cornfields as you fly
  soar high
    little dreamer
  soar high:
    circling the air in your paperwish boat,
    and building tomorrow within your soul –
      for come the sunrise, you will inwardly know
      the magic that'll free you
        free you
          yes
        free you!
      from a dull drab workaday world,
      and you'll see a new beginning:
        new hopes
        new pathways
        as yet unfurled

but now set a new tack and sail away,
kissing a sunset glorified,
over cliffs of conscious thought
and sinking back to mother earth
  where then
  little dreamer
you'll awake, my child –
leaping and laughing, you'll arise!
  dancing on earth
  what was skipped in heaven
  deep in the realms of a midnight sky

night-time travellers
grow up to be
  little dreamers
  like you and me

    so dream your dreams,
    don't set them apart –
    remember them always
    and lock them in your heart

For this evening's flight is tomorrow's reality
and twilight hopes are sunrise actualities

9

The Burning of the Witches

Young dreams are often broken when the cold light
of adult day slices through your life. It happened to
me recently.

My friend – whom I shall call Paul – and I had been
boyhood pals since as far back as I could remember;
as kids we'd gone everywhere together and people
thought we were more like brothers than friends.
Although Paul was olive-skinned with dark brown
eyes, and I was as white as a lily, we both had
jet-black hair and the same lean build.

He was my boyhood best friend; we were two
young lads who confided childish thoughts and secrets
in each other as well as meeting after school, playing
and passing the carefree days of youth in laughter,
fun and games. On special evenings I'd really look
forward to visiting his house way up on the steep
hill because in his garden he'd set up a telescope;
and there, on bright cold nights, together we'd gaze
in awestruck wonder at the huge silver-faced moon,
both excited over anything to do with space and
astronomy. Amazement was our constant companion
whenever we approached the stars.

'I can see the moon's craters!' My breathing almost
stopped as I moved aside and Paul pressed close to the
eye-piece.

'The colours are *brilliant*!' he exclaimed.

'And they're shining, like angel's wings.'

'Do you think there's life up there, Stephen?'

'Oh I don't know,' I said, languishing thoughtfully on the soft evening grass, as Paul relinquished his window on the universe and joined me. For what seemed like an eternity we laid back gazing up at the twinkling stars. 'It didn't look very lively, did it?' I said, at length.

'No, but I bet there's life on Mars.'

'Can you see it through the telescope?' I asked, excitedly sitting up, already half on my feet and eager to view the skies again.

'Yes – it's great! I'll show you – ' and Paul was now standing beside me, positioning the lens. 'It's only a flickering light but it's a kind of red colour. There it is – see!'

And I put my best eye forward and steadied the telescope with my trembling thrilled hands, totally absorbed in the wonder of the orange planet, as I felt Paul leaning on my shoulder while I relished every sparkle of the twinkling crimson dot in the cold night sky. And, as children are, we were made breathless by the sheer beauty of it all; captivated by the splendid majesty and grandeur of outer space.

How we dreamed, we boys, of 'walking' in space and visiting distant planets. We were two little dreamers, completely spellbound by the vastness of the universe.

Paul and I had some great times together – everyone needs a buddy and we were real chums, until the day our childish dreams vaporized on the sad afternoon we parted, when our youth vanished into the strange world of 'growing up'.

We were both eleven at the time, and had successfully passed our 'eleven-plus' examinations which allowed us the honour of attending grammar school. In those days there were a few to choose from and I secretly hoped we'd go to the same one.

'Where will you go, Paul?'

We were sitting on the high school wall on a hot summer's afternoon, wearing our short trousers and dangling our legs in the sunshine.

'Don't know ... there's three, but my Mam wants me to go to ...'

He paused.

The words were obviously difficult to find and suddenly the air between us stood still. I knew he was going to say something dreadful, something upsetting; my heart thudding against my ribs told me so. Paul was my best friend and bad news was coming. I jumped from the wall and stood silently, waiting in the sunshine and awkwardly tracing the pavement lines with the toe of my shoe ...

'I'm going to a different school than you,' he said.

My body froze.

I'd known it; I'd felt it.

I was silent: we were saying goodbye; and I hate goodbyes.

In those quiet harrowing moments I think I experienced my first powerful blow to the heart. As all young people do, I'd innocently and trustingly invested emotions in my best and closest friend, and the parting was painful.

After what seemed like forever, our eyes met again and I could see he was upset too, so, falteringly I managed to say:

'Will you keep in touch?'

'Oh ... yes ... of course ...'

Then we went our separate ways, looking backwards at each other over our shoulders and giving a boyish wave. But, from that day onwards, though many memories of my friend Paul moved many times within my thoughts, I didn't see or hear from him again ...

* * *

It was seventeen years later that I opened the letter; I was twenty-eight then. I had sat down to read it, which was just as well. It was written as a result of seeing me interviewed on BBC's TV news about a mediumship meeting I was taking in aid of blind and handicapped children. Scanning the bitter lines I was shocked by the comments – penned by a Christian.

How on earth could sensible people say such cruel things?

'What you're doing is fundamentally *wrong*,' continued the writer. 'I married a Baptist woman and we know your work is contrary to God's teaching and the Bible, and you should stop.'

And the letter was signed – by Paul . . .

There are moments in one's life when the mind is so profoundly stunned that feelings, thoughts and words seem utterly absent. This was one of them, presented to me by my closest boyhood companion and best friend.

But this wasn't the first time, and it won't be the last, that I and other mediums have been placed in the stocks and had narrow-minded religious bigotry hurled at us.

Regrettably, and to the great shame of Christianity, history reveals that in the Dark Ages the early Christian church led an enthusiastic crusade against countless psychic sensitives and nearly succeeded in extinguishing the psychic light from Earth. Behind these actions was a Bible text which reads *'Thou shalt not suffer a witch to live.'*

This phrase (the origin of which is still regarded by some Biblical scholars as unclear, and it's now widely thought to have been a latter-day 'addition' to the text) seemed to grant the early Christian church absolute power to maim, imprison, torture, persecute and burn to death countless healers, psychics and mediums for fifteen hundred years or so.

It's impossible to place an accurate figure on those who lost their lives, but it surely must number in the millions.

'Witchery' was possessed by individuals who, by any means other than practices acceptable to the established Christian church of that time, healed the sick, saw visions of the future, found lost objects or persons, or conjured up the spirits of the so-called 'dead'. These acts were pronounced evil and linked to the Devil and his adversaries; whereas, in fact, all these psychic abilities are perfectly normal functions of the spirit body and are exercised by naturally sensitive people.

Today's Spiritualist Church still actively encourages mediumship within its religious ceremonies, gifted sensitives being allowed to conduct public services and relay spirit communications via their gifts of clairvoyance, clairaudience and clairsentience (clearseeing, -hearing, or -sensing of the presences of loved ones from the Next World). It's all so naturally delivered, and is often an extremely beautiful, dignified and simple service to witness.

But despite the sincerity of many mediums, since early in history it seems we poor sensitives have never had an easy time of it. A case in point is that of the world's most famous sensitive: The Maid of Orleans – Joan of Arc – who heard spirit voices which guided her to lead the French army to triumphant victory in battle.

Her supernormally heard voices angered the Church of her day, but even when she was under threat of agonizing torture she refused to deny their existence.

Exasperated by her sincerity, when but nineteen

years old, in 1431 at Rouen the Church applied the aforementioned text and accused her of 'sorcery and heresy'. She was tried and found guilty, then chained to a stake and burned to death – watched, it's claimed, by more than 10,000 people. Afterwards her blackened and charred remains were thrown into the River Seine.

Poor Joan.

She was, and always had been, a devout Catholic girl, and witnesses claimed she uttered forgiveness to her ecclesiastical accusers, even as she died. As the flames destroyed her youthful body, the last words issuing from her lips were said to have been: 'Tonight, by God's grace, I shall be in paradise.'

But it took 477 years before Joan of Arc was officially beatified by the Christian church on Earth, in 1908, and twelve years later in 1920 she received the honour of sainthood.

Such tragic trials and persecution of the psychically gifted continued unabated for centuries. On British soil, in Scotland, the story of Bessie Dunlop from Lyne, in Ayrshire, is a case in point.

It was in 1576 when Bessie was accused of being 'a witch' and then burned, mainly because people claimed that near her 'the voices of the dead' were heard to speak. Bessie was obviously one of those rare and gifted individuals who possessed what we now know as Physical Mediumship. A physical medium is someone in whose presence the spirit people may manifest in a complete or partly complete, temporary physical body. In Bessie's case the communicators would have constructed, by thought, a 'mask' made of special bodily fluids and plasma – known today as ectoplasm – which would have been withdrawn from the medium and others in the vicinity. Into this they would then have pressed their vocal organs and hence vibrated our atmosphere, and spoke. Bessie Dunlop was what we now call today a Direct-Voice medium.

Paranormalists have long understood these wonderful phenomena and there have been many books written about them, notably an informative array of writings by the brilliant historian and spiritualist writer Arthur Findlay: just two of his excellent titles are *On the Edge of the Etheric* and *The Rock of Truth* (Psychic Press Ltd) both of which are well worthy of serious study.

Such powerfully gifted sensitives like Joan of Arc and Bessie Dunlop are indeed rare individuals and because they stand apart from the crowd they're therefore misunderstood by those with little or no real knowledge of how psychic gifts work.

The last 'witch' may have been burned in England in 1712, but even in modern times psychics have still not escaped trial and punishment, mainly because British law was set against the practice of mediumship since the inception of the two archaic Witchcraft and Vagrancy Acts: 1735 and 1824 respectively. Under these, sensitives could be prosecuted and 'suffer imprisonment by the space of one whole year without bail', for the 'pretence' of 'witchcraft, sorcery, enchantment or conjuration' or even for claiming to 'tell fortunes'. Incredible as it seems today (especially when one thinks of the long lines of palmists at popular seaside resorts), the prison sentence was implemented in the case of modern day Scottish medium Helen Duncan, on 3 April 1944.

Helen was a Spiritualist and a very fine and powerful physical medium in whose presence the 'dead' fully materialized themselves in temporary physical bodies (constructed of the previously mentioned ectoplasm). Her abilities were scientifically tested and proven genuine many times.

Mrs Duncan was arrested by the police while in a state of deep trance during a seance in Portsmouth; such violent action towards a sensitive in a heightened nervous state is always dangerous – in her case this caused her to haemorrhage; nevertheless she was still charged under the Acts and later sent for trial at the Old Bailey in London.

And even though over forty witnesses testified on oath that their loved ones had physically appeared to them, spoke with them and kissed them during Helen's remarkable seances, British law allowed no defence, for it simply didn't recognize the existence of genuine mediumship under the two archaic Acts.

In her defence, Mrs Duncan even offered a courtroom 'test seance' so that the judge and jury might witness her exceptional psychic talents for themselves but – incredibly – this was denied, and she was found guilty of 'pretence' and imprisoned for nine months.

Helen Duncan became known as 'The first martyr of Spiritualism'.

Until the Witchcraft and Vagrancy Acts were more or less 'replaced' in 1951 by the Fraudulent Mediums Act – a much fairer statute which at least recognized that genuine psychic phenomena can occur – the police would often stand at the back of public meetings and sometimes arrest the medium!

Times have changed, thank God, and nowadays we live in a far more civilized, open-minded and educated world. But, thankful though we mediums are that we're no longer burnt, I'm afraid we're still occasionally tortured – mentally, of course.

Even though we're in the Age of Aquarius and the 20th century it's incredible to think that some sensitives still find it necessary to stand up and be counted: and I'm no exception.

In June 1990 I took part in a discussion on Tyne

Tees Television that was transmitted 'live' to millions. The Church was represented by a middle-aged and bespectacled Reverend David Holloway. Why on earth the media invite the clergy to criticize mediums completely baffles me: what has mediumship – the fact that communication takes place between two different states of being – got to do with religion?

Communication has nothing to do with faith – it's a psychic science; a fact, not a belief.

Anyway, let battle commence:

Holloway: It was quite clear when Christ came on earth that there were manifestations of evil. Now I don't believe that a lot of what goes under the name of Spiritualism or mediumship is all genuine. Some of it is bogus, some of it is fake. But there clearly are occasions when certain things happen which are true – but, the Bible makes it clear that we're not to dabble in it.

Presenter: Is it dangerous?

Holloway: I have to say that I believe it is. Some of it doesn't seem so, necessarily, at the beginning. I mean, it's a bit like drug addiction. I mean, you may start with marijuana or something that's innocent and then you gradually go down that line. I mean, a lot of it is very, very innocent ...

Presenter: So presumably, the more you do it the more chance you have of getting into sort of, serious difficulties?

Holloway: Yes, I mean, I would say, of course, as a Christian I believe that Christ is greater than any of the forces of evil and therefore there's release in Him.

Presenter: Well, we have with us tonight, Reverend Holloway, one man who – if I might say – has done it many times before. If I'm not mistaken, Stephen

O'Brien, you've contacted some thirty thousand people, I'm led to believe, who are on the Other Side, as it were: you are a medium. Who is it, or what is it that you make contact with?

Stephen: I make contact with the minds, the spirits, the souls, the personalities of people who have lived here in this world and have now finished with this world and gone into what one man called 'the Kingdom of Heaven'.

Presenter: So in that particular –

Stephen: There is life after death –

Presenter: – yes, and so you agree with Reverend Holloway?

Stephen: No, I don't agree with *everything* he has said. (*Addressing the clergyman*) First of all I would like to say to you I think that the viewpoint you've put forward is very narrow, because Christianity is *not* the only religion, in this country or the rest of the world. There are Buddhists, Mohammedans, there are Spiritualists. Spiritualism is a state-recognized religion registered at the Home Office, with its own ministers. They are ordained, they can conduct naming services, marriages, funerals and – in many cases – don't get paid for it like the Church of England do.

Holloway: . . . Yes, but, I mean I would have to say that . . . I agree, of course . . . there are other religions . . . but as a Christian I believe that Jesus Christ is the way, the truth and the life; and one of the things he came to do actually was to destroy the works of the Evil One. Now, again, I'm not willing to sit in judgement on anybody, but, the question is: 'What is truth?' . . . And . . . one of the reasons why I'm a Christian is because I do believe that Jesus Christ rose from the dead on that first Easter Sunday morning –

Stephen: – So do I –

Holloway: Yes, but what he did was, he made it quite clear, through his apostles, that we're not actually to deal with this sort of thing.

Throughout the above, at no point did I say, or even imply, that the clergyman's belief was similar to 'drug addiction', or that it may have been linked to 'the works of the Evil One', nor that it could be 'bogus' or 'fake'. However, he levelled all these accusations at my calling.

I find that very sad.

It's also worth noting that most of the currently respected spirit guides agree with the opinion that today's Christian Church has strayed so very far away from its origins, and hence the Beneficent Power of God – the exercise of the Living Gifts of the Spirit – can no longer find a dwelling-place within some of its walls or, more importantly, in the hearts of many of its people. But in antiquity, contact with eternity was a reality for the early Christians, as the following startling extract from an ancient book proves. It's taken from *De Anima*, believed to have been written in AD 211 by Roman lawyer, scholar, and early Christian, Tertullian (AD 160-230).

For seeing that we acknowledge spiritual charismata, or gifts, we too have merited the attainment of the prophetic gift. We have now amongst us a sister whose lot it has been to be favoured with sundry gifts of revelation, which she experiences in the spirit by ecstatic vision amidst the sacred rites of the Lord's Day in the church. She converses with angels, and sometimes even with the Lord. She both sees and hears mysterious communications. Some men's hearts she understands, and to them who

131

are in need she distributes remedies. Whether it be in the reading of the Scriptures, or in the chanting of psalms, or in the preaching of sermons, or in the offering up of prayers, in all these religious services, matter and opportunity are afforded her of seeing visions.

After the people are dismissed at the conclusion of the sacred services, she is in regular habit of reporting to us whatever things she may have seen in vision, for all her communications are examined with the most scrupulous care, in order that their truth may be probed. 'Amongst other things,' says she, 'there has been shown to me a soul in bodily shape, and a spirit has been in the habit of appearing to me, not, however, a void and empty illusion, but such as would offer itself to be even grasped by the hand, soft and transparent and of an ethereal colour, and in form resembling that of a human being in every aspect.'

This was her vision, and for her witness there was God, and the apostle Paul most assuredly foretold that there were to be spiritual gifts in the Church.

In my opinion this woman was obviously a practising medium: she was a gifted psychic, healer and clairvoyant who used her abilities to serve the people of her faith.

Tertullian exhibits far more courtesy, intelligence and common sense than many modern-day clergymen when he states that the medium's utterances 'are examined with the most scrupulous care' to find any truth in them. It's also noticeable that the woman's inspiration wasn't ignored or pronounced demonic and evil, neither was it immediately alleged to be 'fakery' or 'against God'.

Two thousand years may have passed, but even today several of my meetings are still picketed by fundamentalists and even one of my book-signing sessions, when the police had to be called to disband them because they were hassling the public and denouncing my autobiography as 'the Devil's Word', a phrase to which I take objection. My work is accomplished through the Power of Love, and it's all about spreading knowledge of the truths revealed to us through spiritual experiences. I also try to bring comfort and hope to people; plus, I believe in God, too – and all roads lead back to the same common Source.

Yet, despite this, many of you will know I've been spat upon, derided, ridiculed in private and public, and in the media by certain Christian Fundamentalist groups – none of whom knew me personally, or had read my books or witnessed my mediumship. If they had, they would have known of my deep respect for the man Jesus, plus his life and work.

'Love ye one another' is not only a tenet I've always upheld but one I've also tried my best to live by. And no matter who criticizes my beliefs, like Joan of Arc I'll stand by what has been revealed to me.

I will never deny the existence of my voices.

Out of interest, let's finally sweep away the incorrect assumption that spirit communication is a modern-day development which has suddenly surfaced under the in-vogue title of New Age Practices.

Here's a very interesting quote from a man who was born about one hundred years before Jesus walked this world: Cicero (106 – 43 BC). He was a Roman statesman, orator and respected intellectual who wrote of eternity and frequent contact with it. But then, the spirit world has always been with us; men have walked and talked with 'Angels' (more correctly translated as 'Messengers') since time began:

> They whose minds scorn the limitations of the body are honoured with the frequent appearance of the spirits. Their voices have been often heard, and they have appeared in forms so visible that he who doubts it must be partly bereft of reason.

Here endeth the history lesson.

10

Two Worlds

Here's an interesting article from my regular monthly contributions to Two Worlds *magazine which features Spiritualism and the Supernormal and was founded in 1887 by Emma Hardinge Britten.*

I've written on many paranormal topics but, after that last chapter, I thought I'd like to share with you this story involving the Teacher Jesus.

It conveys a powerful message to all those who claim to follow or represent Him on Earth.

Waiting for the Master
A Tale of Love, Re-told

The old fisherwoman was very excited as she fussed around her humble kitchen near the shores of Galilee. She tidied and meticulously swept out each of the tiny rooms which were her home, merrily singing away to herself as she went.

Her mind was so full; she could think of nothing else but the wonderful news she'd heard. A great and noble Teacher was to pass through her village some time that day: Jesus was his name – and many had called him a mighty prophet and seer.

And with each sweep of her brush she convinced herself that without doubt it would be *she* who would receive an honoured visit from him. He would stop and rest awhile at *her* home – she was sure of it. She'd prayed so hard for it to be so, and her great faith made her strive all the harder; she wouldn't be found with an untidy home.

As dawn blossomed into mid-morning she wiped her tired brow and ran to the foot of her dusty garden where she leaned over the creaky gate, searching the horizon for her special visitor. But he was nowhere to be seen.

Just then, her gentle eyes fell upon a wizened, thin washerwoman whose back was bent under the weight of the huge basket of wet clothes she was carrying. The old lady laid down the heavy load, stopped at the gate and said:

'I've walked so very far on my shaky old legs, all the way from the stream in the valley. Please, I'm very hungry. I don't wish to be any trouble, but could you possibly spare a crust of bread that I might eat?'

'Oh, I'm so sorry,' said the agitated fisherwoman, 'but I can't stand at the gate all day – I've such a great deal more work to do before my guest arrives. You'll soon be home, old woman, and then you can cook a grand supper for yourself. But please call again when next you come from the stream.'

And the fisherman's widow scurried up the path into her little house, leaving the hungry washerwoman to trundle back up the steep hill towards her own place, where there was no food in the larder.

By tea-time, the small house was spick and span, but still there was no knock at the door and the busy woman started to fear that the Master Teacher had passed her by. She fretted and moaned: 'I've missed him. But he *must* visit me. I've cleaned my house from top to bottom and warmed it especially for him.'

All at once there was a sudden knock at her back door and her heart leapt up for joy! *'He's come!'* she exclaimed! *'He is here!'*

But on opening it she saw only a poor ragged boy with no shoes on his aching sore feet, and she noticed the large blue veins standing out on his hungry thin frame. And she felt so sorry for the lad.

'Please,' he pleaded, clasping his hands in front of her, 'I have no family and I've walked so many miles, so very far since dawn. Can you spare me a small piece of fish, or perhaps some water or wine?'

Now, although her kind heart went out to the little lad she instantly became aware of time swiftly passing, and therefore gently explained how busy she was. Then – half against her good nature – she slowly closed the door on him, while promising that if he came back the next morning she would milk her prize goat and give him fresh fish and bread to eat.

Then she dashed around to finish off her chores in preparation for her guest. But by night-time there was still no sign of the Master, and all at once she began to reel, her mind falling into dark despondency, fearing that she really had missed him or that he'd passed her humble dwelling and visited a wealthier hearth than her own. Then there was a sudden noise – a scratching at the wooden door.

She jumped to her feet, elated, and in a surge of inexplicable joy she ran across the room, unbolted the latch and swung open the door: only to find a wounded stray dog looking up at her mournfully. Its paw was badly hurt and bleeding and its eyes were full of want and homelessness.

'Oh you poor thing,' she said, gazing pitifully at the creature.

But then her business-sense grasped hold of her and she quickly panicked, suddenly remembering she'd not yet made up a new straw bed for the Master. So she said to the dog:

'You may sleep outside by my barn tonight, my friend, and I'll dress your wounds and feed you tomorrow when I have more time.'

And she latched the wooden door, made up the bed, and afterwards she slumped into deep depression and disappointment at being overlooked by the Teacher, who had not come. Utterly exhausted, she lay down on her soft warm bed and then fell into a deep, deep sleep ...

Then, in a vision, the Master stood before her.

His form was glowing with golden rays.

'Oh!' she cried in delight! 'My Master! I thought you'd forgotten me!'

'No, my child,' replied the Teacher, 'I did not forget you. *Three times today* I knocked at your door and begged for your help. And *three times today* you turned me away, without the love I needed.'

11

The Professional Sceptics

Take One

'I'm in a terrible quandary,' said the pretty young reporter, casting her brown eyes towards the floor and brushing her long blond hair aside. 'I really don't know what to do, Stephen.'

'What on earth's the problem?' I asked, sympathetically.

'Well, as I told you on the telephone, I didn't believe in you or your powers – I was a confirmed sceptic. But after seeing tonight's meeting and the incredibly detailed evidence you gave to all those people, I'm convinced it's true; we can't die.'

'So what's the problem then?'

'Well, I have a report to write and my editor's told me to rubbish this meeting.'

There was an incredulous silence between us. It's a good job I was sitting down at the time, or I think I would have fallen over.

'Stephen, what do I do now?' she asked anxiously.

I took a deep breath, and replied:

'You must follow your conscience, my dear ... and the truth,' I said, sensing gloomy storm clouds gathering on the horizon.

And, as you might have already guessed, her highly favourable report was passed to the newspaper's editor, altered, sensationalized, and the final result was a very slick and thorough hatchet job!

Over the years I've lost count of the times I've been seriously misquoted, misrepresented, or painfully shocked to read words purporting to have issued from my cautious and highly sensitive lips. My press files are choked with articles incorrectly stating some of the simplest facts: my name, age, book titles, and even my nationality. Everyone knows I'm as Welsh as a leek, but one national paper claimed me as a New Zealander!

Sometimes I wonder whether we can believe *anything* we read, don't you? Investigators should always question everything – especially the printed word!

However, not all the gentlemen and ladies of the press are man-eating ogres: there are many who've been very kind to me and featured my work favourably, the *Hull Daily Mail* being a good example:

After causing a regional stir by telephoning Christian clergy in Humberside to get their comments and create a story out of my intended visit to the city hall, the newspaper added to the hoo-hah by later reporting my clairvoyance in what, for the press, must surely be regarded as effervescent terms!

But even though it reads well, it's worth noting the underlying cynicism, such as the phrases appearing in inverted commas, or the tongue-in-cheek headline of 'Haunting Night Out':

> After explaining how he managed to get in touch with people 'on the other side', Mr O'Brien started 'hearing voices' with a remarkably high accuracy rate.
>
> Rene Tailor was the first, an elderly woman who was 'contacted' by her father who had died of a chest illness.
>
> He was with Ada, an auntie, and Mrs Roberts, one of the street's gossips. But when the microphone passed to Rene's granddaughter the messages became a bit woolly.

> There was a shaky start with the next contact, but
> he soon had the woman in tears when he discovered
> she had lost a baby, but that it was with her grand-
> parents.

No doubt, thousands of discerning readers must
have asked: why didn't the journalist simply *report*
the messages, facts and details, and the recipients'
responses? Why indeed? For, as it stands, we only
have the reporter's opinion alleging the messages
became 'woolly'.

I think I've made my point! While I'm 'alive', why
take somebody else's word for it? Come and see me
for yourselves.

But in fairness to this reporter he did reproduce my
comments delivered to the '1,300 punters' I'd 'pulled
in' (oh dear!). I'd mentioned his newspaper's conduct:
'I think it is disgraceful that they contacted the vicar',
I had said.

But the following week, events took a surprise
turn when reader's letters, defending my abilities,
were printed in the *Mail*. So on this occasion, at
least, a balance was struck when two ladies wrote:

'I find it most annoying that the press are always
quick to condemn people like Stephen O'Brien. The
reporter seems a cynic, and tended to put down
everything Stephen O'Brien achieved.

'Attending this meeting was a remarkable and
uplifting experience for myself and no doubt many
others.'

And another woman's husband, who'd entered the
city hall 'unsure' of life after death, was then declared
by her to have altered his opinions: 'He now has no
doubts and is a believer,' she wrote.

Isn't it nice to know that the press who have, in
the past, so often given paranormalists like me such

a hard and cynical time, can – and sometimes will –
be fair enough to bow to public opinion?

Full marks to the *Hull Daily Mail*!

Recent statistics undoubtedly show that the public voice does support mediums and the belief in a
life after death, something verified when Britain's
popular *Woman* magazine tracked me down for a
two-page picture feature on Life After Death. I was
'for' it (naturally), and Barbara Smoker, sixty-seven,
and President of the National Secular Society, was
most definitely 'against'!

But poor Mrs Smoker came in for some stick
because she'd branded all Spiritualists as 'unconscious
or conscious frauds' and 'fakes', and furthermore
she declared them 'dangerous and cruel, playing on
people's weaknesses'.

Dear Barbara and I have clashed a few times
on TV and in one Central Television discussion she
astounded me with the outrageous statement that
mediums earn great amounts of money and 'launder
them away through the Spiritualist Church'. (What
a cheek!)

Following these hurtful attacks, I'm pleased to
say that the public won the day, for *Woman* did
a follow-up readers' poll which seemed to present
a balanced view of what their readers thought.

One astute soul from Leicestershire reflected, I
believe, a great majority of *Woman's* readership
when she penned:

> I am not a Spiritualist, although I do believe in
> life after death as taught by the Church of England,
> but I judged the feature on Spiritualism simply from
> the impression I got of Barbara Smoker and Stephen
> O'Brien.
>
> They are two people with very different views.

Barbara came across as narrow-minded and self-opinionated. Many people, particularly the recently bereaved, would have been hurt by her words.

Stephen, on the other hand, appears to be kind and caring, with a genuine desire to help people which I found more convincing.

This kind observation was further highlighted in my personal postbag; scores of similar comments came in. (Incidentally, I wonder how many letters Mrs Smoker got?)

However, just like Barbara, or anyone else in the public eye, I've sometimes had to dig in my feet against detractors, such as the occasion when Dr Stephen Donnelly, editor of *The Skeptic* (a magazine I'd spent thirty-six years never having heard of) asked if I'd submit my psychic abilities to his non-specified 'scientific' tests.

'I'll publish the results,' he said.

'Why?'

'To validate your work as genuine.'

'Thousands already know it is.'

'But this would give you credibility.'

'I already have it.'

'And other sceptics would accept my results.'

'No they wouldn't, they'd say "Stephen O'Brien duped you", and demand to test me themselves. And before long I'd be giving all my time to disbelievers when my energies are better spent helping the grieving and brokenhearted.'

There was a scratchy, academic pause.

'I've been tested by the media several times,' I said, 'and I'm on trial every night when I stand before a thousand strangers and try to join Two Worlds. My job is to serve, and as long as there's *one* soul burdened by ignorance, I'd rather give my time to them than to you, with the greatest respect.'

And that was the end of that, until the sceptical good doctor and I clashed a few more times on TV, the most prominent occasion being the BBC early-morning chat show *Gloria Live*, hosted by celebrity Gloria Hunniford.

Dr Donnelly and I were plonked into two chairs, awaiting battle, while Gloria interviewed the father of the first British woman to go into space. Halfway through the chat, the doctor – who really does have an excellent sense of humour – leaned over and whispered to me: 'I was short-listed for that, you know. I was amongst the final hundred and fifty applicants being considered for the flight.'

'What a pity you didn't go up,' I said drily, and we both smiled as the cameras turned on us.

Gloria introduced the topic and then showed a very short but successful clip of some TV mediumship I'd done, then quite a long section from that fated *Wogan* message.

The doctor then claimed that when delivering my spirit messages I was just 'playing the laws of probability' and hoping for success, which I immediately scotched with:

'You've never actually seen me live in a demonstration in front of a theatre audience, so I don't know how you can say these things.'

Then came our morning surprise: a nationwide phone-vote on my abilities. And what was the do-or-die question to the British people? Well, it was very specific:

'*Can Stephen O'Brien contact the spirit world? Yes, or No?*'

After the *Wogan* clip, I confess to feeling like one of those quacking, tin fairground ducks, jiggling along a painted river and expecting to be shot down again.

But, while we were waiting twenty minutes for the computers to record the votes, the BBC switchboards were being completely jammed. They received over 8,000 calls – that's seven calls a second. And the result? A resounding victory:

'Can Stephen O'Brien contact the spirit world?'
Yes: 82% No: 18%

Later *Psychic News* quoted my manager Jeff saying, 'The BBC had overlooked that Stephen is well-loved by the British public. They respect him as a medium, bestselling author and popular media celebrity, and the loyal support of his countless followers is strong.'

I've also done public battle many times with several 'anti-paranormalists', that peculiar breed of Homo sapiens which denounces the existence of all psychic phenomena, because it doesn't suit its thinking. Sadly, I've discovered many of them to be narrow-minded bigots, full of their own self-importance and biased opinions, who refuse to accept any evidence of it. No matter how inexplicable, they take great delight in explaining it all away, especially phenomena relating to life after death.

It seems they work from the following premise: *The paranormal does not exist, therefore all evidence of its existence is faked.*

Instead of thorough scientific investigation, painstakingly and carefully undertaken (i.e. sifting through *all* the facts and thoroughly researching every claim), they prefer to loudly and publicly denounce all mediums, psychics and sensitives with cruel allegations of 'uncaring fakes', 'charlatans', or 'irresponsible conmen making pots of money off the backs of the bereaved and the vulnerable'.

I think it's significant to report that I've never yet met a 'professional (paid) sceptic' who treated me as an intelligent being, possessing a genuine concern for people. Still, 'I ain't dead yet!', as the octogenarian vamp Mae West replied to seemingly impossible new sexual conquests. (She was an ardent Spiritualist, by the way.)

Let me give you a secret peek into one of my behind-the-scenes clashes with anti-paranormalists and glimpse for yourself some of their unpublished *real* attitudes. The 'sceptic' in question cornered me – along with five of his colleagues – after a public meeting:

'Now Stephen, you don't *seriously* believe what you gave the public was evidence of survival, now do you? You *know* exactly what it was, just as well as *I* do. I mean, all those little tricks you used are well known to people like me.'

'I beg your pardon?'

'Those techniques you fooled the crowd with: you know what I mean.'

'No I don't. Are you accusing me of fraud?'

'You *know* exactly what I'm saying: and what good will it do them? People are gullible enough to believe you and then base their lives on dangerous ground rather than knowledge.'

'My mediumship is genuine and I'm trying to bring comfort and hope to people.'

'But of what *value* is it?'

'I'll say to you what Jesus told his accusers: go and ask the people I've helped, what my work has meant to them.'

Undeterred, a twisting smirk slithered across his mouth as he continued in a 'Come on, Stephen, you know I've caught you out' smug voice:

'Look, why do you wrap it all up in a God Message?

146

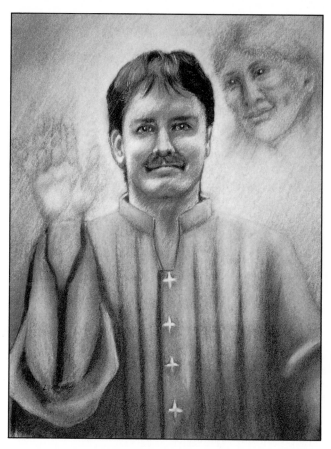

Stephen O'Brien and his Spirit Guide, White Owl: an artist's
impression in pastels by Lin Martin.

Civil Rights Leader, Dr Martin Luther King Jnr. told Stephen, from the Beyond, that his work for freedom continues. © *Bruce Davidson/Magnum Photos*

Singer and actress, Bertice Reading, sent a loving message
from the Beyond to her husband Philip.
© Rex Features

Adam Taylor, aged five, who died after open heart surgery, contacted his parents at a Manchester meeting. They later wrote: 'We thank you from the bottom of our hearts for the comfort we have received by getting proof that our son lives on in another place.'

Stephen with his Tour Manager, Jeff Rees Jones, sorting through one of the many boxes of fan mail at the Voices Management offices.

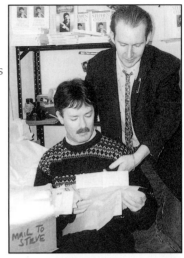

Stephen with some of his youngest fans at a W H Smith book-signing session.

Early morning queues waiting to enter the Wembley Conference Centre, London, where Stephen was to make a guest appearance. Over two thousand people attended. (*Photo: Ray Taylor*)

A quick dust-up for the bright lights and TV cameras.

Stephen relays a spirit message to one of the many
thousands of strangers who attend his meetings each year.

Stephen O'Brien. 'God, who dwells in silence, knows I've always tried my best. He will send me His strength. He will not let me down.'

What has a god to do with all this nonsense? Why link it all up to God and religion?'

'Because I believe in God. I accept a Creative Mind in this Universe that's far greater than ourselves. Far greater than you or me.'

'But you can't *prove* there's a life after death.'

'Really? Can you prove there isn't?'

'Oh, now come on, Stephen, don't play those silly games with me. You know it's impossible to prove a negative.'

(Well folks, my brain might barely fill a thimble but if someone said 'Prove that two and two do *not* make four,' I think we could all manage it.)

For sanity's sake, let's 'leave him stew in his own juices' as my old grandma used to say ...

Swift to chide and slow to bless, anti-paranormalists are ever-eager to brand mediums liars, fakes, cheats and charlatans, especially on the media – and more especially if they're getting paid for doing it. Sometimes, they'll even denounce sensitives sharing the same studio with them (!) many of whom they've never previously met or witnessed in action.

Bitter experience has revealed to me their profound disregard for other people's intelligence; they wrongly assume the public 'can't think', are 'gullible', or 'need protecting from psychics'. (They mean *you*, dear reader!)

They accuse mediums like myself of relaying 'common' names and giving out 'too many boys killed on motorcycles'. But what's in a name? The name isn't the important factor, it's what comes with it – all the other facts which jigsaw together, making perfect sense to the recipient.

And as for motorcycle deaths, I was watching TV the other day and statistics were screened saying that the highest form of mortality on British roads were motorcyclists. That supports the spirit messages, not denies them, doesn't it?

Anti-paranormalists can be easily identified by their swiftness to vilify, which displays an obeisance to four despotic masters: *intolerance*; *self-importance*; *stubborn self-righteousness*; *and the devious art of ignoring or twisting the facts*. But by far the worst of these mental plagues is intolerance – a deep-seated unwillingness to recognize man's right to freedom of choice.

Society's far from perfect and there's much in it with which I strongly disagree, but if *you* want to join those causes – fine, go ahead: you have a right to choose. And this is the rock upon which noisy anti-paranormalists and I part company: I respect your intelligence, while they do not. I *know* you can think for yourselves.

And just because some of these people have attained university degrees or self-styled grand positions – often trotted out as subtitles, probably in the hope of lending authority to bigoted opinions – obviously doesn't mean their views are 'right' for everyone.

Passing examinations doesn't confer wisdom upon the candidate, nor common sense, or even common decency.

Take Two

The telephone rang (when does it ever stop?) and it was a researcher from Granada Television who were planning a national series and would I be kind enough to appear and work with my colleague, psychic artist Coral Polge? I agreed, but little did we know then how troublesome it would all be, the programmes eventually sending the British psychic scene into storms of protest.

The series was being made by Open Media and *Psychic News* carried their advertisement for exponents to display their skills 'before a sympathetic audience'. But, being a canny lot, it wasn't long before the Spiritualists realized what was happening, and the same newspaper front-paged their protests because it was discovered that the man who had been previously referred to as an ex-escapologist, conjuror and psychic de-bunker was involved with the shows. He was James Randi, a Canadian who had strong connections with an organization generally much disliked within Spiritualist circles and known as CSICOP (Committee for Scientific Investigation into Claims of the Paranormal).

I don't remember being informed of his involvement, not in the advert or initially by telephone. Several 'possible' participants made a strong protest – and in fact many psychic exponents withdrew their services.

I did not; and neither did a few other respected mediums who, like myself, fully realized this series could turn out to be a well-executed hatchet job whose cutting-edge was aimed directly at the main arteries of the paranormal. (We are sensitives, after all! And Mr Randi's reputation was already well-known to us.)

The series was called *James Randi, Psychic Investigator*, a title to which I took objection because in my opinion the shows didn't *thoroughly* investigate the sensitives' claims, and – certainly in my own case – failed to transmit certain evidential facts which were later verified by my recipient in the studio audience, facts I relayed during my mediumistic link. If one is going to investigate properly, then a thorough search must be undertaken and *all* the findings should be presented to the public, even those which don't support an investigator's views.

Psychic artist Coral Polge and I agreed to appear despite our gut-feelings, plus the fact that our efforts were to be edited before transmission; we'd suffered from this several times before and knew the ridicule to which we might be exposed. Coral, still concerned, rang me a few times, and even the night before filming:

'Stephen, I don't like the idea of Randi taking part. Should we cancel? What do you think?'

'Well, the studio's booked, the show'll be recorded with or without us, and if all the reputable mediums pull out, who'll be left? He'll take others who aren't experienced in the media and they'll freeze before the cameras.'

'I see . . . well, if you think it'll be OK, we'll go ahead. Anyway, perhaps we're the right people for the job; we've done TV so many times and we certainly don't need the publicity.'

'Exactly, and whatever happens we'll represent the spirit world with dignity,' I replied. Coral agreed and off we went to the Manchester studios, one cold day in March . . .

The green room was a buzzing hive of activity when suddenly mediums Maureen Flynn, Coral Polge, and psychic 'detective' Nella Jones and I were plonked in front of Roger and Sally: photographer and reporter from the *Sunday Times Magazine*. Roger bustled about with his pterodactyl-like silver umbrella and bright arc-lamps, as Sally puffed on her cigarette and yelled across:

'Now come on boys and girls, give us that famous paranormal look!' at which point Nella Jones plunged forward like Ethel Merman in *Gypsy* – arms outstretched and eyes popping – with shouts of 'Tarrah!'

Click!

Nella's a real tonic. She has swarthy Romany looks, big, twinkly eyes and such a direct and forthright manner, all wrapped up with a marvellous sense of quick-fire repartee. She's been featured extensively in national publications for the psychic advice she's given Scotland Yard detectives which helped to solve several crimes.

We noticed Mr Randi was nowhere to be seen.

'Where's the old man, then?' winked Nella.

'I don't know,' I said, 'but being conspicuous by your absence is something a polite host should never be.'

'Quite right, my darling,' beamed Nella, arm around my shoulders. 'Who's missing him anyway?' she shrugged.

(Henceforth – to save space – I'll refer to Mr Randi by his stage-name initials 'JR'. He once held the self-appointed title of 'The Amazing' but I avoid using it as I personally do not regard him as such.)

Back to the studio: the plot thickens (or is it the Thick Plottens?). However, the air – psychically – certainly *was* thick with unfriendliness which prompted a wittily dry and rasping Nella to light a cigarette, puff at it madly like a steam engine in reverse and fill the room with clouds of smoke while wheezing like a caustic Bette Davis: 'Look out, my loves! We're in for a bloody hammering!' And you didn't have to be psychic to know she was right.

Suddenly we were all whisked away into the studio set – a mysterious 'occulty' affair with billows of dry smoke and large white glass balls, trees, and magical symbols painted on the floor! – where we were grouped around a chair upon which sat JR. Nella whispered confidentially into my ear: 'Ah, there's mine host. He looks ever so serious, the poor love.' Then looking disdainfully around the peculiar setting she added mysteriously, 'Where's the cortège?'

Following this, the whole rigmarole of pose, smile and flashlight-palaver was repeated again by Roger plus a TV publicist who also took dozens of shots 'for about a hundred and twenty publications around Britain: there'll be huge publicity for this nationally networked series.'

'Oh dear,' I thought, as I clearly picked up somebody's fear of imminent ridicule.

'Lambs to the slaughter, dear . . .' wheezed Nella, through the dry smoke.

'I'm desperate for a cup of tea,' I said. 'I'm spitting feathers. Come on, Nella, let's get back to the green room.'

So we disbanded and trouped off while a silly comedian 'warmed up' our rather serious audience by inanely mimicking a young Shirley Temple singing 'On the Good Ship Lollipop'. (As a matter of fact, he did it better than Shirley used to do it.) But on our way out, Coral quite rightly remarked:

'Dear me. It's hardly the right attitude to have when approaching some of life's deepest mysteries.'

'They treat it all so shallowly – as if it were an entertainment. They've no idea what we're trying to do.'

She nodded, as we entered a set of corridors, and a conversation.

'Apart from irreverence, my biggest concern is the editor's scissors,' I said. 'In recorded programmes my best work nearly always ends up on the cutting-room floor.'

'That's happened to me *so* many times over the years, Stephen,' sighed Coral as we pushed through the green room doors . . .

'How's the tea, Stephen, darling?' quizzed cheery Nella.

'Like sheep-dip,' I said, and we shared a much-needed raucous laugh, after which Sally – the *Sunday Times* reporter – overheard me asking Maureen Flynn, Coral and Nella about JR.

'Well, who is he anyway?' I asked.

'A silly old sod,' said Nella.

(Sally was quick to pick this up and subsequently featured Nella's quip several times in her article.)

Later, back on the smoky set after we'd received what I thought was a lukewarm introduction from JR, Coral began sketching a portrait of a spirit-woman's face while I tried to obtain evidence, quite haltingly at first because the conditions for contact were so very difficult. I just couldn't hear the link as clearly as I would have liked.

I'd received the name 'William Butler' which a young man whose surname was Butler claimed, but as Coral and I progressed further into the message, neither of us were happy that the contact belonged to him.

'Don't make it fit,' advised Coral, wisely, and we didn't. Contacts *must* go to the right people and unless we're fortunate enough to hear the recipient's name or exact location in the crowd, we can only work with what we get. (In hindsight, it's a living wonder we received anything at all under such stressful, unsuitable conditions.)

Then suddenly a man in the back row responded to the details I was giving. I addressed him concerning my description of someone linked with Coral's picture which I'd also just given:

'Is this making sense to you: a lady who passed away as I described with a possible heart condition – angina – and I feel she went silently, quietly, in her sleep, after quite a bit of illness ...'

'I know a man called William Butler, whose wife

passed away with angina,' he said, 'but I've got to say that the picture doesn't look like her.'

This sometimes happens, and when it does, recipients are asked to research the portraits – in this way better evidence is frequently obtained because telepathy on the part of the mediums is ruled out. He concluded:

'Everything that Stephen has said rings true, but unfortunately the face doesn't.'

(That was about as much as the public saw of the link. However, in the interests of true investigation, on both Coral's and my own behalf I suggested that the TV studio personnel should follow our recipient back home and check to see if the picture resembled a snapshot there. I don't think anyone could have been fairer than that. But, as far as I know, this line of investigation wasn't pursued.)

In fact, just as my connection was establishing itself properly and more details started to flow through, the floor-manager whirled his arms around like a demented windmill and broke my link.

'It's no good asking me to stop,' I announced, 'I've got to place the message properly.'

Then suddenly JR 'appeared' and, very loudly I thought, declared we'd run out of time.

'That's it,' he said, which disgruntled me.

'But you were given at least four attempts to record the show's opening remarks,' I protested, 'why can't we have more time?'

'Because it's run out!' he returned, his tones stinging my ear.

'But that isn't fair. Why don't you ask the audience if they think we've had enough time?' At which point (like the first lone snowdrop of spring) only *one* voice shouted back from the crowd: 'Yes you have!' I regret it belonged to the good Dr Donnelly, whom we've already encountered. However, sections of the audience were now muttering amongst themselves, as my temperature rose and I blurted out:

'Well, I hope you're all very happy with that, because I am not!' and I stalked off the set, leaving a bewildered Coral standing chalk in hand beside her easel, and JR full of smiles but to me he seemed hot and bothered.

I plonked myself down in the front row of the crowd, next to Spiritualist National Union President, Gordon Higginson. Such a lapse of manners was so unlike me. But then I've always railed against unfairness, and – glancing back – why *should* we put up with it?

'Don't worry, Stephen,' said Gordon, 'you've done your best; leave it at that.' He was there to give his expert opinion yet privately confided, 'I don't mind speaking on these programmes, but I wouldn't work for these people.' (Once bitten – twice shy.)

Then suddenly there was a lot of muffled activity and the floor-manager came over.

'Look, we've got to finish this shot ...'

I returned a rather innocent look.

'Stephen, how about going back over to Coral?'

'How about another minute to finish off the link?' I quizzed, which momentarily took him by surprise.

'We can't – we've run out of time.'

'Well you're not being fair,' I said.

There was more whispering through radio-mikes, shuffling and to-ing and fro-ing, and muffled comments buzzing his ear-piece, then he turned and said:

'Thirty seconds.'

'One minute would be better,' I said.

'But thirty seconds is all we can give.'

So, very reluctantly, I acquiesced. (Aren't I silly? Looking back, I should have sat it out.)

However, in the finished show (in which our item

155

had been cut and shortened by Mr Editing Scissors)
my last close-up says it all: I sweep the floor with my
anxious eyes, where I suspected sections of the link
would end up.

I was not disappointed.

A few months later, Mr Randi brought out a
book on the series in which he recorded some rather
upsetting remarks about almost every sensitive who'd
appeared in the series.

In it he pointed out that during our item, Coral's
and my recipient was a medium himself. So what? He
might as well have been a coalman or an insurance
broker, for neither of us knew him or had ever met
him before in our lives. In fact, it was only when
Psychic News later reported the show that we found
out his profession.

Our recipient, Mr Byrne, informed us that the
psychic portrait Coral had drawn had been fully
placed and accepted with the evidence by his mother
when he had taken it home.

*Now, if that doesn't indicate paranormal activity
– what does?*

However . . .

Here goes the telephone again:

'Hello, Stephen?' – it was fellow medium Maureen
Flynn who'd delivered mediumship on the same show
as myself, and whose recipient (a middle-aged woman)
had become quite emotional while receiving a message
from her husband on the Other Side. 'Stephen, have
you read that Randi's book?'

'Unfortunately, yes – and it bored me to tears,'
I replied, yawning.

'It looks like he's pooh-poohed everything paranormal in it. Are you surprised?'

'Not a bit! Printing anything in favour of the
paranormal throws doubt on his case, and I don't

think that's the kind of image he wants to present.'

'I couldn't agree more, Stephen. Did you read the final comments in his book?'

'Yes, I've got them here. He says, "We stepped through the looking-glass in pursuit of strange forces, and they were not there." Somebody'd better tell the hundreds of parapsychologists, professors and scientists who study and support the paranormal in all parts of the world!'

Maureen and I chuckled away over this, and then shared great laughter because we'd decided that after reading Mr Randi's book, anyone with an atom of sensitivity would very soon get a pretty good picture of his ideas.

'Anyway,' said Maureen, cautiously, 'he may not have heard the last of this.'

Maureen's call made me crystallize again my definition of what a sceptic should be: an open-minded person who thoroughly investigates all the evidence, meticulously sifts it, seriously following through every lead and completely exhausting all avenues of research before reaching final conclusions. I have no objection to any intelligent enquiry, providing it respects the truth and is also willing to publish it, even if it's at variance with the investigator's own opinions. Anti-paranormalists, however, are simply out to ridicule.

You can make up your own mind about which category James Randi fits into.

Even as I write, I'm fully aware of groups of anti-paranormalists hatching up future schemes to publicly ridicule me. Certain 'sceptics' have been ordered out of theatres I've worked in because they were tape-recording the meetings – something contravening all copyright law. They've actually sat there, breaking that law – so, before we glance at any of their 'findings', let's remember they entered my 'shows' – as they disrespectfully call them – under a web of deceit.

When all is said and done, people like Harry Houdini, the well-known, prolific psychic de-bunker of yesteryear, are professional 'magicians' of sorts, or, to put it another way – paid deceivers and illusionists.

We should remember that when viewing their 'evidence'.

So, all you up-and-coming mediums: beware! And here's a tip: be very careful which media engagements you accept, and agree *all* the arrangements well before filming day, for events have a peculiar way of suddenly turning on their heads! And there's often an inevitable 'rabbit-out-of-the-hat' emotional shock, intended to throw you into embarrassing confusion as well as to challenge your abilities. Like it or not, that's the way today's media often work.

By the way, I'm not a crotchety old cynic, just a realist speaking from personal experience. And I'm not alone, it seems. Professor Arthur Ellison, one of Britain's leading figures in the Society for Psychical Research, leaned across to me after we'd done a TV chat show together, sighing over the studio applause: 'It's so sad, Stephen. All they want is entertainment, not serious discussion at all. Isn't it a load of old tosh?'

Speaking of which, back to the series! *News of the World* TV guest columnist, Jonathan Ross, said he'd tried to like Mr Randi in his programmes but he 'comes across as so sinister and impersonal that I'd almost rather be ripped off by one of the many "fakes" he seeks to challenge than have him in my front room.'(!)

Anyway, one of the best things about doing that show was meeting the wonderful international singer, actress and film celebrity Bertice Reading who was also a studio guest.

Bertice ('I'm big, black and beautiful, honey!') was absolutely incensed by Mr Randi's attitude:

'What right has he to destroy another person's faith?' she seethed.

'None,' said a cameraman.

Bertice went on to explain how the media had often tried to deride her belief in Spiritualism (she attended meetings quite regularly).

'They'd like to laugh at me,' she warned, 'but I don't allow it. If they want to mention my interest in psychic things I *insist* on dignity, or no interview.' She also frequently cautioned journalists: 'If you so much as *try* to ridicule me, I'll sue you. But if you *really* want to know, I'll tell you all about it.'

Happy in each other's company, we swapped addresses and telephone numbers, and she and her husband – healer and astrologer, Philip, a quiet, tall young man – promised they'd come to my next London appearance at the Lewisham Theatre.

Bubbly Bertice gave me another cuddly bear-hug and after chatting for four hours at the hotel, the last thing she said when we parted at the lift was: 'God bless you with your work, Stephen.' And she glanced over her shoulder and added sincerely, 'I like you; I really do.'

But the next I heard of dear Bertice was very sad news indeed: a few months later she suffered a massive brain haemorrhage and collapsed into a coma. In a critical condition she was immediately placed on life-support systems and her husband, Philip, kept constant vigil at her bedside. I was terribly concerned, and my healing prayers immediately went out. Then I rang their London home and left a message with a friend.

'Please tell Philip I'm praying she'll make a speedy recovery, though ... I don't feel too hopeful, I'm afraid. But the healing might ease her suffering and, if necessary, help Bertice to make a pain-free, dignified passing. Please tell them both that my prayers are with them. God bless you.'

I couldn't say then, but I knew she'd never regain consciousness, for her time had come.

Hours later, the nine o'clock news reported the world of entertainment had suffered a tragic loss when Bertice Reading had died peacefully that evening. She was just fifty-eight years old ...

Quietly, within my mind, I spoke to her that same night, wishing her well in her new home and thanking her for the joy she'd brought to millions across the world.

But strangely enough, that wasn't the end of the story, for two days later I suddenly awoke in the hazy light of dawn, and ... well, here's a note to her husband:

Dear Philip,

At 5 a.m. this morning (Monday 10 June) I awoke as the downstairs clock was striking the hour; and I was so very aware of Bertice near to me. I sent her my thoughts and greetings – feeling she was trying to communicate something important.

I then said: 'If you can, Bertice, give a little sign to prove your presence,' – and within moments the main light fitting and cloth shade with fringes on it, in the centre of the ceiling, started to swing back and forth, then stop, then swing gently again.

(There were no windows open anywhere in the house.)

Then I heard Bertice saying 'Will you write something for Philip?' I agreed. She asked me to tell you that she was safe, and said:

Tell him I love him, and he made me so very happy.'

160

I can't convey in words her feelings of gratitude to get these words across to you, except to say that just after the above she put her hand to her mouth, hunched her shoulders a little and her eyes filled up with tears.

God Bless you – both.'
Stephen

(She's OK, Philip, and as her contact faded out I had a strange feeling that somewhere in her soul she 'knew' something important was going to happen in her life a little while before her passing came. I'm positive she'll contact you again sometime.)

Later that morning I broke my journey to a BBC radio interview and posted Bertice's message by express mail, accompanied by a card with my poem of thankfulness for special life on it ('Do Not Forget Me'), in the hope it would comfort both her and Philip.

Inside I wrote: *God is near.*

Between probing, and sometimes facile, questions at the interview my mind kept fluttering back and forth, remembering Bertice and her vibrant personality, large bowling eyes and smiling face. Every so often, a picture of her charismatic presence floated back to me and stayed strong in my mind's eye, until my host displaced it by referring to the sceptics. With intense brow-knitted intensity he asked:

'And now Stephen, about all those hard-headed realists listening to you out there. They're highly sceptical of your powers and have no belief whatsoever in the paranormal, an afterlife, or your teachings and revelations. Tell us – what do you think of them?'

'Poor souls,' I replied.

12

Dear Stephen . . .

When all's said and done, what matters most to
me is helping people, not the self-opinionated views
of academics and anti-paranormalists.

The following letters are just a few of thousands
I've received from several parts of the world, and they
strike a perfect balance to the scathing condemnations
of the sceptics. Reading them shows just how much
mediumship dramatically affects the lives of millions
of ordinary folk who certainly don't need professional
de-bunkers to do their thinking for them.

Normally, I'd have removed the glowing compliments, out of modesty, but I'm going to ask your
forgiveness as I place my embarrassment aside,
because I think it's about time the public's true
voice was heard.

I hope you'll agree, and here we go:

Dear Stephen,

I am writing to thank you for the communication
from my late husband which you gave me from the
spirit world.

You asked was there anyone that had 'links with
Swalwell, and with an old gentleman?' Well, my late
husband and I used to visit an old gentleman at
Swalwell and had many wonderful times with him.

You then went on to *describe* my late husband,
and said he was 'pointing to the left eye and laughing,
saying "Do you remember the fun we had?"'

My husband had a slight cast in his left eye and

at times he would tell our son, John, that because of the cast the eye was loose! He would place his hand over the eye and pretend to put it into his hand.

When John looked for it, he would pretend to drop it and John would spend quite some time searching on the floor!

You also went on to say about 'tummy pains' my daughter was having and that my husband advised me 'to have her seen to as it isn't what you think it is', being her age.

Well, she attended a local hospital, and sure enough she needed treatment, and is now fine.

Many thanks Stephen, for your wonderful work.
Kindest regards,
Mrs T
Washington

Dear Stephen,

After seeing you at Winchester I just have to write to you.

Can you remember me? I am the lady who had a communication through you at the end of the evening. My dearly loved brother came through with the following facts:

He took his own life by locking himself in his car in the garage of his home last December 26th. He attached a hosepipe leading from the exhaust through a rear window and sealed it, so the fumes filled the car and poisoned him.

He said he was sorry, wasn't in his right mind at the time, and now he was happy with his son X on the Other Side.

The work you do is so important. God will bless you for all the comfort and hope you give to so many people, and, like many others, I pray you will be blessed with good health and strength to carry on.

Yours sincerely,
(name and address supplied)
Hampshire

Dear Stephen,

I believe you will be interested to know that an appointment made by Spirit, through you, was kept.

I attended your meeting at Southampton where you brought my father to me and gave accurate evidence. At the end of the message you said, 'Your father says he will be with you on 25th August'.

I suddenly remembered I was booked to go to Stansted Hall (Arthur Findlay College of Psychic Studies, in Essex) for a week, on the 24th August. I was taking my mother with me and we would be in the Sanctuary on Sunday 25th for the usual service there.

The 25th arrived: after a beautiful service, the clairvoyance started and Margaret Pearson (the medium) asked if anyone knew of someone just about to go in for open heart surgery – I physically felt a push in my back (from the spirit world) and I put up my hand, as only two days before a friend told me her husband had been called by the hospital. Superb evidence was then given to me and then Margaret said 'I have your father here,' and he proceeded to talk with my mother and bring back lovely memories, all exactly correct.

I was asked to tell the full story during one of the lectures that week, to show that indeed Spirit can make appointments, and although we have free will, they are certainly aware of arrangements we make and can plan to be there.

All good wishes for your continued work with Spirit,

Sincerely,
Mrs M M
Hythe

Dear Stephen,

Where to begin?

You visited Tunbridge Wells, Kent, and the *first* message you came through with was from a very talkative, very urgent little boy of eight years old called 'Ben'. Dear Ben, despite his meagre years, managed to 'muscle' his way to the front that night!

Ben, as you accurately described, 'was hit by a car on his way to school, crossing the road'. As you described, 'the damage was all to his left side and he was blind in one eye'.

His parents, who are my next-door neighbours (and dear friends) are people who you would describe as 'the salt of the earth'.

I gave his mother Ben's message and it brought her overwhelming comfort. I cannot express in words how much!

His mother was able to verify all the names you gave, etc. and she was relieved that 'he felt minimal pain', because she had feared this.

How can I begin to express what one can only feel? Ben's communication through yourself has brought sunshine back to the lives of two very special people.

God bless you, Stephen.

J: (name and address supplied)

Surrey

Dear Stephen,

I am a psychologist engaged on research. May I say I was *very* impressed with your work tonight at the Lewisham Theatre, London.

I deal with the laws of probability and tonight the evidence you produced would stand up to statistical significance tests.

You have nothing to fear from investigation, and nothing to gain.

Yours sincerely,

A.T. (Research Psychologist, full name and address supplied) London

Dear Stephen,

Last year I was fortunate enough to see you on stage at Watford. The first lady you called out of the audience, unbeknown to me at that time, was coincidentally my friend's Mum, whom I did not recognize, even though all the evidence that you gave her about her son in spirit matched up.

Afterwards I told her daughter about it and she confirmed that it was her Mum.

As you may be aware, the sceptic critics really tried to pull you apart in our local newspaper, but her Mum wrote to them, and they published her letter which stated that she was most certainly not planted in the audience.

I have seen many mediums but have never heard so much proof in all my life; you were spot-on.

Congratulations on the wonderful work you are doing.

Yours sincerely,
Miss J
Watford

Dear Stephen O'Brien,

I felt I had to write to you saying how much I enjoyed reading your two books *Voices from Heaven* and *Visions of Another World*. I was moved to tears many times reading every word on every page.

I have to say that these books have changed my life in so many ways. I have learned that the things we all worry about from day to day, and the things that we let upset us, are not so important after all.

They have taught me that the most important things in life are love for mankind, and richness of thought and spirit.

If people who put all their time into making money and who are wrapped up in their own selves could see what the other side, and the spirit world, was like, I am sure we would put less importance on material gains.

There are many people in the world who, if they wanted to, could help many other people improve their standard of living.

God bless you, Stephen.
Good health,
S.F.
Kent

Dear Stephen,

You have helped me so very much, I thank you with all my heart. As with your first book, your second book just jumped out at me off the bookshelf.

I don't really know how to put into words how your books have made me feel.

They have made me laugh, cry – so many things I have felt, but I think most of all they have helped me to find me.

I thank you once more, Stephen, for what you have given to me and so many others. May God bless you always.

May your work of Love carry on for many years to come.

God bless you.

Yours sincerely,

Mrs S.M.

Peterborough

Dear Stephen,

I admire your work greatly.

I have always feared 'dying', but after reading your books and attending one of your meetings, I find all my fears have gone.

Thank you so much, Stephen.

Take care of yourself and keep up the good work.

Best wishes,

Mrs C.A.

Hants

This next lady came to my meeting hobbling on a crutch, and her arm was in a sling. She'd dismissed herself from hospital just to attend.

Dear Stephen,

Hi! I don't know if you remember me, I was the girl who came in after the Norwich show and had had a motorcycle accident the previous night. This will probably sound stupid but when you gave me a hug I felt such a surge of absolute Love rush through me, it was incredible.

The most unbelievable bit about it all was that all evening my arm had been hurting quite a lot, but, by the time I got home and went to bed, it hardly hurt at all. AMAZING.

Thank you
VERY MUCH
Lots of Love,
Helen T.
XXX
Norwich

Dear Mr O'Brien,

I'm very pleased I attended one of your evenings at Carlisle. Although I wasn't fortunate enough to receive any communication from the next world, I was deeply moved and so very pleased for those who did.

I want you to know that this has brought me so much comfort and I no longer feel so alone. I no longer fear death, for I know there is no such thing.

Afterwards, when you were signing your books, you asked me what I'd been doing, for I was walking with the aid of a crutch. I told you I'd had multiple sclerosis for twenty years. You mentioned spiritual healing; I'm very interested in this but don't know of any healers in my area.

Finally, Mr O'Brien, thank you so very much for coming to Carlisle and for showing me, along with so many others, that there truly is life after death. Thank you for sharing your wonderful gift and for the caring way you convey all the messages from the spirit world.

I wish you peace and happiness and hope that you continue to bring peace to those who are grieving; on both sides, for many years to come.

God bless you
J.P.
Cumbria

(Note: Spiritual healing can be transmitted across continents and worlds, distance being no obstacle to the soul powers used. While every effort is made to help patients, healing should always go hand-in-hand with medical treatment delivered by qualified doctors. Ultimately, of course, all lives are in God's hands.

The Harry Edwards Sanctuary, a world-renowned charitable organization, undertakes much commendable voluntary work in this direction. For help, write with a stamped addressed envelope to my friends: Ray and Joan Branch, Harry Edwards Spiritual Healing Sanctuary, Burrows Lea, Shere, Guildford, Surrey, GU5 9QG.)

(Those wishing to write to Mr O'Brien, please be thoughtful enough to enclose a stamped addressed envelope, without which he cannot reply.

Please keep your letters brief and be patient for a reply, as the medium receives vast quantities of mail which can take a while to receive attention.)

13

Questions and Answers

The public avidly thirst for knowledge and though I've covered a wide range of interesting issues in my previous books, still they want more.

Over the years I've been asked thousands of perplexing questions, and here – by public demand – are more of my answers addressing some fascinating paranormal issues, drawn, of course, from personal experience.

Is there sex after death?
If you wish it. Most experiences can be duplicated in the Next World, except the formation of physical bodies. Physical bodies are created from physical matter for specific use in the physical world.

In all worlds, every activity is mentally perceived and experienced and can therefore be recalled and reproduced.

What is sex?
Don't you know? (laughter ...) If you mean the purpose of sex, it's the means whereby two physical bodies multiply the species. But the soul comes from the Great Spirit.

How would you explain hermaphrodites: people with the outward appearance of both sexes?
This is simply a genetic peculiarity. Their inner essence, the soul, is the most important attribute.

Is it possible for a person of one gender to feel they've been born as the wrong sex and feel trapped in the wrong body?
Yes, I think so. Memories of previous lives or powerful present-day desires play a large part in this. We're told by Spirit that we've lived more than one life and therefore we have previously incarnated as either sex.

So when we die, do we remain male and female? What is the sex of the soul?
The soul is genderless. What matters is the mind, the experiences, the evolution, the thoughts and feelings. Each incarnation adds maturity, depth and understanding to the whole being.

Some say that practising mediumship affects a person's sexual balance. Would you agree?
Not entirely, but the working of the psychic or soul senses certainly does affect the body's nervous and hormonal systems.

Some teach that female mediums accentuate their masculine characteristics, while males enhance their feminine qualities.
I think there's some truth in that, but it's not entirely due to the mediumship. Women taking public meetings have to call upon their stronger, more positive side to get them through the ordeal. Men, on the other hand, like the women, must express the love of the communicators, and it's not easy to prevent this affecting your delivery.

We must remember that mediums of both sexes are *sensitives* in all senses of the word and we shouldn't get caught up in the stereotyping of individuals. Bodies are only temporary physical coverings, it's the soul that matters; and that, in essence, is both 'negative' and 'positive', or 'masculine' and 'feminine'.

Is it wrong for two adults of the same sex to love one another?
How can love be wrong? If two people genuinely care for each other and share their lives to the mutual benefit of each, then those experiences will obviously enrich them.

Then why do some people condemn these relationships as 'against God', 'evil' or 'perverted'?
Because they're narrow-minded bigots who are ignorant of the true nature of God – the universal laws. Bigots of all persuasions believe only their thoughts are 'right'; and you can often recognize them by their loud voices. (Applause.)

Do the planets affect our characters and destinies as in astrology?
Everything in the Universe influences everything else to greater or lesser degrees because all life is interconnected. It's well known that the moon's gravitational field affects our tides and also, some claim, the fluids in our bodies.

Regarding astrology, if you're speaking of the tabloid press columns advising you not to cross the street or you might meet someone in a red coat who'll upset you: no, I don't accept that.

Neither can I accept that because of certain planetary positions our lives and characters will be shaped. The vibrational fields of the Universe at the time of our birth will probably have an effect upon us, but not to that extent, for the soul is eternal and when we're born the constellations are actually being viewed as *pictures of the past*. Light takes millions of years to reach us, so when viewing the night sky we're actually seeing the Universe as it used to be, not as it actually is now.

The most important thing to remember is that whatever influences are about us, our human spirit can triumph supreme over any obstacle in the Universe which challenges it.

We are the masters of our own destinies and there is no force so great that it can remove this right to govern our own lives.

Is there intelligent life on other planets?
Yes, there has to be. Think of the billions of stars and planets in our own galaxy, then in millions of other galaxies, and then in universes beyond these. Statistically there's bound to be life elsewhere and the Spirit World confirms this: there are planes of existence (other worlds) far ahead of us intellectually and others which have yet to reach man's status.

Have you ever spoken with God?
Yes, every day. God is Infinite Mind, a Consciousness permeating all levels of Thought and Being throughout the Universe. We speak with God in everything we do.

Have you ever seen God?
Every day. All things animate and inanimate are manifestations of the God-Force: you are, so is a flower, a child, a stormy sea, the bright shining stars. We can only see the manifestations of God.

Have the spirit people seen God?
Yes, but not in the way you might be thinking. God isn't a man, and the spirit people, like us, are aware only of the Creative Mind's manifestations.

Why do you think we've been born on Earth?
To develop our souls; to hone the character and experience further conscious awareness of who and what we are. Earth is a growing place and no perfect beings have ever incarnated here. Here we may progress physically, mentally, emotionally and spiritually through meeting challenges which mainly stem from our inter-relationships with others.

The world's people are so cruel and selfish, I feel it would be so wrong to have a child and make it suffer.
But *your* child might be the one to change all that.

Are any new souls ever created?
The soul, or rather the Spirit which motivates it, is ancient. There has never been a time when we were not. Our mind-force or Primary Essence of God has always existed, but it's only in this present characterized state that we're conscious of our current identity. So when we talk of old and new souls we should remember there's nothing new in this Universe. It has a wonderful way of recycling itself: energy changes its form continually, but it springs from an ancient power.

What is soul affinity?
The mutual attraction of one soul for another, or for its group-soul.

What is a group-soul?
Several individuals – sometimes on both sides of the veil – joined as a group and working together because they belong to the same frequency or wavelength of soul evolution.

Like attracts like whether we're on Earth or in Spirit, and the power of attraction is Thought: motivation and feeling. We're all part of various group-souls, all independent yet interconnected at one and the same time.

What is recognizable as ourselves in this physical life is just the tip of a vast iceberg; by far the greater portion of our Mind exists beneath the surface.

My sister was pregnant and tried everything to abort the foetus but her son was born healthy. Why?
Because where a soul is to come into the world it cannot be stopped.

But what if she'd been successful and lost it?
Then the child would have been born elsewhere. The soul comes because its spiritual blueprint dictates it.

But then it would have different parents and a different upbringing.
It seems so, but not in the deeper sense. Souls choose the circumstances whereby they might progress. Time is of little importance: if one opportunity passes another will soon present itself.

There is always a Divine Plan at work even if, at first, we fail to perceive it clearly.

You say the spirit body leaves the physical body after death, but I've heard we have several bodies. How many do we have?
At death we pass into the Astral Plane, those worlds of Thought nearest Earth, and express ourselves through a spirit body which will eventually de-materialize to reveal another vehicle of expression beneath it.

As we progress onwards into higher planes, spirit

guides tell us that rather like shedding the skins of an onion we shall inhabit many more spirit bodies which are within us.

If we've lived before, why can't we remember who and what we were?
Because when taking on the flesh there comes a cloaking-down effect which often obliterates many memories. The physical brain is far too simple a computer to register the entirety and vastness of the mind.

You maintain there's no such thing as possession, when one soul from the next world totally controls another person in this world. Can you prove this?
I'll try and explain: Each night countless billions of people sleep and move out in their spirit bodies into the Next World. When they return in the morning, why hasn't somebody else 'possessed' their bodies while they were away?

It doesn't happen because your spirit blueprint, your mind, soul and body are all intricately woven to make the one and only individual which is you.

Your body is yours, it comes under the direct control of your own mind and spirit, and no-one else can ever assume that role.

What about your guide when he entrances you? Surely he's possessed your body?
No; trance operates in varying degrees from the light and almost imperceptible to the deep and cataleptic. But even in deep states it's still a close impression of the mind, not a domination.

The medium's spirit is close by and co-operating. Trance is a *blending* of personalities and minds, rather than an annihilation of the medium's right to govern himself.

I've sat for forty years in a psychic development circle and never experienced anything profound. Why is this?
Either you've been trained incorrectly or your psychic abilities are so deeply buried within your soul that they're not ready to surface yet.

But forty years haven't been wasted; your soul will have become more sensitive and if you view your unfoldment more objectively, you'll be surprised at the progress you've made.

Flowers only bloom when the seasons are right. Likewise, soul unfoldment can't be rushed.

There's no such thing as instant soul attainment.

Why can my cats and dogs follow my deceased relatives around the room when they visit me, while I can't?
Your pets should be up here taking this meeting! (laughter) Animals are usually far more sensitive than humans; their psychic perceptions are much more acute. A dog hears frequencies of sound way beyond our capabilities.

Do spirit people remember everything, or do they write it down?
They're quite fallible like us. They have books in the Next World. In fact, there are vast libraries of works in every known and now-extinct language. They have copies of all Earth publications there; places to study them in and special ways of permanently recording events for future reference.

They most certainly *don't* know everything. I recall several occasions when people at my meetings have informed the Other Side that a friend has just passed over, only to get the reply, 'Oh, has he crossed over to us? I'll do my best to locate him.'

Why do some religious people condemn your work as being 'of the Devil'?
Because they're steeped in ignorance and trapped by superstition and fear. (spontaneous applause)

Empty vessels make the most noise.

Why do you think some sections of the popular press misrepresent the life and work of mediums?
Because they often print what they *think* the public wants to read, not necessarily what the public would really like. Some newspapers are only concerned with circulation figures and coins chinking into the bank. These publications will 'dig up the dirt' on anyone they can find.

I would caution everyone to never accept as the absolute truth anything they read; God gave us minds to think.

Why are people allowed to die in earthquakes?
No one 'dies' before their time, and earthquakes strike because the planet is evolving just as we are. Those people are there for a purpose at that time of tragedy.

My brother was stabbed to death but his murderer hasn't been caught. What will happen to the man who killed him when he dies?
He'll receive his judgement. Judgement is automatic: the soul moves into the world for which it has fitted itself according to its acts, thoughts and deeds.

In the same way as a fish can only live in water, and not on land (because it can only exist in its correct place), so does the soul move into a sphere of life which it's earned for itself during Earth-life. The soul finds its own level.

The murderer, like everyone else, will inherit a

keener mind on passing, a sharper memory and perceptions which make him aware of broader viewpoints. Then there will come a time when the pain he inflicted on your brother will disturb his conscience and, one day, he'll have to face your brother. After this, the 'wrong' will have to be made 'right'; usually through service.

A medium brought a message from my father in the next world and Dad mentioned his own birthday. You teach there's no calendar time Over There, so how did he know it was his birthday?
He must have picked up your thoughts: they don't follow the clock or the seasons in Spirit so that's the only way he'd be aware of his anniversary. Thoughts are living things, and our loved ones are only a fingertouch away, you know.

Have you ever been on stage and received no spirit messages?
Never – but I've struggled through very difficult meetings, many times, when the contacts were tenuous and quite unclear.

There are over 1,500 people here tonight; let's imagine each person brought in ten relatives or friends with them from the Other Side, which makes roughly 15,000 communicators. A few of these are bound to have some degree of success, providing the medium is closely attuned enough to register them, of course.

Why don't the spirit people give you their full names and those of the people they wish to contact?
Many do, sir, but I'm not always sensitive enough to hear them properly.

On good nights when reception's clear I've received

full street names and addresses as well as other precise facts. But linking two worlds is never easy which is why every attempt should be viewed as an experiment.

A thorough investigation should be made before reaching any conclusions about whether or not life is eternal.

My grandmother was very shy. Would this prevent her from communicating tonight?
If her desire is great enough nothing will stop her trying; but forthright personalities tend to push their way to the front.

I've been to a number of good mediums but my husband has never sent me a message, and he died twenty years ago. Why is this?
There could be several reasons:

> He has no desire to communicate.
> He's tried but been unsuccessful.
> He might prefer to speak to you at night when you're asleep and out in the spirit world beside him.
> Or it might be against his beliefs.

Keep investigating and giving him as many opportunities as you can to reach you, perhaps by regular visits to a Spiritualist church where communication occurs at most public services.

Is it right for mediums to make a living off the backs of the bereaved?
Oh, I think you've got your wires crossed there: you're talking about undertakers, not mediums. (applause . . .)

Everyone at this meeting has chosen to be here and share this spiritual experience. (more applause . . .)

14

Life Before Life

I was about to undergo another spiritual experience. It was a blustery winter's day and I was visiting my old neighbour, Florrie, by making the usual climb along a high path overlooking a steep grassy bank with trees dotted here and there, so I had to be careful where I was stepping.

The crisp cold air caught in the back of my throat as my eyes glanced down lazily at my tired feet dragging along, when – quite out of the blue – came a vivid vision: instead of seeing my faded blue jeans and white trainers, my present-day body had completely vanished from sight and now, in its place, was a long brown monk's habit swinging in the breeze above bare sandalled feet. The vision was so real, I could even feel and hear the rustling of the thick cloth as it brushed against my legs; and see some long plaited cords which were dangling from my waist on the right hand side.

I blinked a few times and suddenly the impressions had gone; but they left sharp imprints in my mind on that frosty December day – and did so again and again, whenever I experienced them on subsequent visits.

Deep inside I 'knew' I'd glimpsed my own past: the grassy bank and path had probably triggered some distant memory of a secluded area I'd lived in long ago, as a Brother in a Silent Order (for I was keenly aware of absolute tranquillity while strolling along). And this made complete sense to me because

I've always been happiest when wandering far away from the noisy world, at peace and alone with my thoughts, alone with God.

Perhaps it sounds peculiar but my soul also *knows* what certain ways of dying *feel* like. I know what it's like to be shot: the impact, the deadening, numbing effect and then the burning pain; I've been terrified by the memory of my body hurtling downwards from a very great height, my arms and legs flailing wildly in the rushing air as I neared the fast-approaching hard ground, where I crashed to my death. I'm very aware, too, of what it's like to be stabbed, garotted, drowned – all these sensations are vividly real because I think they could be connected to my previous lives.

Traumatic events linger in the memory-banks much longer than everyday occurrences. In my life as a monk, for example, I'm aware of the rainy day when I slipped on the high muddy path and fell 300 feet below the monastery walls where my broken and bleeding body rolled into some thick bushes. My ribs were broken and one of my lungs was punctured. I was in desperate pain but too far away from my Brothers to be heard. They believed me to be in my cell, fasting in prayerful seclusion, and hence they didn't find my body until a week later. It was in an unpleasant state of decay because I had 'died' on the morning of the third day, in dreadful agony and racked with heaving pain . . .

I can't offer documented evidence of this spiritual experience for it took place far too long ago, but I can present my utter conviction that it happened, and how it felt. Some cynics might find this difficult to accept, but trying to measure spiritual things by material means rarely works.

The idea of living again on Earth is now becoming more and more widely held; hardly one of my meetings passes without someone mentioning it. It's long been a deep-seated belief in Eastern countries, of course, but only a recent innovation in the West.

But is reincarnation a truth, a Universal Law? Can we return to Earth as a completely different entity? Have we been here before? And if so, what exactly happens to our individual survival after death? And where are our loved ones who have already passed over? Are they still in the spirit world, or reborn?

Many are anxious for answers but, to my own mind, there'll always be room for heated debate and uncertainty simply because we're not all-knowing and can't possess every jot of absolute truth. The whole question remains perplexing because the cases for, and against, reincarnation are just as convincing and in many instances are equally as strong as each other.

On the lighter side, of course, some people make fun of the issues, while others have claimed several previous lives – often exotic and not at all commonplace. One young man wrote, asking:

'Why does my Aunt Sybil – perfectly sane in every way – suddenly lose all her marbles when reincarnation comes up? One sniff of it and off she goes into lurid recollections of previous lives prancing around as a Persian princess in silky, revealing veils, or wickedly "crook-and-flailing" peasants as an all-powerful Egyptian prince. Why is she never the smelly slave girl who slopped out the pigs?'

Why indeed?

(By the way, I wouldn't rule out engaging a reputable psychotherapist for Aunt Sybil, would you?)

Such outlandish claims bring to mind another true but very witty story concerning a well-endowed, pompous London medium who was giving a sitting to a thin woman. Trying desperately to impress (because her mediumship was failing) the clairvoyant haughtily announced: 'Of course, I was Cleopatra you know, in my *previous* life.' To which the affronted sitter immediately snapped: 'Don't be so silly, woman – *I haven't come back yet!*'

But returning to the serious side, there's now such an immense wealth of genuine evidence for rebirth scattered throughout the world which suggests, at the very least, that it's probably a fact. And not all the recollections are glamorous, lurid or linked to famous royal lines either; there are many folk who've claimed very ordinary pre-life memories when placed under hypnotic regression.

Other extraordinary past-life experiences also merit quite serious study and consideration, such as the incredibly detailed recollections of Joan Grant. Her 'Far Memory' series of books revealing her previous lives makes riveting reading. In one of them, *Eyes of Horus*, Joan recounts her days as a man – Ra-ab Hotep – the son of a high-ranking Egyptian official who lived approximately 3,500 years before the time of Jesus.

In this gripping life story, Joan recalls graphic stomach-churning details of how an elderly royal embalmer – named Yiahn – prepared a male corpse for mummification. It's an amazingly vivid description with such an incredible ring of authenticity attached to it that, as you scan the passage, you feel you're almost present, watching ...

Joan writes of how the dead man's head was treated prior to embalming: the physician used 'a narrow strip of flexible metal' which was inserted in through the corpse's nose and then 'released ... so that it held the nostril wide open'. Then the embalmer grasped another instrument which had 'a handle the length of his palm and at one end were two metal hooks curved like a leopard's claws. Up the nostril he thrust the claws; there was a grating sound like a mouse gnawing'.

She then watched him 'scraping the brain out through the nose; thick whitish curds flecked with blood and mucus; carefully transferring them to the first of the jars'.

Pretty powerful images, I think you'll agree, the details of which impressed Egyptologists who were studying possible methods of mummification.

Of her fascinating autobiography, *Far Memory*, Joan Grant wrote: 'During the last twenty years, seven books of mine have been published as historical novels which to me are biographies of previous lives I have known.'

Thought-provoking comments, but no more so than another extraordinary case of reincarnation concerning ancient Egypt – this time stemming from the mind of Dorothy Eady who was born in Edwardian London in 1904. When she was three, little Dorothy had an accident, falling head-over-heels down a flight of stairs, and she was promptly pronounced stone-dead by a doctor.

But imagine her family's deep grief suddenly changing to astonishment when they later entered the child's bedroom and found her sitting up in bed, having regained full consciousness. The doctor was amazed. 'But she was *dead*!' he exclaimed.

After this, young Dorothy began to have strange recurring dreams which later turned out to be visions of ancient temple monuments in Abydos, in the Egypt of long ago. She also perturbed her parents by constantly declaring: 'I want to go *home*.' Distraught, they couldn't make her understand she *was* home already, but Dorothy would have none of it. Then stranger things happened.

When they took her to visit the British Museum, the four-year-old girl further perplexed her family by throwing herself at the feet of the mummies, announcing with fervour:

'Leave me! *These* are my people.'

As time passed, Dorothy began recalling quite remarkable details of a former existence as an Egyptian temple priestess – named Bentreshyt – who was also a secret lover of Pharaoh Sety the First, about 3,200 years ago . . .

She said she had met 'His Majesty' (as she always referred to him) and promptly fallen in love with him in the spacious temple gardens at Abydos, where – as the fourteen-year-old Bentreshyt – she had often walked amongst the flowers. Asked where this unlikely mini-paradise was situated she instantly replied, 'To the south of Sety's Temple.'

The idea of luxurious trees and flowers in a desert setting seemed quite ridiculous to the experts, but they were soon to eat their own words. Surprised Egyptologists later *did* discover and then excavate this ancient garden in the *exact* place where Dorothy Eady had located it. They even found an avenue of very old tree-stumps and their deep root systems, plus a well and its irrigation channels for the lush green plants and flowers.

Pretty impressive facts.

In adulthood, as a citizen of Egypt, Dorothy took the now-famous name of Omm Sety, and as well as becoming a noted scholar of the ancient Egyptian religion and antiquities, she also helped the authorities to translate many hieroglyphic writings, aided by her amazing far memories.

Up to her death she maintained an absolute conviction in an afterlife, even writing in her private diaries that the spirit of the 'dead' Pharaoh Sety regularly paid her night-visits in a fully materialized physical form.

Both Omm Sety and Joan Grant are well worth studying.

But before turning our full attention to the spirit people and hearing their opinions on reincarnation, first let's take a look at further evidence – offered this time by my colleague, psychic artist Coral Polge who believes her mediumship has proven the existence of rebirth.

Coral is undoubtedly one of the world's best-known exponents of psychic portraiture; her sketched likenesses of so-called 'dead' people (when compared to photographs of them taken in life) are quite startling, as featured in her book *Living Images*, where her psychic drawings are brilliantly verified by corresponding family snapshots. Coral's mediumship has been tested like this worldwide for decades. She's drawn pictures for total strangers from nearly every country you can think of, and several sketches seem to confirm that reincarnation takes place.

Here's Coral on life before life:

As a psychic artist my work has been mainly concerned with the portrayal of people who have departed from their earthly bodies and are returning to greet their loved ones still confined in this material existence. But what of those souls who are now seeking to return to the Earth, not just in a portrait but in a new body? Are they looking around for a suitable family to incarnate into, visualizing what they may look like, planning a life-pattern to tackle?

A number of drawings have convinced me that souls do choose their future parents, and sometimes do so a long while ahead.

My first experience of drawing a before-life personality happened many years ago, but it was a considerable time before the recipient discovered what I had done. The picture was of a small boy with very large blue eyes and a quiff of reddish hair. Confident that he was part of her family, I was surprised to find that the picture meant nothing to my sitter and that no one in her family had red hair.

Many years later we met again and she told the strange outcome to this story. At something like ten years after receiving the portrait, she was informed by a young spirit that he was coming to be her new baby; something she had no plans for at the time, her existing children all being in their teens and she in her late thirties. But he was already on the way, she discovered . . . and who did he turn out to be, but the little redhead I had drawn so long ago.

And here is another tale with an even stranger twist.

A boy who had been miscarried came to be drawn for his father. I told the sitter that his wife had had two miscarriages and that on both occasions it had been the same child trying to join their family.

'He will make it on the third attempt,' I explained.

The sitter didn't think his wife had lost a second child – but a few months later, she did.

Encouraged by my statement that he would eventually come into the earth world, they tried again, and this time all proved to be well.

But the nicest part of this story was the father's comment that they now loved him so much, knowing how hard he had tried to join them. 'It makes him so much more precious,' he said, when writing to tell me the outcome.

My pre-birth pictures convince me that we all choose our particular life, hard though it may be to understand.

Without doubt, these experiences raise deep and perplexing questions, as does this next snippet which also concerns a young spirit child, but this time one who contacted his parents to *correct* their thoughts of reincarnation.

The youngster's message came through during a rare private appointment with an anxious couple who'd lost their only boy through cancer. He was just a toddler, but told his surprised mother, who was now heavily pregnant again:

'I'm not coming back you know, Mum.'

Afterwards she explained:

'I thought this new child I'm carrying would turn out to be my deceased son, reincarnating as another boy.'

She then told me that she and the lad's father had been privately discussing this days before, but the bright-eyed spirit lad must have heard their ideas and arrived at the sitting to 'put them right'.

She later gave birth to a beautiful girl.

Staying with the theme of children for a moment, here's an intriguing story of a previous existence and how it strongly affected the subject's current lifetime, as told by a teacher named Val. It started in 1965 after she and her husband had walked up a spiral staircase in Pembroke Castle's Norman keep. Val went up the stairs fine, but at the top she was gripped by a sudden irrational fear:

> I was heavily pregnant with my first child, but having always been fascinated by castles I enjoyed the climb up a spiral staircase in Pembroke. I'd been in many castles as a child, going up and down stairwells, and had never had any bother at all, but on that day I was very apprehensive and frightened.
>
> My fears were all linked with *coming down* the spiral staircase.
>
> I know it sounds silly, but I couldn't help it.
>
> But eventually, I gathered my thoughts together and, being practical, put it all down to normal

pregnancy fears and descended carefully. After that, I thought no more about it.

Ten years later, Val wasn't pregnant on this occasion, but she was visiting another ancient monument when a strikingly similar experience befell her:

My husband and I had been sightseeing in York and, of course, the ancient Minster was a *must* on our list of things to be seen.

We climbed the spiral staircase to the roof of the south transept, over a hundred feet from the ground, in order to have a good view of the historic city. I had no problem going up, in fact I never even gave our ascent a second thought; but when we turned to come down the narrow winding stairway I was seized by an uncontrollable fear.

I was petrified.

I didn't want to go down, but one cannot stay forever on a cathedral roof, so the terror had to be faced, even though I was momentarily 'paralyzed'.

'Hold tightly to me,' encouraged my concerned husband, 'and we'll make it together.'

I felt so dreadful; my legs went like jelly, I was shivering and sweating profusely and my stomach was churning like mad, and I felt that all the blood had drained out of my body.

I couldn't move: I froze to the spot in terror and it was only my husband's persistent and gentle persuasion which eventually led me down the staircase, very apprehensively. But even then, I was so terrified, and I can remember the fear being so strong, that I was scratching at the walls with my nails as I descended.

My husband said I was green-faced by the time I collapsed into a chair at the bottom. I was quaking all over and fit for nothing ...

Val desperately wanted to return to their hotel, where she flopped, exhausted, onto the bed.

My husband, seeing my unsettled emotional state and being a hypnotherapist, suggested he should relax me and try to find the reason for this intense and sudden fear. I agreed and an amazing tale spilled out of my mouth . . .

Under hypnosis I claimed I had lived in a Scottish castle, centuries ago. I had clear memories of being up a flight of spiral stone steps and gazing wistfully out of a very high window across the horizon.

I then became aware I'd just got welcome word that my husband, in that lifetime, was returning home unexpectedly, so I excitedly ran down the spiral staircase to greet him. I was very pregnant and all of a sudden I tripped and fell heavily on the steps, tumbling right down to the bottom of the winding staircase.

I didn't remember any more . . .

Yet, oddly enough, as I was recalling this dramatic incident during the hypnotic regression, my current husband was simultaneously visualizing and recollecting this entire scene: in his mind's eye he could 'see' it all.

He said I was attired in an elegant full-length gown and wearing a tall pointed wimple with a long, flowing, white gossamer train. Furthermore, he realized my heavy pregnancy was six or seven months advanced.

Five years passed and Val was now involved in a very active teaching career, when she gradually realized she was ill:

To my absolute amazement my doctor discovered I'd recently been pregnant and suffered a miscarriage in its very early stages.

I was deeply shocked and disturbed because I had no idea I'd been expecting a child, especially as I was then in my forties when pregnancies can be medically difficult.

Not only did the news of losing the very-early-stage foetus stun me, but it also completely drained me of

191

energy. Although the doctor said I'd be back to normal in a fortnight, I just couldn't seem to get better. In fact I became so poorly and unwell that one night, while feeling terribly ill, a strange fear crept into my mind, an irrational fear which my intellect couldn't dismiss or explain away.

I was frightened enough to wake up my husband with some disturbing news, expressed earnestly:

'I feel dreadful,' I said. 'I feel as though I'm going to die.'

And then – I was immediately struck by a peculiar thought: this experience might be linked in some strange way with the pre-life memory of my miscarriage in the Scottish castle centuries ago when I'd fallen down the steps. So straightaway I asked my husband if he thought I'd died in that incident. Without hesitation he replied:

'You must have done, for you were six or seven months pregnant and it seems highly unlikely you'd have survived such a harrowing experience in that day and age.'

Then the strangest thing happened. As soon as I had linked these two similar events – connected across the centuries – *my fear of expecting to die completely disappeared* and was replaced by the realization that, subconsciously, I'd thought I was going to die after *this* miscarriage because I'd done so before, in my previous life.

This incredible thought suddenly and instantly released my irrational fear of death.

Val now realizes that once the *key* to a fear is truly discovered, the owner can then unlock its cruel grip on the mind.

Psychologists share her views.

Now she's convinced that she really did live before as a pregnant woman, centuries ago in a Scottish castle:

I now believe that not only do we have many different

lives, but also that any truly traumatic experiences we've undergone in past existences can, and sometimes do, trigger off similar effects in this life – right now.

What, then, can we make of all this? Is reincarnation a fact? People say that if anyone knows the truth it would surely be the advanced souls on the Other Side. Well, I wouldn't necessarily agree because it all depends on the mind you're questioning; even in the Beyond they're divided on this vital issue. Some claim it as an Absolute Truth, while others hotly deny it. Older spirit guides usually state reincarnation is a Universal Law, and it therefore does occur, but when you ask why other spirit people refute this, they reply:

'Many souls have not yet sufficiently evolved to appreciate its existence. Knowledge comes only to those who have unfolded their awareness to the point where they are ready to receive it; the right to know has to be earned.'

As for myself: I believe in God, and that with God all things are possible. Not very scientific, I know, but then does everything have to be? There are so many inexplicable mysteries in this vast universe of ours, how can we who are physically *finite*, fully comprehend the spiritually *infinite*? We cannot – which is why all intelligent people should keep an open mind.

So if reincarnation is a law, *what* comes back? I don't believe *you* as an individual, a personality, a characterized soul will return to Earth. But what *can* be reborn into flesh may be another aspect of your eternal mind.

There's a great difference between your Personality and your Spirit. The Personality is everything we are in our physical consciousness – whereas the Spirit is the everlasting essence of us, the direct Life-Force which links us to God, the Great Spirit. So in our current individual form, as *this* particular individual, I don't believe we'll ever return to Earth, but we will pass into eternity, forever.

However, another portion of our Spirit, our Mind, might be characterized into flesh again as a different entity at some future time. This means that our separate individual survival is assured.

Concepts like these aren't easy to grasp, but perhaps we can be helped by likening the Spirit to a many faceted diamond, segments of which are personalized into Earth consciousness as individuals – each part having a life of its own, but all derived from the same Life-Force. In this way we have a centralized core of Mind – *us* – while at the same time there are fragments of the diamond shining in different Earth locations at one and the same time, each aspect adding its lustre to the centralized Mind.

Here's an easier picture: a bicycle wheel portrays the centralized mind as the hub of the wheel with all the spokes projecting outwards to join the continuous Circle of Time: each spoke is a separate life which touches the time-stream at different points in Earth's history.

All are interlinked, yet 'separate'.

However, I don't think reincarnation can be successfully proven, even though there's a vast array of startling evidence put forward, for there are many other possible explanations which can nullify facts concerning 'previous lives'.

Neither do I think rebirth is as common an occurrence as some lead us to believe. If it does happen, then the individual realizes there are valuable lessons to be learned or special tasks to be accomplished on this planet and, because of free will, undertakes the incarnation itself.

I can't accept the idea of higher authorities *making* souls return. Either we have personal responsibility or we don't. I believe we do.

What, then, could be the other explanations for pre-birth memories? Several things:

1. A vivid imagination.
2. A secondary personality of the subject, surfacing under hypnosis and claiming to be a different individual.
3. An ancient spirit entity linking with the subject's mind and relaying, through thought transference, or mediumship, its past memories.
4. The subject could be tapping into what Carl Jung called the 'Collective Unconscious', referred to in the East as the 'Akashic Records' (a kind of complete cosmic library of thoughts, feelings and deeds recorded since the beginning of time).
5. Remote viewing (mentally perceiving the past, then dramatizing it as a living present).
6. Out-of-the-body recollections, or astral projection memories, where the travelling Spirit Body sees places and people while the physical body is asleep. Then, when awake, the subject may later recognize them again.
7. Genetic memories. Some claim ancestral memories may be passed down with the genes of the body.
8. Cryptomnesia: the recalling of films/TV/all reading matter/conversations etc, heard or seen when younger, and now surfacing as a dramatized 'life'.
9. Multiple personality: a psychiatric condition

where one individual may have several different personalities, each manifesting at different times; and it's even possible for each persona to be ignorant of the existence of the others and their acts.

Any one of these could broadly nullify rebirth memories, which is why I don't think the issue will ever escape doubt – though personal conviction is good enough proof for those who have undergone the experience.

If we still doubt it, how could this last baffling case be explained away? It's one of the most fascinating stories in favour of reincarnation I've ever heard, related by professional hypnotherapist, Elizabeth Bowen, BA, Dip Ed, CC, CHP (College of Hypnotherapy and Psychotherapy).

The case came to her attention in the early 1980s and concerns a young, healthy man in his twenties who was totally blind and had been since birth. As a newborn baby he'd been placed in an oxygen tent and too much gas was delivered, which caused the malady.

He approached Mrs Bowen because of 'unsettling dreams' he'd been experiencing which seemed to 'centre around the brilliance of the sun'.

She then regressed him when, suddenly, much to her amazement, he exclaimed: '*I can see!*' and then went on to describe himself 'inside a wooden hut, in natural light, roughly carving the butts and handles of rifles so that the men could later shape them to their individual shoulders and physiques for comfort'. His visions were in full colour and he could even see and describe in accurate detail 'the trees and the forest outside', objects he had never seen before.

Quite a remarkable feat; but even more so when Elizabeth regressed him further back into what he could also 'see' was some kind of ancient tribe of which he was a member. They were worshipping the sun and had been instructed by the elders 'not to look upon the disc' as it rose. Being 'curious' in that lifetime, he disobeyed the law, was seized and then 'sacrificed on a stone altar'.

At the end of these incredible experiences, upon return to normality, the young man was once again blind. 'It's one of the most interesting and baffling cases I've ever come across,' said Mrs Bowen.

I would certainly agree.

She ended by asking, 'How can this be explained, except that my client must have had some kind of previous existence in which his eyes functioned correctly?'

Finally, I'd never be forgiven if I didn't allow my spirit guide, White Owl, to address this issue; but it's worth recording that while I keep an open mind on the topic, he, it seems, is totally convinced of its existence.

Here's how he answered the question: *If there are previous lives before this one, why?*

Because the soul can only build its experiences through the crucible of learning.

Earth is a training-ground for souls; it presents unique opportunities to interact on a physical plane with many and varied other beings at differing levels of soul-growth to one's self.

In my world, the spirit plane, souls are naturally and automatically grouped together according to their evolution and growth, but in your world no such formal grouping takes place – your planes of thought are comprised of millions of beings all at different stages of evolution, all together, all interacting in one place, all growing through their challenges, struggles and experiences.

As a conscious being, first you are partially aware, a Divine Spark clothed in a beast; then you walk erect. Maybe you are poor, after which you are materially wealthy; sighted, then blind; ignorant, then intellectual; maimed and then whole; you are a male, then a female; lost and wandering, and then finally secure in your knowledge of self and God.

After this comes the greatest lesson of all: the soul learns to climb upwards towards the light, until it fully knows and expresses the true meaning of service, love and kindness . . .

You cannot learn all which Earth-life has to teach in one incarnation, for the Great Spirit has ordained that wisdom may only be possessed by the wise.

15

A Purpose to Living

Some of Life's Certainties

Do we now possess more wisdom because of all our enquiries into the world of soul? Where have our investigations led us?

In the turbulent sea of life's uncertainties and doubt: birth, life, death; life before birth; life after death – of what can we now be sure? Well, I believe there are a number of things:

No soul is born without a purpose, a complicated spiritual blueprint which it brings with it into Earth-life. This deep, soul-pattern may have been built up through several incarnations, many life-experiences, all of which add to the completeness of the whole individual.

Birth provides an excellent opportunity of returning to an existence where mankind and the animal kingdom are both thrown together in a miasma of confusion caused by the interaction of beings at all different stages of evolution; each soul struggling to develop its innate qualities alongside others trying to do the same. And out of all this will eventually emerge further spiritual growth and order in the human race.

But while we exist within this seeming chaos, if we examine our lives carefully, we can see that the broad outlines of our days are planned – by us; for we lead a double existence: twelve hours on Earth and twelve hours in the World of Spirit where we truly belong. In our sleep-life older minds impart wise counsel to us (should we desire it) about what we were born to attain, our past achievements, where we are now and – probably the most important of all – where our present thoughts will lead us.

So when next we wonder 'Where on earth am I going?' let us remember:

The Inner Self knows everything, and if we learn how to touch our own Higher Mind – that elevated part of our consciousness not ordinarily perceived without effort – through stillness, meditation and prayer we'll discover priceless inner guide-posts which will not fail us.

All the answers are within.

Even so, countless souls still remain pathetically lost and sadly wandering in the dark absence of knowledge, still painfully unaware that they've chosen their lives and could really be at peace with themselves, if only they would seek it.

A young disabled man I know – he's wheelchair-bound – deeply searched his soul for many years, desperately trying to come to terms with his illness and the reasons for it. With all his might he valiantly fought his disabilities every inch of the way, until eventually he won his reward. It was a harsh but, paradoxically, kind dawning of realization:

'Now I finally know,' he said with resignation, 'I chose this unresponsive body because it's taught me lessons I never would have learned otherwise.'

Following this, a great well of peace was released within his spirit, the life-giving waters of which rose and completely bathed him in inner contentment. He immediately ceased to fight himself, saw the spiritual benefits of his misfortunes, accepted them gracefully, and now he's a much happier man. He even looks forward to waking in the morning, whereas previously he dreaded each new dawn.

Because of the increased tides of peace and power within him, gradually he realized a Constant Truth: *we can blame no one for our lives, but ourselves.*

When others emotionally hurt us, we are to blame – it's our own fault, for we've allowed them to cause us harm. By opening ourselves to their poisonous arrows we have received them squarely in the heart (and sometimes all too willingly).

But in every life, suffering is inevitable, for Earth-souls are constantly battling against one another, struggling to survive, expand and mould the character. As human beings we're also forever fighting our own selves, within. The beast of flesh seeks power over the spirit, and the soul endeavours to come into its own and thereby vanquish the enemy. The eternal part of ourselves does everything in its power to master the physical temple and all its frequently selfish, narrow-minded thoughts.

We're engaged in ferocious mental and spiritual warfare within ourselves, a conflict which unbalances the triune being we truly are: body, mind and spirit. The war challenges the mind and builds up soul experiences: and thus we learn and slowly evolve.

Earth-life provides wonderful opportunities to develop ourselves ethically, morally, spiritually, physically, mentally and emotionally; and no-one can escape these forces. All life-forms have their eyes filled with tears, their hearts wrenched with the pain of loss, and their minds confused by the trials of the spirit as it seeks to overcome its past and mould its future more fruitfully.

Without exception, every soul must know the torments of adversity.

And as we travel forward it's absolutely certain we can't always agree with our fellow-creatures, which is why our judgements should be guarded. Unless we've walked in the other man's shoes – intimately knowing and feeling his every inner struggle, joy and personal despair – we cannot pass judgement on the quality or meaning of his life; though many believe they can, and frequently do.

The wicked act of condemning others is nothing more than a simple psychological mind-trick: by casting suspicion away from ourselves and on to someone else, our own faults will avoid detection.

But this is a lie and our time would be more wisely spent on examining ourselves instead of others.

'*Man know thyself.*'

This vitally important concept will help us to find our peace in this world. We can pray until kingdom comes to obtain 'a purpose to our days', 'happiness', 'our heart's desire', or any other 'possession' we'd like to 'own' – but none of these will ever be granted as a gift.

All soul qualities must be earned. This is a Universal Law which cannot be abrogated or cheated: *Cause and Effect* decree that we can only receive exactly what we've earned for ourselves; we reap only what we've previously sown.

And during this eternal quest, every single scar or moment of joy is indelibly registered on the soul. Nothing is ever wasted or forgotten. The mind is a picture-making, recording substance: an Essence of Spirit Consciousness Itself which, when we think of something, 'images' it as a reality. Rather like a 'living' movie, our thoughts are projected onto the screen of our lives.

We are the originators: we create the plot, write the script, engage the other participants, direct the action, and also play out the drama ourselves.

And because each line of dialogue is forever stored, filed away in a vast living memory-bank (an ever-accessible library of eternal experiences), not one idea or expression is ever lost: they remain 'alive', deep within the furthest reaches of the mind.

Nothing is ever 'finished', 'lost', 'irretrievable' or experienced without some 'hidden' purpose.

As we evolve, this experience-gathering mind of ours soon recognizes that life is full of comparison: light as well as shade. Who wants to live in a world where the blazing-hot sun never stops shining? I don't; I'd desperately miss the cool of the night. And how could we treasure the peaceful harmony of a healthy body unless we've first known the misery and heart-break of pain? How could we appreciate the Earth's beauty from a high mountain peak unless we've first won the privilege of viewing it by scrambling up the steep and craggy hillsides, fingers bleeding as we grasped for hand-holds?

Only on the mountain-top can we know that we've risen from dark and miserable valleys below, places which were once our homes before the powerful Light of Progress urged us forward.

But we must always seek, before we can find.

Life involves change, evolution; a journey of the soul from the darkness of mental slavery into the effulgent light of self-government and spiritual realization. And, like it or not, we'll definitely encounter numberless hardships along our way; that's why we're conscious. But we can make the road much easier for ourselves.

By removing Negative Mental Forces and adopting Positive Thought we can *welcome* our challenges. When we're truly grateful for them, they cease to be enemies and become treasured friends which teach us priceless spiritual lessons, both here and in eternity. (Life in the next world isn't easy, either, and progression is an everlasting process.)

Destructive Negative Forces thrive in the moanings of 'Why did this terrible thing happen to *me*?' Or 'Why didn't someone else suffer this tragedy?' Or 'Look at others – they've lived a privileged life; nothing bad has ever happened to *them*'. All these are shallow-sighted lies, for the sea of life tosses everyone hither and thither in a turbulent mass of conscious experience, no matter who we are, or who we might *think* we are.

Discontented souls are inexperienced beings who are out of touch with their higher selves, their true purpose and motivations. What these people are actually saying is: 'I don't want to mature; I don't want to evolve and change for the better – I want everything my own way.'

This is the hidden child speaking in us; an undeveloped being who wants the hardest tasks accomplished for him, without taking any of the responsibility himself.

So many people make their own lives, and those of others connected to them, utterly miserable by carrying huge amounts of 'excess emotional baggage' within themselves. This usually takes the form of crippling negative emotions and energy-consuming worries which they point-blankly refuse to drop.

Much physical illness is generated psychosomatically – by an overall negative attitude of mind. If we would just release these disharmonies, we could be free of all disease, and subsequently, much happier beings. There's a marvellous story which illustrates this:

Two saffron-robed monks were walking quietly along a riverbank, deep in silent contemplation, when all of a sudden they came upon a distressed old woman who wanted to cross the stream but felt she was too frail and fearful to do so. The younger monk lifted her into his strong arms, carried her across and deposited his grateful charge on the opposite bank. He then re-joined his colleague to continue their journey.

They walked on for a further mile or so in silence, but the older monk was inwardly very upset, boiling with anger because their religious order forbade any contact whatsoever with women, and his younger colleague had flagrantly disobeyed this command.

After another mile, the furious elder suddenly broke his vow of silence and severely and aggressively reprimanded his friend, to which the young monk calmly replied:

'Brother, I put that woman down two miles back: why are you still carrying her?'

Without doubt, the deeper problems of the soul are infinitely complex, so there are no easy answers, no instant solutions. This makes the path of soul attainment a long, slow and arduous one, with treasured prizes being garnered only one at a time, through struggle and personal effort. There are no short cuts, just hard work and, finally, the indescribable joy of self-discovery which brings greater awareness of our own consciousness and the way to control it, and with it – our lives.

We are personally responsible for our lives, actions, thoughts and deeds: no church, no book, no creed, no belief, no 'magical formulas' or divine beings can remove this law. We cannot live utterly selfish lives and then, upon 'death', expect our actions to be wiped away and 'forgiven' by anyone except the souls to whom we have caused the suffering. We ourselves will have to 'right' all the 'wrongs' we have committed.

We reap exactly what we sow, *every time*.

This is Divine Justice.

We are the masters of ourselves, the conscious captains of our own destinies; and there's nothing so insurmountable that it can obstruct or prevent us from steering the ships of our lives through peaceful waters, if that's what we really want.

And at the end of the journey, there is no such thing as death. Within us is a Spirit Body, through which we will continue to be conscious in a world nearby.

Progression – evolution – is open to every soul; and I believe the way forward is through expressing the powers of love and compassion.

And so the pageant of life continues.

The great adventure is a never-ending pilgrimage, a ceaseless struggle towards perfection ...

Although I'm often categorized as 'a man in contact with another world', the implications of my work reach much deeper than this. Through all aspects of the written and spoken word, plus mass-media appearances, there's been a far more important message underlying my voice than the fact that we survive death: and this is the conduct of the soul of man.

I've never been one bit concerned about the 'dead', for they're quite able to take care of themselves. It's the so-called 'living' who need our attention: the millions of people thronging the Earth who need encouragement to seek peace, tolerance, brotherhood, love and understanding; harmony, friendship, kindness and compassion; mutual respect for other life-forms and for this small planet on which we must all dwell together.

Only by expressing these qualities in our own lives can we ever hope to affect and change the lives of others for the better. These concepts are far more important to me than the fact that we cannot die.

What really matters is that Man learns to live at peace with himself and others.

It also matters that the animal kingdom should finally receive the love and respect it deserves, and that it shouldn't be exploited, tortured, maimed or 'scientifically' experimented upon by those who foolishly believe that progress can come by the shedding of innocent brotherly blood.

My message is far from new; many seers and prophets down the ages have advocated it. But if only all the family of Earth, every race and nation, all sects and creeds, the rich and poor, believers and non-believers, would strive to light a lamp of understanding, brotherhood, love and peace within their hearts – what a wonderful world this could be.

The Wise Ones in Spirit consider it a privilege to serve, so much so that they've willingly renounced their places in exalted spirit spheres to return and teach us more of these concepts. And, why? – *because they love us*.

Despite Man's constant foolish attempts to blot out their pristine Truths of the Spirit with unnecessary creeds and dogmas, some shining pearls of wisdom still remain, thank God.

Like countless voices before me I've asked mankind to stop, think, change and spiritually progress. But at the end of the day, like everyone else, I'm simply a messenger whose message is far more important than its deliverer.

One day, when your life here is thankfully over and you happily return to the realms from whence you came, your finite body will crumble into dust –

back into the heart of the Great Mother who gave it – but, in the Next World, your soul will rejoice in the knowledge that somewhere, somehow, your experiences – like mine – will have added something to the evolution of the human race.

In the Next World, I guess I'll be grateful for the privilege of spreading knowledge of some of life's spiritual realities to friends on Earth.

But what about you?

How will you view your time on this planet?

Only you will be able to answer.

But however you'll feel about it, the same rules will have governed us all: we will have realized there's no such thing as Chance, only Cause and Effect, and that what we have sent out into the Great Stream of Life is exactly what has returned to us, in full measure.

This vast Universe is ruled by highly-organized Ancient Mind, of which we are each an integral part. We are the Eternal Sons and Daughters of the Living Light; brothers and sisters; gods-in-the-making, using the magnificent and inexhaustible Power of the Great Spirit's Thought and materializing it through our individual lives on Earth, and in Spirit.

The Great Spirit is Indestructible and Everlasting – and so are we.

The Great Spirit

And in bewildering confusion, Man looked up and cried out from the depths of his Being: 'God, who art Thou?'

And as silent as a whisper upon the wind came a mind-voice, speaking:

I Am all that Is.
  I Am in all things,
Through all things,
  Behind all things:
The Fire of Life
  Within a babe;
I shine behind your lover's eyes,
  A power, crystallized.

I Am the Positive
And the Negative,
  Good and Bad;
  Love and Hate.
I Am black and white,
  And a myriad shades of grey.
I Am in the rolling thunder and the fire-fly's light;
  I Am the morning
  And the night;
The darkness and the light.

See me in soft gentility,
  And also in every cruel act:
For I am Everywhere,
  In Everything;
Within all life-forms, no matter what they lack.

Neither male nor female I,
  But Spirit, Soul, Consciousness,
  A pulsing Breath of Life and Mind:
    the Beginning, which never was;
    the Fleeting Now;
    And the very End – which man will never find.

Find Me in a flowering bud
  Or glimpse Me in a looking-glass;
I am the Unlovable, the Untouchable; the Intolerable –
In Everything which comes to pass.

The 'Is' Am I:
  A set of Laws,
  Laid down Fast, Immutable,

Unchangeable keys to all doors.
I am discompassionately Sublime,
   Mathematically Perfect;
   I Am the Beater of Time.

And those attuned to Me,
   Harmoniously,
      Find peacefulness and ease;
But to those ignoring Me
   comes disharmony
   and dis-ease.

For I Am all Causes and their precise Effects:
   I Am inside the All,
And outside the Everything you know;
   I fill the Nothing,
And yet I Am the Nothingness also.

And I need no worship or genuflection,
Nor petty appeasements:
   For I Am not an 'I' –
   I simply Am all things:
And you are my reflection.

And unto you is granted
A measure of My Power,
   For use, according to your Willing;

*For You and I are One –
And We are Mind,
Evolving.*

PART TWO
The Man Behind the Mask

16

A Spirit of the Times

by Jeff Rees Jones
(Stephen O'Brien's tour manager)

In response to thousands of fan-mail letters requesting 'inside information' about the real man behind the mask of publicity, Stephen O'Brien 'couldn't do it' himself, but as his tour manager, would I?

'That depends,' I said, 'on how much freedom I get with the text.'

'Complete,' he replied (with a caution not to include too many profanities!).

Out of respect for his many followers, I agreed, and was given *carte blanche* to write the following, 'warts and all'.

I gave it serious thought and decided by far the best method was to record events which the medium's public would never, under normal circumstances, be aware of; aspects of his private life and self, plus his backstage personality.

I titled this chapter by borrowing a headline from a celebrity interview *Wales on Sunday* published about Stephen, which I think is perfectly apt.

Backstage

Both my family and I have known Stephen for about fourteen years and he's certainly no angel. He's an ordinary man with a well-developed sense of black humour, precision comic-timing, and a willpower of steel. Over this period, we've watched him rise from virtual obscurity (my mother used to send him food parcels in the 1980s) to becoming a household name whenever mediumship is discussed.

What the public never sees is his excellent business-sense and keen intellectual mind. But he can also be tetchy, stubborn and intransigent, steadfastly holding his ground without the least sign of weakening against any opponent. Stephen O'Brien would stand to be killed for something he truly believed in, yet, paradoxically, he can sometimes appear ridiculously anxious over the slightest concerns which wouldn't affect others.

Like all true celebrities, he has a sparkling personality, but is somewhat of an enigma.

Undoubtedly, he's gentle, an animal-lover, a vegan, and almost a recluse who is many times kind – without the glare of publicity attached to the good works he does. For example, very few people know he sponsors the education and medical health of a ten-year-old African girl from a poor district in troubled Uganda, sending regular financial aid and correspondence to her through the Christian Children's Fund of Great Britain, in Bedford Row, London.

These kindnesses, however, don't make him a saint. His choice of language covers a very broad spectrum! He believes 'words are there to be used – nothing's exempt,' which he frequently proves. I've heard him use many expletives and this, I believe, is the free spirit and writer in him being expressed; after all, he comes from a working-class background and wasn't born with a silver spoon in his mouth.

First and last he's a man who loves the silence and loathes being 'idolized' by over-enthusiastic fans.

What really irritates him is the way strangers embrace or kiss him, particularly when he's signing autographs.

'Aren't they aware of personal zones?' he frowns.

I sympathize, but add: 'That's the price of fame.'

Stephen can hold his own in any discussion and he's never yet been stumped for words. His ever-present witty, and often cutting, sense of black humour is a great delight which his books fail to adequately convey because of the sensitive subjects he tackles in them. He'll make fun of – and laugh at – anything, especially himself. His small circle of friends thoroughly enjoy his quick repartee, often being the butt of it:

Once, when he had to decide what gifts to buy two very dowdy, wrinkled people he knew, he drily announced:

'Oh, I know, I'll get them a cucumber face-pack each.'

He also has a peculiar habit of blessing people with his own amusing nicknames, some of which I couldn't repeat! One old medium – whom he's seen working hundreds of times and who has yet to receive a 'yes' to any of her information – is comically referred to as 'Madame No'. And his cat Sooty is called anything which pops into his head, like 'Flea-bag'.

One thin young woman, who'd obviously fallen under the spell of his platform charms, would – each time she saw Stephen – wiggle voluptuously around him 'like a giggly schoolgirl with full motors running', fluttering her eyes adoringly and licking her lips. One day, in mid-wiggle as she approached him, he whispered to me quickly out of the corner of his mouth, 'Quick, open the back door – here comes "Eyelash"!'

I remember another amusing episode when he posted some surprise accommodation money to an English lady-friend of his who'd provided him with his own single room for a few days on tour. He sent her a banknote plus a scribbled message: '£20 enclosed for the use of your bed: full story appears in the *News of the World* next Sunday!'

As well as ready wit, he seems to also possess what some have termed as a 'magnetic presence', and I wonder if this might be something to do with his often childlike innocence and naïvete?

Once, while out on a business trip, I popped into a supermarket for a few groceries and left Stephen at the checkouts. When I'd paid for my items, imagine my surprise to see a small crowd gazing towards one corner of the store, and seated inside a tiny Cartoon Cabin was Stephen, with two young children and their father gathered around him, all having a good laugh at one of his favourite cartoon characters, Daffy Duck. ('The greatest star in the universe.') As he placed another coin in the machine, I grabbed my shopping, walked past the Cabin and hissed out of the corner of my mouth, 'I'll meet you back at the car.' At the exit someone asked me: 'Do you know him?' 'No,' I said, loftily, as I sailed out of the doors.

But what about the private man, far away from the public spotlight? Well, oddly enough, he's a quiet person who doesn't mind appearing *before* thousands of people, but loathes being *in* crowds. Many times I've seen him leave a busy pavement and walk in the road, preferring to take his chance with fast traffic, just to avoid people, and when frequently recognized in public, he's usually embarrassed and makes a quick getaway.

Paradoxically, he loves absolute silence but also

good music: both composing and listening to it. He likes opera and has written volumes of deep, thought-provoking, spiritual poetry.

One area of his life is strictly out of bounds: his home. Positively *no-one*, except his closest friends, is ever invited or admitted. Journalists meet him in hotels or other people's houses, and no photographs of Stephen's possessions or surroundings have ever been published. 'I've been photographed to death. My home is the last piece of privacy I have left in the world,' he laments. He rarely goes out, hates pubs and parties, and all this highlights the intensely private man who's 'loved from afar by thousands' but has very few personal friends – you could count them on two hands and maybe have fingers to spare.

Whenever I call on him to settle business matters, he's either playing the piano, watching a video, listening to music ('thrilled' by Pavarotti or Shirley Bassey), 'just having a nap' on the couch (with his cat, Sooty, lying across his knees), writing, or reading – he devours scores of books. In fact, the first places we both seek out on tour are second-hand bookshops, and once he's in, you just can't get him out again.

At home, he's invariably in a 'sloppy-Joe' loose jumper (either somebody else's cast-off or bought at a charity shop) and sporting baggy trousers. He's usually unshaven and flopping around in carpet slippers, one of his habits from childhood. ('My mother trained us all to take our shoes off as soon as we came home and to put our slippers on straightaway. I wear them till the soles fall off before getting another pair'.)

In his spare time, when he gets the opportunity he loves walking in the open countryside or near the rolling sea, but he's a man who seems to exist in a world of his own and he's frequently stated, 'I don't really belong here, on Earth'. Some of his habits back this up: he never buys a newspaper (because 'it's all so transient') and he even reads someone else's *Psychic News*. But he's an extremely selective television watcher. To the humdrum soap operas (many of which he loathes) he exclaims:

'Oh my gawd! Switch the bloody thing off! All the horrible people you never wanted to meet, all shouting and bawling at each other in your own living-room. No thanks.'

His favourite programmes are nature documentaries and comedy shows. He likes 'intelligent' humour, and comedians Frankie Howerd, Ken Dodd, French and Saunders, Dame Edna Everage, and *The Golden Girls* series, amongst others, are a must whenever their shows are screened.

Old feature films are also firm favourites, like *Whatever Happened to Baby Jane?* He loves to watch Bette Davis, finding her screen presence 'captivating'.

I've called on him on more than one occasion, at a particularly emotional point in a film, to discover him lying on the sofa, watching it, and making no noise whatsoever but with tears rolling down his face. This is guaranteed during *E.T.* (The Extra-Terrestrial), one of his favourite movies.

Touching upon another world, it's quite a commonplace occurrence when around Stephen O'Brien to suddenly hear him muttering replies to phantom questions. Quite out of the blue he'll say something like: 'No, I've told you; I'm not going to do that.' Or 'All right, all right; nag, nag, nag. I'll see to it tomorrow.' Far from slipping into dementia, he's answering the spirit people who are obviously in conversation with him.

I know the medium's greatest ambition is to have a small place of his own in secluded countryside, 'away from the masses', something in keeping with his deep and profound respect for nature, in all its forms. I've been in his company when suddenly an electric thunderstorm began to rage. Without asking, he immediately switched off the light, opened the curtains wide and marvelled at the lightning hitting the distant hills. The look on his face was similar to that of a young child opening gifts on Christmas morning. In passing, he doesn't uphold with sending cards or presents simply because of Christmas: 'We should love people all year round,' he says, 'not just on one day.'

(He has very little contact with his relatives, but they always receive telephone calls from him on Christmas afternoon, wherever he might be in the country.)

My family and I have always found Stephen to be direct and honest with people. He'll tell you *exactly* what he thinks, without any malice. If he knows it might upset you, he asks: 'Do you really want to know?' And if they do, he tells them straight. I suspect he's lost the acquaintance of certain people in this way, but then – as he says – 'People who can't take objective criticism, especially when they've asked for it, aren't friends anyway.'

How do you measure a person's kindness?

Well, I believe the answer's to be found in what he does, and not what he says he does.

Once, while returning along a motorway late at night after a discussion with the manager of the world-famous City Varieties Theatre in Leeds, the fast traffic came to a sudden halt. Hazard lights were flashing as Stephen stopped the car, saying seriously, 'It's an accident,' and he immediately got out and ran to the front of the action without a thought of what he might find.

A small car had crashed into a lorry which had completely smashed in its front. In the frosty night air the engine was producing clouds of steam, and inside the car lay an unconscious elderly man in his late seventies, with deep gashes on his forehead. His blood was freely flowing and steaming in the cold wind, covering his face and body. An annoyed Stephen said afterwards: 'Ten men were standing around the wreckage doing nothing. No-one was interested in the old man. Someone was telephoning for an ambulance and that was it. I couldn't believe it!'

But Stephen prized open the smashed rear door, sat awkwardly among the shattered glass and twisted metal and spoke with and comforted the man, as he wiped the blood from his face with a shirt. And he stayed there, beside him, until professional help arrived.

Although the victim (named Hector) was badly concussed and extremely lucky to be alive after having fallen asleep at the wheel, through his confusion the elderly man managed to stroke Stephen's hand and say: 'You're doing a grand job, son . . . Thank you . . . You're doing a fine job.'

With similar quiet dedication Stephen also answers thousands of letters, personally (he has no secretary at the time of writing, though this move is contemplated for the future), and I know that many a sad person's day has been brightened by an unexpected reply from him.

But, as his manager, this concerns me, for there isn't enough energy in him, or hours in the day to accomplish all this work without undue stress: so many people make heavy demands on his time, in many cases without so much as a 'please' or 'thank you' or even a stamped addressed envelope.

But his dedication to his public and, more importantly (as he sees it), to the spirit world, is total and uncompromising. He won't consider failing them.

I remember he was once extremely ill on tour in Northern England, promptly producing the contents of his stomach six times. Violently ill, dizzy and miserable when he retired, he was aware that at 6 a.m. the next morning he had to motor down from the North to the Midlands (about a three-hour drive), where he was to appear at a sell-out demonstration in Birmingham Town Hall that night. The meeting was going to be filmed by the BBC as part of an interview for the *Daytime UK* TV programme.

As sick as he was, he was the first in the house to rise at 5.30 a.m. waking everyone else up. He helped to load the car and then drove to Birmingham where he conducted the filmed meeting under great (and invisible) stress – all without so much as even mentioning his illness to the audience. They never knew.

The meeting was a good one, and the televised clairvoyance caused a great deal of interest in the country. 'I've *got* to be there,' I remember him saying. 'People are expecting me and I can't let them, or the spirit world, down.'

I've also known him show such concern for lesser creatures. I've seen him pick up a twig and raise sluggish earthworms from scorching-hot paving stones and transfer them onto damp earth nearby, muttering as he did so: 'There you are; dig in! That's much better isn't it?'

In addition to this commendable concern, he can also call upon great strength, directness and positivity. In all the years I've known him he's never been afraid to speak his mind, which can be quite embarrassing, especially when things go wrong at meetings.

I remember his surprise at one Welsh venue

when we discovered there were no technicians. The manager was a small, round and pompous man with an obvious arrogance. This, plus Stephen's concern for 'organizing things properly' and his deep dislike of 'ignorant and coarse' people, brought about an embarrassing red-faced clash. The manager patronizingly informed him that 'sound and lights had been cancelled' and there'd be 'no-one to operate them anyway'.

Stephen called out: 'Jeffrey! Pass me the contract please!'

(I'm always summoned as 'Jeffrey' when a bombshell is about to be dropped. So I handed it to him then stood back, waiting.)

Stephen waved the paper under the man's nose, proved him wrong and told the official it was his 'job to provide them'.

When the man said 'it's too late now, mate; there'll be no bloody electrics', the medium immediately commanded: 'Oh yes there will, and *you* will set them up!'

The manager loudly complained that he 'didn't go to college for seven years to set up poxy microphones and lights'.

Stephen replied: 'Well, you'll be doing it tonight. And what's more, you'll do it now, because the public will be here in fifteen minutes.'

The manager's response is unprintable, but the equipment was grumpily provided forthwith!

Tony Ortzen, author and editor of *Psychic News*, which has frequently front-paged Stephen's mediumship and also published articles by him, asked the medium if he'd agree to his handwriting being analysed by graphologist and astrologer, Peter West.

Some might find this excerpt, published on 15 June 1991, quite interesting:

Stephen enjoys playing a high profile in the public eye and can cope with the benefits such activity brings.

However, he will prefer as much privacy as he can get. He can be inconsistent at times and may have a lazy streak; he could well operate in fits and starts.

Occasionally, modesty may be a problem, but by and large both feet are firmly on the ground.

Stephen can be quite chatty when he chooses . . . There is a lot of energy. The pressure of the pen on the page is so strong that the writing can be deciphered from the back of the paper.

I would imagine when Stephen first enters a room he fills it with his personality . . .

I've seen this happen many times; when Stephen arrives, all eyes turn on him, even if he's not speaking.

This kind of intangible charismatic presence is difficult to define or fully understand, but celebrities either have it or they don't: Stephen O'Brien does.

Two Welsh journalists summed it up like this:

I met Stephen O'Brien and was greeted by an affable character whose smile and handshake I immediately warmed to. He spoke softly and eloquently and, like the packed audiences he holds mesmerized, I was captivated by his personal magnetism. It was quickly apparent that Stephen is very much a 'real person', nothing celluloid or pretentious, rather a mixture of sensitivity and vulnerability.

Wales in Action

Mr O'Brien certainly knows how to hold an audience – 500 people were like putty in his hands. Mr O'Brien's popularity is easy to understand: each message is delivered with compassion and humour. He is relaxed, sympathetic and confident – even the most sceptical could not fail to be impressed.

South Wales Echo

Author Linda Williamson has met the medium several times and once shared the platform with him at a London venue. Linda featured Stephen's life and work in her informative and successful book *Mediums and their Work* (Robert Hale, 1990).

She touched upon his 'magnetic presence', which could well be linked to some of the other qualities she mentions:

> Stephen has a very quiet and reserved manner, in fact when I first met him I found it hard to imagine him handling a large audience, but I was surprised to discover that he has a great charisma on the stage. His gentleness and sincerity evoke an immediate response, and there is obvious conviction in the way in which he delivers the messages from the Other Side of life – but fame has not brought him wealth, as he explains.
>
> 'The proceeds of my early public meetings went to charity, either to help in the Third World, or for needy children, or for the handicapped. I didn't make money from them, in fact I was often out of pocket. I know what it is to be poor.'
>
> Some of the organizations Stephen has supported have been animal charities such as the RSPCA and PDSA. 'Animals are our brothers,' he states. 'They have souls, and they too survive death.' For this reason he is a vegan, touching no animal foods or produce.
>
> He sees his writing as a further opportunity of getting across his message of peace, brotherhood and survival to a much wider public. 'A long time ago,' he told me, 'I made a pact with the Spirit World to serve them, and I will honour this. All I ask is that God will give me the strength to complete what I was born to do.'

When I asked him his views on what gives a person charisma, he said it was 'a soul emanation, psychic light and energy surrounding certain people, shining, unhindered, from the centre of themselves.'

Some other matters are worthy of note. For example, he always wears dark glasses when driving – even on overcast and rainy days because 'soul sensitivity reflects on the physical body; bright daylight hurts my eyes because they're more sensitive than many other people's. My hearing's very sharp too.'

This is undeniably true. Once, when discussing business he pulled a face and grumbled: 'Isn't that music awful? Can you hear it?' When I said I couldn't, he seemed surprised, adding incredulously, *'Can't you?'*

After stilling myself and listening hard, I then picked up the very faint but distant sounds of someone's car radio which, to Stephen's ears, had obviously been quite distinct and annoying.

Though such a private person, when he has no choice but to mix with strangers he'll speak to anyone. At BBC TV Birmingham I went for some coffee and when I returned to the green room he was merrily chatting away with Hollywood film star Richard E. Grant and television presenter Judi Spiers, as though they were all long-lost friends. This kind of warmth is typical of the man.

But, essentially, underneath the public persona, Stephen O'Brien is a cool-minded, emotionally detached Aquarian who possesses amazing energy levels and a strong will. Most times he has uncannily accurate foresight, and works tirelessly until all his strength is spent, sometimes pushing himself to the very brink of physical and nervous exhaustion.

He gives every atom of his abilities to serve the public who flock to see him, and the care, concern and sincere kindness which shine through his personality never fail to captivate his audiences.

On Stage

Stephen doesn't play the 'psychic superstar' or 'prima donna' as some have wrongly assumed. In fact, far from it: he takes a major role in formulating every part of his tour schedules right through from their inception to conclusion, and he isn't afraid of hard work.

He's a good organizer, but wrongly believes he's the only person who can do the jobs to his own satisfaction which, quite frankly, makes me realize how easy it would be to commit murder! Touring is always a strenuous enough experience without Stephen's added perfectionism.

Normally, at 5.30 a.m. a telephone call comes from him and we soon meet and are loading up his car with books, cassettes, programmes and suitcases – and sometimes Sooty. Then we're off. I don't drive, so this thankless job is left to him while I snore away in the passenger seat (management does have its little perks).

Between catnaps we work in the car, preparing things like the text for his bestselling cassette *Life After Death, What Awaits Us in the Next World* which was dictated by him on the motorways somewhere between Wales and Brighton. 'A pity to waste time,' he says.

We also discuss advertising, business, his next book manuscript and suchlike until we arrive at our destination where, at the guest-house, we unload the vehicle. The digs (tea and coffee extra) are usually cheap places.

There are often radio or press interviews for Stephen, then, back at the venue, he instructs the stage crew, precisely, on the levels of light and sound – insisting on being visible from every part of the auditorium, and also that the reproduction of his voice is mellow and pleasant. Sometimes technicians are difficult 'know-it-alls' but he's a perfectionist and persists until he gets exactly what he wants, or the best that they can offer. If the crew are difficult, he'll often comment to me: 'They're supposed to be professional people. Why don't they give me what I'm asking for?'

The medium has never visited many of the tour cities prior to his first meetings, and his audiences are always complete strangers to him. From the time he locks himself in his dressing-room until he appears on stage, he has no contact with the public, so theories of collusion are ruled out.

(Nonsensical sceptics have even been silly enough to suggest mediums visit graveyards to pick up names! What rubbish that is; besides, Stephen's evidence often contains many personal details which no gravestone could offer.)

Backstage, before entering, sometimes he'll slowly pace the boards, or else he sits quietly. On occasions he'll say concernedly, 'I haven't got a link yet.' He likes to establish his first contacts from the Other Side as early as possible in the theatre; I suppose this gives him extra confidence that his psychic powers are working proficiently and the evening will be successful.

I say to him: 'Are you ready?'

'No. I'm never ready,' he replies. 'But let's get going.'

(But despite his public calmness, sometimes he can be irritable and tetchy which has led to minor disagreements between us, both before and after

227

meetings. But his is a stressful job: he only has his spirit voices to carry him through each meeting, unlike show-business performers who know exactly what they're going to do.)

On stage, he's always warmly welcomed, though some audiences are, as he graphically phrases it, 'dead from the neck up', meaning they just sit and stare and are afraid to respond.

However, his excellent sense of precision comic-timing has controlled very large crowds on hundreds of occasions, sometimes having them laughing in the aisles – at just the point when he wants them to.

He speaks to his public for about twenty minutes before attempting communication, and he certainly knows how to induce a relaxed atmosphere. One of his favourite true stories which helped him in this concerned a man standing on a soapbox at Hyde Park Corner in London. He was shouting abuse about the Russians whom he didn't like, screaming out things like 'The Russians are evil!,' 'The East is Red!,' and 'The Russians are Communists!'

Among his small group of listeners there was a priest who stopped the ranting man with:

'Excuse me, but have you ever *been* to Russia?'

'Well – no,' replied the shouter.

'Then don't talk about things you don't know anything about!' admonished the priest.

At which point, 'quick as a flash and bright as a button, the man on the soapbox said to the priest: "Excuse me, but have *you* ever been to heaven?"'!

That anecdote never fails to get a good response, and often produces spontaneous applause from his audiences, achieving its purpose of breaking down the considerable tension one finds in large gatherings of newcomers to mediumship.

This same expert timing and ready intelligence is

employed when dealing with the very rare audience heckler. Once, in Sunderland, a young Christian Fundamentalist in the crowd seized a microphone and started quoting the Bible at everyone, infuriating the audience who stamped their feet in disapproval. Stephen announced:

'I believe in the power of love and kindness, and I'll tell you this: I could never do to *you* what *you've* just done to me!'

The crowd's reaction was electric: hundreds of people immediately rose, enthusiastically clapped their hands above their heads and whistled and cheered.

I've never seen anything like it before, or since.

The medium, however, was obviously shaken by the uproar which had placed him under greater stress, but he soldiered on. With an occasionally shaking hand, as it raised a glass of water, he didn't falter (though he was upset). Whatever happens, he's a complete professional to the end. 'If the stage falls down, I'll carry on,' he says, 'and I won't come off until I've finished.'

(He continued working even when his father was gravely ill.)

Each night, with charm, he explains his beliefs and how his abilities work: how he hears spirit voices, sees communicators, senses their presence and emotions, and how some aren't quite successful in getting their messages through. He makes it quite clear he's only human, and that obviously he can 'and probably will' make mistakes.

'I'm not a computer,' he says. 'Some of the contacts are very clear, others aren't – but whatever happens, I'll do my best. Mediumship is always an experiment.'

His messages, however, are sometimes so very moving that recipients often burst into tears, or laughter. Sometimes the links are very comical.

While the messages are being relayed, the audience usually sits in silence, listening to every word.

When the link is particularly tender, say, a child returning to his mother, they react accordingly: sometimes those who aren't personally receiving the message have been heard to cry because it's so emotional.

And the detail is usually very good, not generalized. People have said publicly, 'There's no way you could have known that.' Gasps of amazement from his audiences are regular features, too, as are full houses.

Glancing through some press cuttings, many hard-headed journalists have also been impressed:

How, assuming he had no previous contact with a packed audience, could he possibly have produced so many intimate details? At times it was astounding, even unnerving, for the recipient.

Recipients ranged from teenagers being ticked off by fussing grandparents, to young mothers hearing from recently lost children as the compelling evening lurched from one emotion to another.

South Wales Evening Post

A complete stranger who knew exactly what I'd been up to . . . A medium rare.

It's hard to be sceptical of the psychic world when a stranger tells you precisely what you were doing that morning, and even days before. And I was startled, almost shocked.

Liverpool Echo

Stephen offers hope of life after death to those who have lost all hope, and he certainly has helped countless scores of grieving relatives come to terms with the death of a loved one.

His messages from the Other Side are often so

direct and detailed that nobody dares accuse him of
fakery, telepathy or showbiz hype.

Wales on Sunday

A man of immense emotional and psychical sensitivity.

Eastern Evening News

This powerfully-gifted young man.

Two Worlds

The epitome of mediumistic excellence.

Psychic News

The public, contrary to media belief, are not easily
convinced: they seek proof in black-and-white terms,
and Stephen frequently delivers it. That's why so
many flock to his meetings – and not just once but
time and again. People travel the length and breadth
of the country just to witness his mediumship.

He's obviously fulfilling very great needs in the
public mind, and demonstrating what he often says
is true: 'We are eternal beings; there is no such thing
as death.'

All my life sceptics have been pitted against me, but
it doesn't matter. A fact is a fact whether you believe
it or not. I don't believe there is a life after death, I
know it.

Stephen in the *Northern Echo*

After the interval ('during which spirits of a different
kind are available!') part two begins with a lively, and
often surprising question-and-answer session which
never fails to interest. Stephen's sound and extensive
knowledge of the paranormal is conveyed so simply,
that this alone, I believe, must place him as one of
Britain's foremost authorities on mediumship.

231

As the evening closes, he dashes to his dressing room, has a quick sip of de-caffeinated Diet Coca-Cola (if he's lucky) then returns to the auditorium to greet the people queuing for autographs or a quick chat with him.

Even though he might be physically exhausted, he speaks to each one personally and doesn't leave the hall until everyone has gone. However, I'm trying to persuade him to stop this practice, for there are already far too many pressures on him.

When the hall's empty, he invariably asks, quietly: 'How did it go tonight, Jeff? Do you think the people were helped enough?'

It's easy to see why this man has endeared himself to millions of people.

Though the experience is over for the crowds, it isn't for him. We both pack up everything and load it back into the car. ('There are no stars in *this* outfit. One day, when I'm famous, I won't have to do any of this!')

Dressing-rooms must then be tidied and he drives us back to the guest-house, where everything has to be unloaded again – usually gasping for air up four flights of mountainous stairs!

It's been another late, late night – 'I'm absolutely shattered,' – and it'll be a crack-of-dawn start the next day, on to the next city, where the whole process is repeated, and his abilities are tested again at the next venue.

Stephen O'Brien is a household name who stands out simply because he's able 'when conditions are right' to deliver some stunning clairvoyance.

What is it, then, that makes people sit up and listen to this man?

That's a difficult question, for it's impossible to capture on paper the medium's charismatic personality, or convey the riveting way in which his gentle voice delivers spirit communication.

Naturally, the man himself is the first to admit that some evenings are more evidential, and therefore more successful, than others, but perhaps this old *Psychic News* report may prove interesting?

It was a large meeting, filmed by HTV Wales in the early 1980s and, even though it dismally fails to establish his presence, it does convey just a glimmer of some of the unusual details he can sometimes receive from his inspirers in the Next World:

When Stephen O'Brien took the platform he linked a war veteran with a relative in the audience. 'His name is William,' said the medium, 'he sailed on HMS *Victorious* in World War Two, but returned unhurt.'

'That's right,' agreed the relative.

Stephen continued: 'He's telling me "We sailed near to Folkestone Harbour".'

'Yes.'

The communicator then referred to the two houses he had left when he passed. 'The settlement will take six months,' added Stephen. 'Does that make sense to you?'

'Yes, it's right.'

Stephen then described Aunt Lizzie, dressed in old-time music-hall costume complete with a feather boa. 'She was in amateur operatics,' he explained.

'She was,' agreed the recipient.

'And she sings here "My Old Man Said Follow the Van". You're moving house?' This, too, was correct.

'You've paid a bill for £60,' Stephen told a young recipient.

'Just this minute,' she replied.

'Your great-grandmother is telling me about this,' Stephen explained, and she says, 'I'm Mary Jane.'

'Oh yes, that's her name!' answered the delighted recipient.

'She says you're thinking of marrying soon.'

'I am.'

'Mary Jane is telling me "He's a good-looking boy. Tell her I approve".'

The recipient's stop-gap method in dealing with a minor crisis was revealed when Stephen announced, 'You've just laddered your tights and made a quick repair job.'

'I tied a knot in them,' confessed the girl to the audience's amusement.

A Protestant and a Roman Catholic returned to one woman: 'I'm the Reverend Harries, looking for Mrs Rees, one of my flock,' said a clergyman. When Mrs Rees was located, he added that he had officiated at her family's services.

'That's right,' agreed the woman.

'And he's brought a Catholic nun with him – Mother Maria,' added the medium.

'I knew her well,' replied Mrs Rees.

Stephen then explained there was an unexpected visitor with the clergyman: 'About thirty years ago he christened a stillborn baby boy in your family, signing the cross in water on his forehead,' he said. 'He's brought the boy with him but he's now a grown man, of course.'

This unusual message was accepted by Mrs Rees.

Another woman in the audience recalled the vagrant hunchback who returned to demonstrate his survival to her. She agreed with Stephen's statement that she had lived near a school when she was young.

'This man slept rough near there,' added the medium.

'I remember him,' she replied. 'I recognize your description.'

The poignant message from the communicator was 'Thank her for smiling at me.'

There are thousands of mediums in the world, but only one Stephen O'Brien.

Stephen O'Brien's talents and abilities have generated wide media and public interest: but what of the deeply private person and his world? What makes the real man behind the image of 'a medium' tick?

The following frank and in-depth interview probes into the mind of the sensitive referred to on radio as 'One of the world's finest mediums', and reveals to us his direct and sometimes controversial and surprising thoughts.

Questions to Stephen are drawn from press articles, media interviews, letters and personal sources.

These Am I

I am a speaker of mysteries:
　　but the pure in heart
　　　　glean wisdom, hidden from the wise.

A toucher of souls am I:
　　a shaker of death, to life.
　　　　A lover of the loveless,
　　　　can moisten tired eyes.
I believe the unbelievable:
　　they make my spirit rise.

A stealer of time am I:
　　so laugh with me
　　and never die.

A Giver of Light I've tried to be:
　　shining rays on darkened truths
　　and revealing hidden lies.

I've never been a picture on a faded page,
　　nor a smiling face
　　without a mind to see:
　　　　And you may know me,
　　　　if you may know me ...

　　　　　　　　Stephen O'Brien

17

Tête-à-Tête

Are you single?
Yes.
Would you like to settle down and have children?
I feel quite settled already. I like the thought of being a dad, but that isn't my single goal in life. If it happens: fine. If not, well I'm not too bothered: there are already far too many unwanted children in the world and not enough good people to love them.

'Continuing my name' doesn't concern me at all; that kind of narrowed vision is meaningless to me. My name's just a label. When I look into a mirror I don't think of my reflection as 'me'.

'I', 'you', we're nothing to do with titles. We're mind; something much greater than anything physical.

People are obsessed with judging outward things: possessions, status and suchlike, when there are far more important aspects to life – inner qualities of mind and spirit, the true person within; service to others. The list is endless.

Do you have a steady relationship at present?
Yes, with myself. I've tried the other kinds and learned you can't find happiness outside of yourself. It doesn't reside in other people or objects: it's *within*. The most important relationship we'll ever have, is the

one we have with ourselves. Every other is secondary.
Even before one with God?
Of course. If you haven't found yourself, you'll never
find God. If a man doesn't know himself, how can he
ever hope to understand others? And if you can't find
yourself, how on earth can you find God, when the
realization of God is within? You can't – it's impossible.
Do you live alone?
No, I live with my cat (!) and I'm perfectly content.
Some people need others constantly fussing
around them for comfort and emotional security, to
avoid being lonesome. I don't. Those kind of emotions
probably stem from man's past evolution – the herding
instinct.

I don't need that kind of attention. It's stifling,
demanding and unnecessary.
Is that because you're an independent Aquarian?
Well, I'm certainly independent – and Aquarian –
but that's not why. I enjoy governing myself.

People let you down, so I've moved away from
too much dependency on others. Of course, if the
right person came along . . .
Yes?
Well, if a soul-partner appeared, that would be
wonderful!
What are your thoughts on marriage?
For some, it works and can be a fulfilling experience. But, as far as I'm concerned, we're all separate
individuals and it's impossible for a piece of paper to
spiritually bind people together. As long as respect
exists in a relationship, it's worth preserving; but
once that's gone, it's over.
You didn't mention the word love.
That's because true spiritual love *never* dies, but the
kind of 'love' some couples share is nothing of the sort.

What is it then, in your opinion?
Oh, it could be many things: infatuation, physical attraction, lust, admiration, emotional insecurity compelling you to seek company. There are many different reasons.

Then what's the purpose of marriage?
If you mean the purpose of relationships, to develop as minds and characters through shared experiences. So many partnerships divide because one person outgrows the other on any of these levels. But it's a soul-growth process.

A great many people would disagree.
Good. Thank God we're all different! What a boring world it would be, if we weren't.

Let's take an imaginary step: picture yourself lying by a quiet pool, and there's music playing. Who's with you? What's the music, and what are you thinking about?
I'm alone. The music is classical: probably Chopin's Etude in E Major. I'm thinking about peace, strength, harmony and being at one with the rhythms of life.

Let's take some readers' topics now: first – your psychic talents. Are they gifts or abilities?
Both. God gives the gifts, but it's our responsibility to develop and unfold them.

Have you perfect faith in your psychic abilities?
No. When they work well, it's marvellous; but when they don't, it's dreadful.

I wish I had more control over the conditions which make mediumship function at its best, but I don't. There are too many conflicting factors involved, mostly connected with the public.

What's the biggest problem with your public work?
There are two: lack of clear reception from the spirit world, and unresponsive crowds. The more psychic energies the audiences give, the less my own

are burnt up; the less they give the more exhausted I get, which makes the results much poorer.

If more people learned to give instead of take, they'd get much better meetings.

What's the biggest problem in your private work?
As far as the sitters go: the biggest stumbling-blocks are cast-iron minds demanding specific details, or hostile people not really listening to what I'm saying.

As far as the medium goes: emotions and mental disturbances impede communication. Tiredness and ill-health deplete mediums' psychic energies, too, making contact harder to get.

Have you ever wanted to finish your work and reject it?
Oh yes, many times.

Why?
Because I do so much of it, it exhausts me and takes up far too much of my life. In the last four years I've hardly had any free time to myself; it's been one endless round of service.

I need a rest now; something the public rarely considers.

If you're such a reluctant medium, why do you do the job?
Because I can't cross Over until my time's up.

Everyone does some kind of work and if we can't help other people, what's the point of living?

Besides, years ago I made a promise to the spirit world to help them – and I always keep my promises.

What's your greatest wish for yourself?
To be a Free Spirit again and have a home of my own. To bathe in the music of silence.

Do you fear death?
No; death is a friend.

Do you fear facing huge audiences and having no messages to give?

No; but it wouldn't please me! I take the platform to succeed, not fail.

You've often spoken of leaving the cities. Why?

Because they depress me: masses of people all functioning on different levels of existence – moral, spiritual and evolutionary – and they radiate coarse vibrations. People can be very irritating and I want to get away from them. I've always tuned in to my surroundings; that's just the way I am. Loud and aggressive people repel me. Very few people radiate peace and positive healthy thoughts – the opposite, in fact.

But in the country, next to nature, great psychic energies soothe and heal my spirit, and I want them in my life.

But surely the cities have good souls in them, offering compassionate services?

Yes, but compared with the selfish masses they're very few. Cities are breeding-grounds for greed, rape, murder, jealousy, anger, deviousness and self-centred vested interests. I don't mind helping people, but that doesn't mean I want to live with them.

When you were a boy you said you felt ill at ease in this world, is that why?

No, more than that. I was a changeling; a dreamer, an idealist – a foreign child who didn't fit into his family. I assumed I was adopted, which of course I wasn't; but my young mind couldn't understand why I was here.

It wasn't easy for me to grow up through all that.

Is that why you said winning a grammar school scholarship, at eleven, changed your life?

Yes. It raised me from the dullness around me and opened up a whole new world of finer thoughts. I can't explain the profound effect this had on me. Education

241

made me feel like a fish in water, instead of gasping for air on dry land.

What about the gasps of your critics? How would you answer those who claim mediums are cashing in on the grief of vulnerable people?

In my case, that's rubbish. I'm not rich with a private income tucked away. Ticket prices meet the expense of funding meetings. Adverts and theatres cost a small fortune.

Unfortunately everything in the Western world has a price on it, even my books. I don't like this, or agree with it, but that's the way it is. In my early days I fought against earning money through mediumship, and only did charity events.

I still help charities.

Why did you write your books?

To share my experiences with others.

But why books, particularly?

Because they have a dogged determination to stay on people's shelves. They have a kind of permanence and they can be studied and read over and over again. I did my articles and tapes for the same reasons.

I love books; they've helped me so much. They're priceless ways of reaching people. I've had thousands of letters saying how much my writings have helped others with their lives, so it's all been worthwhile.

Were they 'ghost-written', if you'll pardon the pun?

No! (Through laughter) . . . I planned and wrote them myself, except the public contributions, of course. I had it contracted that the final approval of the text would be mine, before going to print.

My voice, my message, shouldn't be watered down by third parties who might not understand my objectives.

Why did you change publishing houses for this third volume of your autobiography?

Because control of my previous publishers changed hands, and this editing clause wasn't offered. There were other reasons, too, but that was the main one.

In your books you say you found it difficult to cope with being renowned, because of your quiet personality. Has that changed?

No. Either you like the limelight or you don't: I don't.

But media work generates this attention. Surely you knew that and pursued it?

No. I've never sought personal publicity: I loathe it. They can cover my work and message, as long as they leave me alone.

I've had to get used to being interviewed, but as for myself: I just want to be left alone.

What would you most like to say to those who've featured you?

Thanks for the opportunity of sharing my message with millions of people.

And what advice would you give them, if they were to interview you again?

First read my books: see where I've come from and what I'm trying to do – and then ask your questions.

There's something else I'd like to say, too: the public aren't as gullible as some of you think. People *can* think for themselves *and* take responsibility for their lives.

Speaking of the public: are you concerned about them living out your teachings in their daily lives?

No. That's their responsibility, not mine. It's up to them to study my ideas, use them if they think they're sensible, or reject them if they think their intelligence has been insulted.

I've never asked anyone to blindly accept my teachings. I've always said, 'Question everything.' How else can we develop our minds?

What about people who continually bombard you with frequent letters and requests? How do you feel about them?

I wish they'd see sense, try and stand on their own two feet, and turn within, to find their own answers. I had to do it; and if I can do it, so can they.

All the answers are within.

I've had my fair share of 'pests' over the years, but we're not our brothers' keepers. We can't be; we can help one another, but Personal Responsibility is the Law.

Neither am I a psychic fortune-telling service; yet still people write asking me to find lost jewellery, missing wills, or even what kind of 'lucky charm' to wear!

Sometimes they demand advice for the future. The future *can* be seen, of course, but it's better they should live it.

What if I foresaw a fatal accident, or injuries causing both legs to be amputated? Or the sudden loss of a parent, spouse or child? Would they want to hear it?

Can these things be seen?

Of course. Every soul carries its future with it. But *please* no more letters asking for predictions by post, because I don't do them and a refusal often offends.

Can you see where orthodox religion is going?

Yes: downhill, and quite fast at present, because it doesn't have the Living Power of the Spirit within it, and it'll continue to fall unless it's re-introduced.

Theology is sterile, just a set of barren words. Only the Power of the Spirit can breathe life into faith, and only true spiritual knowledge will satisfy the evolving minds of future generations.

What's your own religion, Stephen?

244

I've never 'labelled' myself, but I've been called many peculiar things!

Love and service are important to me. Without the living expression of these, all religions are spiritually dead.

I value the right to think for myself and the freedom to speak my mind, as well as make my own quest.

My work is my work. Why do we need a label on it?

In the British Spiritualist Movement I met people who helped me towards greater realization of self and the purpose of existence.

But I've never belonged to any national religious organization as an affiliated member. I've always avoided signing membership books and distance myself from narrow views that might suppress my mind and spirit.

I work for the Great Spirit's Children, and I belong to One Cause only – I belong to God.

Whom do you most admire, and why?

'Admire' isn't a word I often use, but I respect people trying to be harmless towards others, the animal kingdom and the environment. And I've a high regard for anyone who, in the face of terrible adversity, can still be tolerant and loving.

Whom do you most dislike, and why?

The list would be too long to print! (laughter) But it would include dictators and tyrants everywhere, who dominate or damage others against their will.

What's the worst thing that's ever happened to you?

Nothing outstanding springs to mind, but there've been plenty of embarrassments and quite a few nasty experiences.

Name one.

No.

Then what's the best thing that's ever happened to you?

In which part of my life?

Personally.

(Long pause . . .) Do you want to know what I'm thinking?

Yes.

'Mind your own business'. (pause, smiling) Well, you did ask!

Have you an unusual memory?

Yes: when I asked Marlene Dietrich if I might kiss her hand. She leaned forward, cupped my head in her palms and kissed me on either side of my face.

She was in her seventies at the time, but still very beautiful.

More readers' questions now: what was your first thought this morning?

'Oh my God, another day on Earth'.

What is your opinion of cryogenics: the freezing of human bodies, or heads, to be re-vitalized in the future?

It's a waste of time and money. Once the body's 'dead', the spirit departs.

Anyway, who wants to 'come back' sewn onto someone else's body? It's a dreadful thought, and I don't think they'll achieve it with full success. At least, I pray they don't. It would be an unspeakable genetic nightmare.

Why do you think you were born?

To evolve, and learn from, as well as share with others, many thoughts and experiences.

In my opinion, we're all born with a soul blueprint, but it's up to us to discover what it is.

What about your critics' opinions? Do they bother you?

No, but they trouble *them*.

What about those who brand mediumship 'make-believe' or 'fraudulent'?

What about them?

Do they unsettle you?

No; they can believe what they like. They only bother me when they hurl insults into my face or print wicked lies about me.

Does it concern you that your message hasn't reached them?

But it has. Why do you think they get so frustrated?

No-one can respond to the call of the spirit until their soul is ready. Spiritual doors stay firmly shut until they're ready to open. That's the Law.

Somebody once said: 'Don't cast your pearls before swine.' I couldn't agree more, and, if you'll pardon my frankness, I'm sensitive enough to recognize swine when I see them.

What are your thoughts on the press?

Well, they build you up one moment, then cut your legs from underneath you the next. They say that's what their readers want, but they're wrong. They believe this sells newspapers, and they're wrong again.

Anyway, I wish they'd actually report what happens at my meetings and not their personal thoughts about the event.

And secondly, religious fanatics?

I think they'd be doing everyone a favour if they stayed in their churches and spent more time trying to develop the soul quality of toleration.

Religious fanatics haven't yet found themselves: they'll *tell* you they have, loudly, but they haven't. What they've discovered is a cloak for their inadequacies, something which offers a false sense of security – and the clasps are made of fear.

And lastly, your thoughts on the 'professional sceptics'?

While I'm here, and even long after I'm 'dead' and gone, the sceptics will still be parading their 'new revelations' and carefully tailored 'scientific facts' aimed at discrediting and denigrating both my character and reputation.

How do you know?

I'm psychic! But you don't have to be sensitive to realize that there's a living to be made out of it, providing you knock the famous whom the public love.

No popular medium has ever escaped their attention. Every successful sensitive has been attacked and criticized, and statistics (coupled with fickle human nature) decree this isn't going to change.

Mediums have always had raucous voices protesting against their work; but we're still here.

In my own case, I've glanced forward and seen what the 'sceptics' will attempt. However, when they launch their attacks, it's only fair to warn them that the battle might be long and painful.

What are your politics?

None: I place no trust in politics or politicians.

Why not?

Because the desire to govern others' lives instantly breeds corruption into the soul.

What about governments, aren't they needed?

Oh yes, I'm not an anarchist. Society needs fair structure. Without this, life would be more miserable for many more people than it is now; but I don't think we've got it, do you?

How can politics be respected when rich countries are burning huge amounts of excess food while poor countries are starving because they 'can't afford to buy it'?

That's a travesty of human rights, a sad example of the lack of spiritual advancement in the human animal.

I suppose politicians are trying their best, but many have forgotten that those who have too much should give to those who have too little.

I'd call that compassion.

Do you think there'll ever be a nuclear war?

Every weapon man's ever invented has been used, and abused, by irresponsible hands.

I wrote a poem about politics and nuclear weapons which sums up my feelings. Would you like to hear it?

Please ...

Sunburst

The earth runs red with deep young blood,
    spilled by greed and avarice;
and the rivers boil with a crimson hue
    for the men who wanted more than you.

And the skies fade black, and the snow-storms come,
    as the daylight dims to twilight night:
        Someone burst the sunshine,
        to crown himself a King
        and subjugate with Might ...

        And a father's tears fall purple-red
        on the lifeless corpse of his baby son;
            a bright light hurt him,
            maimed him,
            killed him:
            A finger-press – and the deed was done ...

Only then did the Nations rise
against the men whose greed had run its course:

            but not before the death of millions;
            not before the children's cries;
            not before the holocaust ...

Does knowing of the afterlife colour your own thoughts on other emotive subjects, such as euthanasia?

Oh yes: I can see a time when legalized voluntary suicide will be accepted in society. The planet's population is exploding, its resources are being consumed faster than we can replace them, and there are already countless people who want to 'die'. One day, euthanasia will be legally available, subject, of course, to stringent regulations.

I believe to take another's life is wrong, but if I felt I'd finished with this world and really wanted to leave it, I'd have no hesitation in accepting personal euthanasia, peacefully and without pain.

The main problem, of course, is that once you legalize the right to terminate life: what is compassion, and what could be construed as 'murder'?

How would you like to grow old?

I wouldn't. Old age holds no attraction for me. I'd rather die young, quietly, and in my sleep.

I'd rather take my life than be nursed or be a burden to anyone.

But having now said that, I bet someone Up There's listening and – just for the devilment of it – I'll be made to stay here forever!

If you die a wealthy man, to whom will you leave your money?

(Through chuckling . . .) Pardon my mild hysterics at the thought of having plenty of money!

But, if it comes, I'd leave most of it to the animals. People can work for their living, but preventing cruelty to animals needs money, and to treat the unfortunate victims.

After your days, how would you like to be remembered?

I'm not bothered.

I expect some may remember me, but many won't; and I've lived long enough to know that no-one's indispensable – absolutely no-one.

What about your teachings?
Nothing is original; there are no new Divine Revelations; they've all been given countless times before, by others.

There aren't any new thoughts, just constant truths, re-designed to meet the needs of different generations.

The messenger certainly is *not* more important than his message. The message will remain long after the messenger is gone: and that's the way it should be.

What about your own farewell, Stephen? What kind of ceremony would you like?
I don't want any fuss – just make sure I'm dead before you cremate me! (Burial is such a dirty business; if more people knew what happened to decaying bodies after interment, they'd be horrified – they're so unhygienic, full of germs and diseases.)

At the service if someone wants to say a few words, don't let it be a clergyman or anybody who didn't personally know me – that would be hypocrisy. Perhaps my dearest friends might wish me well.

Make it a happy, musical occasion: play 'Going Home' as they carry me down the aisle and then sing some soul-stirring songs, like 'You'll Never Walk Alone'.

Then, carry on with the great adventure of living.

And if someone sheds any tears, cry because you loved me; cry for joy and not for sorrow – because I'll be free, and Home at last.

PART THREE
Life in the Beyond

Glimpses into Eternity

Earth is but a Fleeting Dream,
Faint Shadows cast by Greater Lights Beyond:

only the Essence
may know the Source;

only the Soul
maps out the Way;

and the Spirit is forever
In Touch with Eternity ...

18

Visits to the Astral Worlds

I

It was a quiet and peaceful summer's night, but I was far too tired to enjoy it. Having been touring Britain for what seemed like centuries, I was feeling quite exhausted and although it was only four o'clock in the afternoon I had to get my feet up on the bed and lie down, just to gather my thoughts.

As I closed my eyes, my legs felt as heavy as lead and my feet were throbbing. Sooty laid down beside me, purring, as unconsciousness crept slowly through my mind and the blackness began to swirl with radiant ever-glowing colours. Then, strangely, the rainbows suddenly swept aside, and beyond them I could see some deep green grassy fields. Their vibrancy was marvellous, so enticing that I seemed to float right across into them, as if they were beckoning me. Only then did I realize I was once more in touch with eternity, having crossed over to the Other Side of Life on another of my out-of-the-body excursions.

The blazing sunshine was beating down on flowering fields, blessing everything with great vigour and making it so alive and beautiful. For a moment I didn't want to walk on, but just wanted to savour the radiant light and drink it in. So I gently rested under the shade of a large spreading tree, perfectly at peace and happy to wallow in the living energies all around me.

I don't know how long I stayed in the cool shade; I may even have slept awhile: there are no clocks in the Beyond or sunsets to indicate the passing time.

I then lazily rose and decided to take a stroll, wandering across some fields and paths towards a building I had spied in the distance. At least, I'd thought it was a building until I approached it, when the sunshine revealed it was a kind of natural amphitheatre, formed from the gently sloping hills. Wanting to enter, I climbed a hillock and approached the powerful voice which I could hear lecturing within.

As I reached the top I could see from my position that the place was three-quarters full of all kinds of people: elderly folk, the young and healthy, and whole families complete with boisterous children, all seated on natural grassy ridges which seemed cut into the very sides of the hill. All different races, creeds and colours were there; the common bond uniting them all was the absolute silence and undivided attention they were giving to an impressive speaker beneath them on the semi-circular stage.

Sweeping several glances over the listening hundreds, I was fully aware, through my spirit body senses, that these were mostly New Arrivals: people who'd recently 'died'.

Then I thought, 'I recognize that deep voice,' and upon telescoping my sight I saw my friend and teacher, White Owl.

I sat captivated by his fine eloquent speech, eager to listen to his knowledge. And, like me, the crowds were enthralled by his common sense and gentle but powerful authority. Even though the amphitheatre was vast, holding some two thousand people, his calm voice carried effortlessly to every listener's ear. And as he spoke, his kind face took in all sections of the auditorium:

'Here, there is no time as you knew it on Earth. Night is unknown because our atmosphere is so high that our sun's light cannot be hidden from us: it is radiated throughout our spheres and we have constant day, with sometimes short periods of twilight.'

'How can that be?' asked a long-haired youth near the front, who was resting his chin on his drawn-up, clasped knees.

'Think of the polar regions on Earth: there, day and night last about six months each because of the elevation of the sun. Here in our world there is a much higher atmosphere than that of Earth and therefore our sun's rays are constantly glowing all around it.

'On Earth, after sunset, if your atmosphere extended much further out into space, as ours does, you, too, would have no night. Your sun's luminescence would be bounced around the high atmosphere all around your globe, giving a kind of twilight; and that is what happens here.'

'Oh,' said the questioner, now pondering on the lesson, 'when do we sleep then?' White Owl continued:

'I have been here for many centuries, as you think of time, and rarely have I ever needed sleep, though I have occasionally rested near streams, and often in the company of good and faithful friends. Sometimes I have changed my surroundings to rid my mind of old habit-patterns, travelling out into the deeper realms of the Spirit World to visit the Shining Ones and the Masters from whom I obtain great soul-strength and an inexpressible peace of mind.'

The crowd listened intently, as I observed his auric and mental fields sensing their immediate needs. My psychic exercise completed, he addressed them again:

257

'So each of my days, as you understand the term, has no beginning and no end, for we exist here in the Eternal Now.

'There is much to occupy us, great service to perform. When I am not taking counsel with older minds I might be called to any point in the World of Spirit, or on Earth, where help is needed.

'How?' asked the inquisitive student again, and, even though he was interrupting, the crowd didn't seem to mind; there were no grumblings. I intuitively sensed they'd already learned patience. In Eternity there's plenty of time to sit and listen. What's the rush when you have forever before you?

'We speak by Thought,' answered White Owl, resplendent in his purple and lilac spirit robes which reached from his broad shoulders down to the pearl-coloured platform. 'Thought and Mind are the powers which link all beings together, whichever plane of life they exist in.'

It was then that his deep brown eyes engaged mine at the top of the hill (though I've no doubt he knew of my arrival long before) and with a smile flickering across his lips he incorporated me into his talk:

'Sometimes, the man who acts as my medium, of whom I was speaking earlier, sends me an urgent SOS call, simply by Thought. It arrives as a small explosion of energy and acts like an alarm call within my mind.'

Then he demonstrated it, as all at once a brilliant blue-gold light – like a sudden flash of electricity – burst into being about three feet above his head. This impressed the crowd and sent a thrill of excitement buzzing through it.

'After receiving it, I am able to retrace its path and home in on my medium's mind-frequency, and in an instant I can be beside him. Rather like physical Man who has perfected missiles which follow a directional laser beam, in the same way I can find my medium.

'By simply *thinking* of our destination, Thought carries us there instantaneously, once we have learned to hold and project the images correctly. But though this sounds easy, in reality it requires much practice before it becomes second nature. But I can also tune in, hear and see what is transpiring at any call's source *without* actually travelling there in my spirit body.'

The crowd began whispering, obviously intrigued by this latest remark, which again prompted the youth to ask:

'Does that happen when we think we can sense an invisible person in the room?'

'Yes, indeed. But instead of our presence, you might simply be registering our thought-rays. It all depends on your sensitivity at the time of transmission.'

There were lively exchanges amongst the people as similar experiences were discussed, and when silence finally returned again, a middle-aged nurse, who had recently passed over, questioned:

'Please, what happens when someone "dies"? I sat beside many dear souls, tending to their sick bodies, but what about the spirit's release? Are special calls sent out then?'

My teacher smiled at the woman and answered her as a loving father might address his child:

'At the points of passing, had your psychic vision been operating you would have seen many from Spirit surrounding the travellers' beds. No-one dies alone. Calls go out in the form of prayers or even just desires and we are in attendance long before the transition occurs.'

'Thank you,' she replied, thoughtfully.

'And would you like to continue nursing?'

'Oh yes ... yes, I would,' she said, thoroughly warmed by the secret he'd read from her mind.

'Then you shall, for there are many aspects of spiritual healing to be learned here. You may be one of the Watchers around beds of illness, if you so desire it.'

'Oh, I do,' she smiled, 'I'd like that very much.'

'Then so be it: thoughts are reality here, and presently someone will come and help you to actualize them.'

Her joy was instantaneous and her beaming face, indescribable.

'Thank you. Thank you so much, my friend.'

'Ah ... ' he chuckled back. 'Friendship! I have many great friends in several worlds, and it is now my privilege to count you as one of them. To be in the company of good friends is a wonderful experience: it renews the spirit, refreshes the mind and brings strength to step forward and serve. Life here is all about service, rendering knowledge and comfort to people existing in many and varied levels of being. Though never easy, it is always a joy to aid those struggling for light.

'I have always been helped in my times of need and now I am repaying these debts. You, too, will render service to others. I know you will.'

'I shall,' smiled the nurse; and the crowd picked up these powerful emotions, vocally agreeing with her.

'To serve is a privilege. This is what attracts me here, and also to my medium on Earth. He and I attune to each other because of the love and friendship we have consciously fostered during our association.'

Then, as his compassionate gaze took in every face among the hundreds, he quietly outstretched his arms, which took with them the many folds of his glimmering purple raiments, and with an open face and utter sincerity he whispered – and yet it was loud enough to be heard by all – 'Know that I am your friend and you are all mine. And whenever you may need me, just call upon my name and I will answer.'

My spine tingled as I felt the great wave of love washing out from the people towards him; they were overjoyed to be in his presence, and I was proud to know him so well.

I was also then aware I'd been 'brought' there to see these aspects of his work.

Then a little coloured girl about eight years old, with black twizzled hair and wearing a red-and-white checked frock, enthusiastically shouted from her place:

'Where's God? I haven't seen Him yet!'

After amusement had rippled through the hundreds and then subsided, White Owl leaned forward and swept her up in his strong arms as though she weighed nothing at all, and smiled at her:

'I have been here such a long time and I have never yet seen a person who might be called God. And no-one else here has either. But I can see your mother's eyes, there. Can you?'

The youngster put her finger dumbly into her mouth and nodded 'yes'.

'Well then, when I look into your mother's eyes I think I can see God shining out of them,' he said.

And with that she wriggled free of his grip and quickly ran to her mother's embrace, as he turned and informed the people:

'All we can experience are the manifestations of God, the many faces and forms of a great power which appear on all levels of being, both seen and unseen. A long time ago, when I was incarnated on Earth, I belonged to the race now known as the North American Indians. We lived close to nature and worshipped the Great White Spirit.

'I still hold this concept: God as a Breath of Conscious Life. I can see no better way of expressing in human terms the Infinite Mind behind All Creation, a Supreme Mind which rules through Perfect Natural Laws.'

'But why can't I *see* Him?' she persisted. 'I'm not an Indian! I'm from Jamaica, and so's my mother!'

'Little one,' he smiled through the audience laughter, 'you will come to know Him, in time. This I promise you.'

'Words,' he said to the crowd, 'are always inadequate when describing Infinite Thought. Man, in physical form, is a Finite being, but God the Great Spirit is Infinite, spanning all eternity, countless universes and galaxies known and as yet undiscovered. God is a Power.'

'You mean, like sunshine and electricity?' said the little girl, much to the crowd's further delight.

'Yes,' he smiled.

But undeterred, she wanted to know: 'Well, where does He live then?!'

'Everywhere.'

Then through various archways, brightly dressed spirit people entered, sought out and then sat next to each group of listeners in the auditorium. White Owl seemed very pleased they'd arrived, no doubt at his mental beckoning. (In fact, I wondered if his earlier demonstration of how a spirit call is sent and received was actually a transmission asking these guides to collect their new arrivals.)

'Our visitors will now escort you to your people, or rest homes, or wherever you might be happiest at present. Trust them and be happy. And the love of the Great Spirit be with you all, my friends.'

And he raised up both his arms and there was instant applause from the crowd. I suppose it was a natural reaction, and one of thunderous gratitude, as he slowly faded from our sight in a vaporous mist, followed by an explosion of bright silver light.

I watched all the joyous listeners leaving with their new friends and helpers, then I walked over the top of the hill, there to be greeted by White Owl who was awaiting me.

Then I can't recall what happened after that; there's a blackness in my memory . . .

II

. . . Recollection returns as we were walking down through the lovely fields I'd first become conscious of at the start of my journey. White Owl was talking:

'Evolved minds can see people and events in different time zones, past, present and future, and also in different spheres without the need to travel there. Like radio sets, they can pick up signals being transmitted thousands of miles away.'

'You mentioned many spirit spheres earlier. How many are there?'

'Some on Earth teach there are seven, but I disagree. There are seven planes of thought near to your planet from which many souls communicate, but beyond these are multitudinous worlds, waiting to be discerned. Each time we think we have reached peaks in our evolution, there are further mountains ahead of us.'

'So there are countless worlds of spirit?'

'Indeed, and I have visited many of them because

I'm quite an old soul. My stage of evolution enables me to travel way up into the higher realms, as well as down to Earth.'

His eyes were clear and full as he gazed across the beautiful fields rolling out around us.

'These scenes bring me great delight. We are quite close to Mother Earth now, but this beauty is as nothing when compared to my true home in the higher realms. It is difficult for me to express its wonder.

'After centuries of soul progression, upwards and inwards towards Perfection and the Light of God, outward shape and form become unnecessary.'

'You mean the Wise Ones have no bodies?'

'Individuality is retained, along with character and soul experiences, but there is no need for any vehicle of expression other than pure Mind.'

'But how do they recognize one another there?'

'Awareness: a soul-knowing. Sight and sound are clumsy tools which are unnecessary there.'

'Have we many bodies before losing outward form?'

'Legion; after which individuality exists only as a focal point, like a distant star on a dark night.'

We were now nearing another location, a sort of open-air hospital or rest-place. I could see colourful beds and couches lying out in the sunshine in a kind of grove surrounded by flowering trees and cool shaded areas. My spirit body instantly registered the deep serenity and healing surrounding everything.

'See! Our destination,' said my teacher, as we reached the place.

'Are these people newcomers, too?'

'You have sensed it well.'

And we stood apart at a short distance and observed certain young spirit women and men in bright robes moving amongst the sleeping 'patients' on the couches.

'Many who are helped to make the last crossing are surprised that they still exist.'

'I suppose few give serious thought to the possibility of an after-world.'

'Ah, but now they *have* to accept it. There is usually great laughter and many tears shed when their loved ones come to greet them. Watch now, and see.' And he turned me towards a shaded grove. 'There: the old woman is waking and her children are around the bed. Let us observe.'

And the elderly, refined-looking woman opened her eyes, stretched her arms up high and then yawned. These were her first moments awakening from 'the sleep of death'. She rubbed her eyes in amazement at the sight of the four people around her couch. Her incredulous tone perfectly matched her surprised and disbelieving expression.

'Arthur? Mavis? . . . Joe? Is that you? My babies? But . . . ' she sat up and leaned forward, ' . . . but, you're all dead.'

'We never died, Mamma,' said Mavis, 'we simply went ahead and waited to greet you again, like this.'

'What . . .? You mean . . .? What? . . . I've . . . ' And the educated woman couldn't for a moment find the strength to speak the word. 'Have I . . . died?'

Three of her children smiled, except the fourth who was a well-built, six-foot tall young man with a thick mane of raven-black hair, with silver-blue sunlight playing upon it. He looked hesitant and then his seriousness broke into a wreath of smiles as he stepped towards her bed.

'And who is this young man?'

There was an awkward pause, during which the tall stranger leaned forward and then gently caressed and kissed his mother on the face. Something inexplicable must have invisibly transferred itself and touched the old woman's soul as his lips met her aged skin:

'Oh . . .' she gasped, dumbstruck, while realization began to blissfully dawn and light up her features. 'Oh . . . Sebastian? Is it you, my darling? Oh . . . is it really you; my baby boy?'

'Yes, mother; it is me. All these years of waiting, but now we are together . . . ' he smiled.

'Oh, my baby! My little boy!' she exclaimed, too overcome to say any more. And she threw her arms up around his neck and embraced him ecstatically while tears rolled down her cheeks.

'How I wished you could have lived, my son,' she said. And I sensed her remembering he'd only taken a few precious breaths on Mother Earth before he had 'died'. 'But how you've grown!'

The kind woman's face lit up with beautiful smiles and she embraced her once stillborn child, now a full-grown man, over and over again:

'Yes, I remember now, my son – I've seen you before, many many times throughout the years. It's all coming back to me now . . . '

'That's right,' he replied, brimming with joy. 'Every loving memory we've ever shared in your sleep-life will return to you, Mamma. Nothing will be forgotten. You're safe now, Mamma; out of your pain and we're all back together again, as a family.'

I can't describe the look of pure wonder on the dear woman's face as she clasped him tightly to herself once more and said from the depths of her spirit:

'Oh my precious, precious boy! Sebastian, my son . . . There surely must be a God, to have given you back to me.'

And her three remaining devoted children stepped

back and cried at their mother's joy in Sebastian's arms. Tears fell like rain on the shoulders of her firstborn, as her love for him, especially, could not be contained for one moment longer.

'There is a God,' she whispered through her tears. 'There is a God . . .'

And both White Owl and I felt we were encroaching on such a personal and private sacred moment that we, in unison, moved quietly away to another corner of the gardens, where an old man had just become conscious . . .

III

'Come and speak with him,' said White Owl as we approached the golden couch he was laying upon and were greeted by his wrinkled, smiling face.

'Hello, my friend,' said the old man, 'I didn't think to see you again so soon.'

'Well,' returned my guide, 'God knows best when to call a traveller home.'

'Oh, I'm so glad to be out of my pain: the tears I've shed; the agony was unbearable, so terrible and great.'

'Yes, but it's all over now.'

And the two friends clasped hands tightly.

'Yes, I don't feel a thing any more, except tranquillity. That big ball of pain inside my stomach has completely gone. It's been deflated!' joked the elderly arrival. And the three of us laughed together.

'This is someone I have known for many years on Earth,' said White Owl, indicating me at his side. The old man lifted a gnarled and bony hand to vigorously shake mine.

'I'm very pleased to meet you, young man. Any

friend of my companion, is also a friend of mine.'

My teacher spoke again:

'Last time we met, when you were physically unconscious and we talked, you asked about the Judgement Day. Do you remember?'

'I do.'

'Well, now it has come.'

My guide sat on a form beside the bed, motioning me to join him, which I did, but I wasn't intending to speak; I was content to just sit quietly and listen to these two friends. And I watched as White Owl took the old man's wrinkled hand, gently explaining about Judgement Day:

'You have nothing to fear, for there is none. When a soul passes, as the spirit is freed the mind dislocates from the brain to express itself through the etheric body, a number of memories are often seen again by the person "dying".'

'It happened to me,' said the enthralled traveller.

'Yes: it's said a drowning man experiences this, too; and in a sense he does, though it is impossible to view an entire life in one second.'

'As I breathed my last, I saw a panorama of some of the more important parts of my life, pictures swirling in my mind.'

'Judgement happens over a long period as a soul slowly re-adjusts to its new life. This world is not strange to New Arrivals for they have passed in and out of it every night during sleep; like Stephen, here. He is not "dead".'

I smiled at the man.

'The higher self is well accustomed to the World of Spirit so there is no shock on passing. Is that not so?'

'Why, yes,' said the traveller, 'I feel I belong here, my friend. Almost . . . almost as if Earth was just a short journey from my real home . . . like a dream . . .'

'And so it is.'

'These astral planes are very similar to Earth, anyway,' I chipped in.

'Yes,' added White Owl, 'because they are populated by folk who have just come from there and they have created this environment by Thought.' He then faced the old man again. 'You are very lucky, my friend, for you have knowledge. The saddest cases of all are those who have held no belief in anything. They find themselves existing but sometimes unable to fully comprehend that *this* is their reality now and not some hazy dream.

'Think for a moment of the many times you have dreamed vivid dreams and recalled them. But what if you were never to wake up? The dream would be your reality, would it not?'

'Yes,' said the man, as though some brilliant light lit his mind for the very first time. His face was full of eagerness and wonder and he propped himself up on his forearms and inclined his head forward, intently, as my guide went on:

'Adjustments must be made, of course, because you will eventually meet a number of people you may have wronged as well as those you dearly loved. So we constantly judge ourselves. Only through a process of purging the mind may we find peace within ourselves, by eventually reviewing and weighing all past acts, thoughts, words and deeds.'

'Tell me, dear friend, what happens next to me, now?' asked the man.

'Oh, you can do as you please,' smiled my guide. 'There is free will here and no-one will tell you what you may or may not do. There are arts, sciences, healing, education, many activities indeed. The choice is yours, unless you require guidance.'

'I may please myself?' he asked, incredulously.

'Of course. But if you attempt activities beyond your current level of soul-growth or understanding, you will fail to execute them successfully.'

'Do you mean we must comply with the Great Spirit's laws we talked of, some time back?'

'I do. They operate automatically all the time and we must all work under their giant umbrella and within the scope of their limitations.'

'I see.'

'However, help is always at hand if you need it. But hopefully, you will learn by your mistakes.'

'How I value your help and friendship,' said the man with shining eyes, as he tightly clasped White Owl's hand. I simply watched and said nothing, content just to witness this interchange of thoughts.

'And tell me, White Owl, for how long must I be old and crabbed like this, my dear friend?'

'Until you decide to change your appearance. Your spirit body is young and at the height of its strength and beauty, should you desire it. Only your old thought-patterns keep you aged.'

'I see,' said the man.

'Concentrate,' returned White Owl.

'I'll try . . . ' And closing his eyes tight-shut he began thinking of himself as a much younger being, at the prime of life when he was a carefree youth – fit, well and happy.

And as he did so, very slowly, a remarkable change took place. Superimposing over the old shell came a much younger image. He was transforming his appearance, by Thought.

And before long the wizened body had gradually dissolved to give way to a well-built, handsome young chap in his early twenties.

Now healthy, strong and athletic, he let out a

sudden whoop of laughter and hopped out of bed like a renewed Ebenezer Scrooge on Christmas morning, after the spirits had taught him their invaluable lessons.

'Thank you, my friend – *thank you!*' he gushed, dancing about on nimble feet and shaking our hands profusely. He was incredibly happy. 'But I mustn't waste another second! No more time! I must go now and find my people! I shall run!' he shouted, dashing towards the fields like a newborn pony kicking its legs with the sheer joy of being alive.

'Yes! Go and be happy!' cried out White Owl.

'Good luck!' I added, loudly, as the light-footed youngster skipped through the multi-coloured carpet of flowers.

Nearby spirit helpers smiled and didn't bat an eyelid, fully understanding his sudden enthusiastic departure; obviously having seen it all before, many times.

I then felt rather sleepy ... or was my vision functioning incorrectly?

What was happening?

Maybe there was some kind of strange magnetic pull from my physical body back on Earth, because suddenly the whole scene was disappearing in a swish of wispy white smoke – and I awoke back in my bed, twisting awkwardly in the night.

IV

I gained consciousness in the Next World right in the middle of a conversation with White Owl:

'Some say animals have no souls,' he said. 'These people are misguided, for even the wildest animals have an etheric body within their physical

271

form. Wildebeest, mice, leopards, tigers, elephants, all creatures have this energy body. Like other life-forms, their physical bodies only hold together because they are built around the blueprint of the spirit body.

'All creatures have consciousness and personality, albeit, in some cases, of a somewhat less advanced order than man. It is the Divine Spark of the God-Force within them that assures their survival.

'These souls have their own worlds but, of course, some creatures have lived with man for so long that through conscious co-operation and loving loyalty they have been helped into a greater awareness of themselves, and therefore have been aided further along the road of progress. Come; take my arm and I will show you.'

And as I obeyed, the whole sphere and greenery vanished and we found ourselves in a dark and dank-looking place. I didn't like the coldness permeating the atmosphere there.

'This is the realm wherein dwell those who have showed dreadful cruelty to animals and human beings.'

'Where are the people?' I asked, noticing no signs of life anywhere.

'Hiding in those caves,' and he pointed them out nearby. 'They shrink from their shame, full of regret and the constantly present cruelty and pain they inflicted on their brethren which plagues their minds and disturbs the deepest peace of their spirits.'

I glanced around and spied several dark caves hewn out of the sheer cliff-face where we had arrived, and near which we were now standing. We were perched precariously on a small rock-shelf. I wanted to go inside a cave and talk to one of the people and my thoughts were instantly registered:

'I will take you nearer, but the rest is up to you.'

And in a twinkling of an eye we were immediately transported up onto a higher ledge in the cliff. I was balanced on a tiny ridge, just big enough for my two feet to creep along, providing I kept my back to the slimy sheer rocks with arms outstretched, in case I should fall. (Isn't it strange how old habits grip us, even in the spirit world?)

Slowly, carefully, I edged my way across towards a dark opening, my head pulled right back so that I could only view the disquietened sky. I was terrified to look down at the 400-foot drop into seeming black nothingness, way down below my feet. I never did like heights.

White Owl stood apart on a nearby larger jutting piece of rock, watching while I gained a surer footing and thankfully slipped inside the cave, into the thick blackness – where I saw no-one at all. Neither could I, at first, hear anything except the steady dripping of water.

'Hello? Hello there? I've come to talk with you. Will you show yourself?'

When the echo of my voice faded, there was silence – but I then sensed that somewhere in the shadows there was a huddled shivering figure of a sad and wretched man. He didn't speak, but I knew he was there. Although he never made a sound, I strangely 'heard' his troubled thoughts, but couldn't make out their confusion.

'Hello?'

'Go away!'

The sharpness slapped me in the face and straightened my spine as if a sniper's bullet had been shot into it. Then I tried again.

'Please, I'd like to help you if I can ... Won't you step forward and talk with me? I won't hurt you, my

273

friend.'

There was a further long silence, and no response.

So I stepped deeper into the dank cave, gradually focusing my eyes until they fell upon the shaking form of a pathetically thin man. He was more afraid of me than I of him, and as soon as he felt my piercing gaze he cowered back as far as the rocks would allow. He seemed petrified of my presence. His eyes widened and he drew his whitened fingers into a knotted fist, closer underneath his chin.

'I won't hurt you,' I said, quietly, 'I just want to help you, if I can.'

Silence again as he curled his slender frame into a tighter ball of fear. It was then that I became aware of the awful sadness all about him. In a flash of a second I knew he was truly sorry for his past cruelty. I also knew what he'd done: he'd been responsible for mutilating several horses and other animals, for 'sport' and 'pleasure'; but these tears were shed out of regret.

'There's a much better world for you to live in,' I said. 'If only you would accept you're ready to leave this terrible place. I can help you to leave.'

'But I . . . I don't deserve to live with ordinary folk. What I did . . . what I've done is too cruel to describe . . . I am, so ashamed . . . '

'I know,' and by now my reassuring hand was resting on his sharp shoulder blades. 'I know everything you did, but that's all behind you now. You can make amends for it somehow. But you can't stay here forever. It's time to move on. The time's right for progress and I've been brought here to take you onwards.'

And the huddled figure began to weep unashamedly, and he clasped my legs and buried his head into them. I bent down and touched his shivering form with my hands. It was then I noticed he could only have been about thirty years old, and his dirty shirt and trousers were covered in dried-up blood stains: indelible impressions of heinous crimes, perpetuated by a horrified mind.

'Come along, now. Follow me, for you've suffered enough. Your memories have plagued you for far too long.' And I gently helped him to his feet, until he was looking right into my eyes. 'I've been sent to place you in the care of others nearby and – if you'll just say the word – a much better life starts from now. All you have to do is *desire* it.'

'I do,' he wept, his shoulders rising and falling under the powerful emotions rising in his breast. 'I do . . . but . . . it can't be this easy . . . not after all the harm I've done . . . ?'

'But it is,' I assured. 'We can walk away together, now, or if you wish, I can help you to sleep and when you wake up you'll be in a much better place. You've earned the right, you see. Just trust me, my friend. Your remorse is spent and these tears prove you're ready to make amends.'

'I am,' he whispered emotionally, his eyes brimming with new hope. 'Yes, I truly am, really . . . And I'll help the animals in any way I can now; I owe them this . . . And I do so want to rest.'

At this point, a smiling, kindly, White Owl walked towards us, outstretching a hand which touched the thin man's troubled brow, instantly causing him to fall asleep, as if some powerful anaesthetic had been miraculously delivered. Then the cave suddenly vanished . . .

White Owl and I stood together once more in the flowering gardens, and the same young man was now resting upon a prepared green couch before us, unconscious, heaving his chest like a tired child overcome by some deep and profound sleep. His healing bed was attended by three nurses and several helpers who were already transmitting energy rays to him, and patiently awaiting his return to balance, health and consciousness.

'Will he ask for me when he wakes?' I said.

'No. But he will never forget you. All he needs now is rest. We can help him again, later, and this time perhaps *you* would like to explain the Judgement Day. Would you?'

'Yes.'

'Good,' he said – and my memory faded out . . .

V

. . . Awareness returned within a dreadful atmosphere of utter confusion and fear which so filled my mind as I became conscious next to my spirit guide that I panicked. He calmed me by his thoughts and I realized where we were. It was a place where animals – mostly cows, pigs, chickens and sheep – were suddenly 'appearing' on concrete-type floors of what could have been some kind of farm outhouses.

The animals seemed stunned, or looked as though they'd just collapsed of exhaustion. Many of them were rolling from side to side with their legs curled up tightly towards their bodies, until they suddenly 'awoke', when they tried to scramble to their feet, terror-stricken in many instances.

The surrounding atmosphere was somewhat darker than in the other places we'd visited, and I instantly knew this had been created as a direct result of the animals' fearful memories. White Owl broke my sorrowful thoughts and spoke softly:

'We are in one of the many places where animals arrive after being slaughtered for meat, on Earth.'

My instincts had served me well, for I'd felt this before I'd heard his voice.

'Are they just arriving?'

'Yes. Shocked and dismayed; stunned, as you can see.'

And I could. And as I took in the dismal surroundings, in one corner of the yard a cow had just 'appeared'. She was rolling on her stomach, on the ground, her legs seemingly quite useless as she lowed loudly, when an attractive young teenage girl – a spirit helper – dashed towards her and started to stroke her body and soothe her distress with fine gentle words and comfort.

'These good souls are kept forever busy here, as you can no doubt imagine.'

I felt so sad I thought my heart was going to burst. I was completely overwhelmed by sorrow and deeply troubled in the spirit.

'Do these poor creatures remain here long?'

'No. This is just the place of their transition. They "died" at the merciless hands of Man, in his abattoirs, and therefore we bring them immediately to these similar man-made buildings. All their lives were spent in similar surroundings and arriving here considerably lessens the shock they receive. They will shortly be taken away to other spheres.'

'Animals have their own planes of thought?'

'Oh yes, except for the *very* domesticated ones, like cats, dogs and other pets of all varieties who stay with their human friends, or members of the family who have passed to this side. Wild creatures have their own spheres of activity.'

'And what will happen to this herd of cows?' I mournfully asked, pointing out into the courtyard where a few youngsters were leading several sad-looking animals further away from the outhouses, into lanes hedged with leafy trees.

'They go with these friends and then into their own worlds. There they will be left to find their own way of living.'

'What about farm animals who've grown attached to their owners and their children?'

'They remain with them, in fields and paddocks provided by the humans. Love is the link. Only love can build true friendship between any life-forms.'

'And the wild animals: is their continued survival assured, White Owl?'

'Yes, if they desire it. Once consciousness is personalized into physical form, it gains an individual awareness of itself – so survival is assured.'

'You seem to imply that some don't have continuous survival.'

'That is so. It all depends upon the level of Mind which the creature has reached in its struggle to progress towards depth of awareness.

'As far as the animal kingdom is concerned, there is what we term the Group-Soul, and its influence is especially strong in their lives. In their own spheres, the individual can lose its identity in the amassed consciousness of the whole of the herd – if it so chooses.'

'But doesn't that contradict the Law?'

'I can only reveal how matters are; I did not invent the Natural Laws, but am merely an observer, like yourself . . .'

VI

I'd tried to doze off in an armchair, but had woken

up to hear the rain sleeting against the windowpane. As I rose to close the curtains, I noticed it was a dark, bleak day outside.

For a moment I stood and watched the sheets of hypnotic rain washing in at forty-five degree angles to the ground, and sweeping in torrents down the deserted roads.

Sundays were always quiet when it was wet.

I wearily pulled the drapes on the grey deluge, turned up the gas fire and took up residence on my soft and comfy sofa, cuddling three pillows around my head like long lost friends.

Everything was so peaceful, warm and snug, and the inky blackness behind my eyes was velvety soft and marvellously inviting ...

... My first memory was of a happy group of children seated under the shady branches of a large and spreading oak tree. I was just outside their circle, but alone, my guide being absent.

I felt I'd been there with him for quite some time, but now he'd left to attend to other pressing work while I observed this playful class.

The tutor was a young slim man in his early twenties; and he wasn't an ancient soul – no, he was as young as his age and, I thought to myself, a relatively New Arrival to the Spirit Side. He had an aquiline nose and deep-set, brown-black eyes, edged with thick black lashes. His face was olive-tanned and very kind. His light brown hair was gathered at the back into a pony-tail. He wasn't wearing classic spirit robes, but an open-necked white shirt and loose-fitting black jeans.

It was all such a natural scene, I might have been on a country picnic; the children gathered around him ranged from the ages of about six to twelve and were quietly attentive in the coolness, listening to him.

'Now we're going to use the power of Thought to create our surroundings,' he announced.

There was immediate excitement in the little crowd who started whispering confidentially amongst themselves. He didn't stop them, but simply waited patiently.

'Right, I'm going to build something in the palm of my hand simply by using the power of my mind.'

'How?' asked a Chinese girl, who spoke with an American accent.

'How do you think?' he smiled.

A young English boy with blond hair, who was aged about ten chipped in:

'Well, whenever I made something back home,' he said, 'I used to gather the materials first, before I could put it together.'

'That's right, Andrew, and it's exactly the same here – only the method of gathering is slightly different.'

'Is it by Thought, Guy?'

'Yes, that's exactly right. Everything is a thought, isn't it?'

'Yes, Guy,' said Andrew again. And there was general agreement amongst the children, after which their tutor continued:

'By thinking hard, and really concentrating our thoughts single-mindedly, we can draw together the necessary substances from the atmosphere and then create something. Thought is more powerful here than it is on Earth; it has a more *direct* effect on our ether, our surroundings.

'But it isn't easy, by any means. It takes a good deal of effort.

'On the mother planet we'd have to physically chop down a tree before we could burn its logs for heat. But even then, we couldn't do any of that without first taking Thought, could we children?'

'No,' they chorused in staggered sound.

'In this new world we don't gather things physically, but spiritually, by using the drawing power of our thoughts. Now – what shall we make?'

'I'd like a pencil,' said the Chinese girl.

'Right.'

'A red pencil!' she added.

'OK. Let's see if I can get it for you. I have to think quite hard when I do this: one small thought isn't enough – it has to be a real effort on my part. I must "see" and hold the form of the solid object in my mind before it can be projected outwards and materialize in my hands . . . '

He then held out his two palms, cupped them together, and closed his eyes.

A silence fell over his captive and fascinated young audience.

He was obviously caught in deep concentration, which delighted the youngsters no end. They pointed at his features and whispered amongst themselves, as children do, as to whether or not they thought he'd be successful and whether he'd get the colour just right. (Because if it didn't turn out to be red, the Chinese girl 'didn't want it!')

After a short time, something started 'hazing' or 'misting' in his palms . . .

The red pencil gradually took shape, became visible and solidified, and soon was permanently present as a tangible and useful object.

The youngsters laughed and applauded gleefully as Guy threw the pencil to the delighted young girl.

'Now you must all try it,' he smiled at his charges; and here I mysteriously lost the class . . .

But between the two worlds, while I suddenly

journeyed back to Earth, I caught my guide's deep voice announcing:

'Tomorrow night, I shall be privileged to accompany you on a visit to a Higher Sphere of Brilliance and Light – and there we shall meet someone very special . . .'

19

The Shining Ones

I

'Hold fast to my hand, and whatever you do: do not let go,' cautioned White Owl, 'for tonight we shall visit deep into the Realms of Light where the Shining Ones dwell and without my power you cannot travel there.'

At this, the misty surroundings of the astral world began to shiver to my sight. Then our hands touched and I felt a tremendous surge of electrical power – life-energy – transferring itself from him to me, power which quickened up the vibrations of my spirit body, and I began to feel nervous.

'Be at ease and enjoy the lightness of soul,' he said.

'I'll try.' But I was still rather concerned about what was happening, for now there was nothing recognizable surrounding us – just pastel colours, swirling and blending together so beautifully and quickly that they took my breath clean away. It was such a wonderful sight, with such indescribable soul sensations that I felt I wanted to cry.

Now I was as light as a feather, electrically 'alive' and so full of awareness because my vibrations had been lifted to such a pitch that every fibre of my spirit body tingled with energy. I felt super-aware, super-conscious, as we seemed to be arriving in some Higher Spheres.

'Do not attempt to speak,' said my guide, 'until you have acclimatized yourself to the finer environment, my friend. And, under no circumstances whatsoever, let go of my hand.'

I nodded, part of me realizing he was my power-link to this sphere and the rest of me mystified by what was happening. He instantly 'knew' these concerns, so with his deep and mellow thought-voice continued advising:

'None here speak with their mouths; we transfer intentions and ideas by Thought. You are to be given a rare glimpse into life in worlds so far removed from Earth that, at first, you may not fully comprehend all you see. But it is enough to witness and remember. Later, you will understand.'

I then 'heard' my own thought-voice, for the first time as clear as a crisp church bell, sounding its automatic response which made my teacher laugh aloud (in his mind, of course). I had replied, 'I shall have to behave myself!'

'You would not be here, if you could not,' was his amusing retort.

'Are we expected?' I thought again.

'Nothing goes unnoticed in these realms; the Power of the Mind is Supreme, as I have always taught you. But here, it's potency will amaze even yourself!' he said, chuckling like a wise old man, after which his deep eyes indicated I should look ahead. I obeyed, as I felt him clasp my hand more tightly, and I responded likewise.

All around us was a fine transparent cloud of pink, green and blue pastel-coloured mists wafting gently in the atmosphere. Then suddenly, and quietly, they swirled aside to reveal a scene of beautiful light.

284

Everything in this place, which didn't resemble a room, a house or even countryside, had been 'crafted', 'sculpted' or, perhaps more correctly, *created* in light. And within this cloudy self-illuminated world, brilliant points of different coloured light, like twinkling stars, were moving gracefully about in all directions: some fast, some very slow.

They were of every known and unknown shade; their colours glowing with an unearthly iridescence.

Through this all-pervading light, I could see no angels playing heavenly lyres (though I confess it wouldn't have at all surprised me if I had; so gorgeous was the scene). No, there was just a soft, yet radiantly diffused glow filling my vision; a wondrous fogbank of pastel energies.

Many questions immediately flashed through my mind, all of which became 'real' the moment they were born.

'Be still, and know that I Am God,' said White Owl, and I instantly thought he meant we were in the presence of – or certainly near to – beings whose task it was to guide the worlds of spirit by Thought.

But I was completely wrong.

'We are approaching only the lowlands of the spheres of light wherein dwell beings whose tasks are to tend various, seemingly insentient, life-forms on Mother Earth. This sector contains elemental spirits serving some of the planet's vegetation and animal life.'

'Are we near the animals?'

'No: you are in the presence of some of the guiding forces of Nature.'

'These beings have no form,' I said, a note of surprise in my thought-voice.

'But they do. You have only just approximated to this sphere and your perceptions are not yet finely attuned. Clear your vision and discover where you are.'

'But I thought we'd arrived somewhere really high in the spirit world.'

'No; that is yet to come. Look again, and see!'

So I sharpened my sight and watched in wonderment as the pastel clouds slowly parted and drifted away, leaving only the bright pinpoints of light dancing in the air, in the midst of a lovely rural scene filled with thick vegetation. The colours of the plants were almost shining and even their foliage was 'alive' with vibrancy which I could acutely sense and feel.

'This is Earth, my friend, and these fields of flowers and hedgerows are near the borders of the South of France.'

'But I thought . . .'

'I've imparted but a fraction of my power to speed up your spirit body to approximate to the rate whereby these nature spirits can be seen.'

'I'm attuned to their frequencies?'

'Yes.'

Excitedly, I looked all around me and saw that within each dancing light (which moved from flowers to branches in all different directions, touching and examining different plants) there was a tiny being at its centre.

'Move forward,' was the gentle suggestion from my guide, when I wondered if I might touch one. 'Stretch out your hand and do not be afraid, for they are easily frightened even though they are sometimes rather mischievous. They avoid creatures whose hearts are impure or whose minds harbour fear or hostile negativity. But they are very amiable little beings, once they have accepted you as a friend.'

Gently, almost without thinking, I slowly extended the open flat palm of my free left hand, rather as one might do when inviting a wild bird to accept and feed on a few grains in it, and, shortly, there was a little flurry of activity nearby and four or five of the dancing lights approached, gliding in the air.

I marvelled at the opportunity to study them at close quarters, incredulously viewing the tiny life-forms within their small, two- or three-inch radiant globes, and noticing it was the bodies of the forms themselves which shed these wonderful auras. The electromagnetic lights were of various swirling hues: golds, blues, pinks, greens, and even some with reddish colours.

Then, quite spontaneously, one of the little people alighted on my hand. To my amazement, I peered into its form and discovered what appeared to be a young, slim, naked woman within the light. Sporting flesh-coloured skin (seemingly made of the light itself, but perhaps containing more pale yellow shades than our skin tones), she was the proud owner of beautifully piercing pale blue eyes. Her long silvery hair, almost platinum in colour and fine in texture, was parted in the centre of her head and long enough to fall well below her waist; she kept brushing it gently aside as she studied my features.

This little nature spirit showed no outward signs of gender, no sexual organs or breasts, but just a pleasing young female form which seemed to glow and project such natural grace and gentleness of spirit.

Gazing intently at each other, we were both totally absorbed by the other's appearance; she, rather coy, while I was completely fascinated.

I noticed she had *four* fingers on each hand, and *four* toes on each foot, and attached to the back of her shoulders there was a pair of almost dragonfly-like translucent gossamer wings which quivered and shook with life. The little person chuckled as I moved my large eyes back and forth, examining her vibrant and perfectly formed body, which seemed to have been created out of nothing more than the ethereal light she was bathed in.

While standing on my palm and seemingly weighing virtually nothing, she turned so that I might see her wings more closely (she was well aware of my interest in them).

Then, with a further faint chuckle, she fluttered them quickly back and forth and suddenly sailed up into the air and over to some nearby flowers.

Like a tiny flock of birds, her friends who'd also come to see me (and they didn't all look the same, some of them being male) instantly followed her and, in a moment, they were flying around the brightly-lit stamens within some blossoms. They were just like busy insects tending to the job of cross-fertilization; only, from their bodies, they seemed to discharge life-energies to the Essence of the flowers, and not pollen.

'They are the divas of these plants,' said my teacher.

'Can they speak?'

'In a manner, but not in language you or I understand. But she knew your thoughts and displayed her wings.'

'I've seen drawings of these creatures,' I said.

'Yes; and why do you think their images have been captured so well?'

And I instinctively knew what he meant: that in everything which, at first, might seem created by vivid imagination, grains of truth might well reside.

Immediately after these ideas occurred, I lost touch with my visions, and can't recall the next steps in our journey . . .

II

. . . But consciousness fades back as both my guide and I were standing at the foot of some very impressive mountains. Their mighty peaks were high and majestic, purple-headed and stunningly beautiful. They seemed to almost touch the sky and were ranged for so many miles about us that I couldn't properly distinguish any horizon at all.

'There is to be a visit,' he smiled. 'Someone who commands great respect in these lands is coming soon.'

'But I thought there was no government here.' I replied.

'And there isn't. Not as you know it on Earth, but we do have hierarchies, respected individuals and groups of ancient souls who are renowned for their great wisdom, knowledge and experience which they have attained through many existences.'

'How long have they existed?'

'Countless centuries, aeons. There are many souls here upon whom it would be difficult, if not impossible, to place an exact age. Timeless in Essence, they administer their wise judgement to any in need of it. And one of the most advanced souls in this plane has informed us of the impending arrival of such a Shining One.'

'Us?'

'The Group of Souls whom I count as my Brothers and Sisters, though not in terms of blood, but soul-affinity.'

'Who is coming?' I asked.

'You will see. In fact, I do not think she will be alone, there may well be a group visitation.'

'Why?' I stumblingly asked, quietly within my own mind. 'Why have I been permitted this honour when I obviously haven't earned it? I have no right to share in such a wonderful occasion.'

'But you have,' he said. 'No-one here is allowed an experience unless they need it.'

'I've earned the right?'

'Of course. You presently cannot remember, but it is no mistake that you are here. Did you think I simply decided to bring you, Stephen?'

I wanted to naïvely answer 'yes', but I felt ashamed of my lack of understanding, a feeling which made him smile all the more.

After an amused silence, during which both he and I took great delight in drawing upon the life-giving rarified air and marvelling at the wonderful purple-headed peaks, he resumed:

'You could not be here in these spheres without my power, and I could not have given it to you without the permission of greater minds who guide these heavens. If your presence here would be imprudent, then I would have been prevented. But, fortunately, they see much further forward into our existences than we can presently imagine.'

He turned his face away from the mountains and looked directly into my eyes. 'There are reasons why,' he said, 'and I daresay these will eventually become clear to us both.'

'How would you have been prevented from bringing me?'

'My power would have been withdrawn; and so would you.'

'Would I have been harmed?'

'No, just quietly removed. You would have woken back within the confines of your physical body and your memory of the effort would have been completely buried, "forgotten".'

'But I understood these kingdoms weren't controlled

by governments like we have on Earth. Politics and temporal rulers are often so corrupt.'

'True; but not here. In these Realms the Great Spirit rules Supreme. God is the only Governor, whose Laws are Just and Wholesome and certainly not corrupt.

'Here each sphere has many progressed minds existing within it who, because of their experience, have naturally earned access to knowledge about which we can at present only dream. So vast are the parameters of these worlds that God has ordained that everywhere one travels there will always be advanced minds monitoring our thoughts and actions.

'In these Realms we cannot escape being fully known and understood; no more than you on Earth can avoid our attention – should we desire to give it.'

I shivered at the thought of all our actions being registered, but fully realized that only when this fact truly dawns in our minds would humanity undertake, in real earnest, the long process of continually purifying its thoughts. I was then compelled to ask:

'Do we have privacy on Earth?'

'Of a kind,' he smiled. 'For the most part a person's Earth-life trundles by in ordained paths without us viewing each act and deed. But there is no-one with you who can prevent us monitoring certain events, if we consider it beneficial to do so.'

'But who permits it?' I asked (rather indignantly, I'm afraid).

'The Great Spirit, who has ordained us with the Power to see.'

Then his speech fell away, for there came a perceptible change in the atmosphere – it shivered, as if an earthquake were about to occur. I discerned this to be the announcement of an imminent arrival, further up at the top of the mountains.

'Quite correctly perceived,' he said, 'and we must go to the plateau where our friends are waiting. We are to witness the arrival of Sheerah and her attendants.'

'Sheerah?'

'One of the most progressed spirits and evolved minds connected with this sphere; indeed an old and wise soul.'

'A Shining One?'

'Yes. Come! We must not keep our welcoming party waiting.'

I knew we would then make the instant journey to the top of the mountains. I was right, and within a microsecond – no, sooner – we were right in the midst of a group of about twenty Enlightened Ones who projected such sincere soul-warmth that I immediately felt 'at home'.

Then something odd happened: as soon as our presence was felt, White Owl released my hand. A little surge of panic made me clumsily reach out to take his arm again, but he withdrew it. Suddenly I realized I was safe within the centre of this circle of advanced souls, who had gathered silently around a nook near to a cave entrance. In the same instant I also knew their collected power was supporting my vibrations and I no longer needed my guide's help.

All at once, almost in unison, every head turned in my direction and the finely featured beings (robed in what seemed like light itself, of differing hues) smiled and strangely nodded in greeting. Pleased, but slightly embarrassed, I returned the compliment by slightly inclining my head, and, as I did so, I was aware of having met, or known, each of these people, but I couldn't quite remember when or where.

White Owl stepped to my side and the entire mountain atmosphere altered again, almost impelling us to face towards the raised, rocky nook nearby. We duly obeyed and then watched as a brilliant golden mist gradually appeared from thin air and gently condensed, until within it we could just about perceive the forms of four people, one standing far forward of the other three.

As the hazy shapes materialized and solidified, there was revealed to us a beautiful woman with golden hair who was wearing a lilac-coloured robe which seemed to be a part of herself. Her eyes were deep blue-green, like unfathomed ocean waters, and her remarkably penetrating gaze conveyed the most wonderful sense of peace I've ever experienced in the spirit spheres.

She was serenity personified.

Slowly, she looked around the small gathering and nodded to her companions in the crowd, who touched their heads or bowed and reverently acknowledged her presence.

Her three attendants in the background were all male, each wearing a long robe which, like hers, seemed a part of themselves: one wore pale green, one pale blue and another in a similar shade to Sheerah's attire. The men were all over six feet in height, but Sheerah was only about five feet tall. Yet she radiated the purest light and the most powerful aura of us all. It required no effort to sense her greatness of heart, or her clarity of thought, or the deep and powerful well of Love carried in her soul for all creation. These qualities were almost tangible.

No one uttered a syllable as her expansive mind stretched out and touched us, enfolding us within her power until we almost felt we were an integral part of her great self.

She was undoubtedly a very advanced soul of great age and wisdom, but concealed beneath slim youth and radiant beauty.

Her compassionate gaze then turned upon me, after she'd greeted all her friends and given each one a personal message of encouragement for the work they had been undertaking near to Earth, in the name of Love and Peace. Her thoughts then touched me:

'There are no mistakes. You have been summoned, for there is much work for you to do.'

'If I can do it, I will,' I replied.

A murmur of approval moved within the minds of the assembly.

'The kingdom of Earth is forever a place of toil and woe. Part of its function in the Divine Plan is to provide searing blows to the spirit which will help it grow. But the human race needs Light.'

'I agree,' I said, within my mind.

'The Planet is daily being abused and systematically ruined. Its forests are being destroyed, and these are the Mother's great lungs which produce life-giving oxygen. Without them, the atmosphere will deteriorate, and life is threatened.'

'I know,' I said, innocently.

'Ask Man to care. Instruct him to plant new trees, purify the air, and do everything in his power to keep the Mother's pulse beating for centuries to come. Global warming spells disaster for the children of the Earth, but still not enough minds take immediate action.'

Rather presumptuously, I asked:

'Surely, it's all part of a plan?'

'Yes,' she returned kindly, 'as indeed is this request, lovingly given to those who follow you.'

Put gently in my place, I apologized for my hasty

remark and asked what else I might do to help.

'Instruct Man to think forward: his actions today affect his Mother tomorrow. The pollution which poisons her veins is speeding up at an alarming rate. Her once-pure streams and soils are now thickly clogged with harmful chemicals.'

'What of her people?' I asked.

'Tend to them lovingly, but I am charged to speak of the Planet.'

'What can I do?'

'Tell all who will listen to care for her. Record our meeting and people will be touched as these warnings are given.'

'But I forget so much when I wake.'

'You will be helped by these powers,' she said, indicating with a graceful arm the small gathering of teachers all around me. 'You will not forget me, or my thoughts. I shall attend to it.'

And with this, a ray of silver light shot out from the centre of her forehead and touched the centre of mine. As it struck, I felt completely overwhelmed by a great peacefulness and also knew that certain information had been 'branded' on my mind; that's the only way I can describe it.

'You will not recall our meeting, until the time is right,' she went on, 'only then will memory surface, and you will write.'

'Yes,' I said. 'I'll do whatever I can.'

Another soul present asked:

'Sheerah, what will be the outcome?'

'I regret,' she replied gracefully, 'I am not yet permitted to reveal this, my friend.'

Respecting her decision, the teacher acknowledged her reply.

She then raised her right arm and from her hand, a soft but radiant bluish-gold light spurted upwards like a fountain of stars, cascading over all the gathering, who straightened their backs under its caress. She spoke again to the group:

'Peace be with you. The work of spiritualizing Man is progressing as it was meant to do. Never tire of your duties, my dear friends; and encourage your charges to serve the race with Loving Compassion, for the work is never over.'

That was then I realized that these teachers were all spirit guides, each connected with a separate medium, or mediums, on Earth.

A quiet respect fell about the group.

'The Shining Ones, higher in status and wisdom than any of ourselves, send you their Blessing.'

Expectancy filled the air . . .

'The Masters of Light are pleased with what has been achieved thus far; even though our brothers and sisters in the flesh are, for the most part, still spiritually asleep, much has been accomplished.

'The Wise Ones will never cease from pouring out their guidance to touch and inspire you, each one of you, in the various spheres of your activity. Personal instructions will soon be transmitted to each one of you.'

Then her wise counsel surprisingly revealed just who these spiritual teachers, gathered in that silent place, truly were:

'Keep the souls of those nations in your charge firmly thinking along the lines of harmony between all facets of the Great Spirit's Creation.

'Renounce all doubts and be glad: the work is moving forward, and we, with the Invincible Power of Love, are winning the battle over materialism, greed and cruelty.

'The Love of the Masters is with you, now and always.

'The Shining Ones will guide each one.

'You have only but to call upon their names to seek their Inspiration, and their unceasing Blessing.'

And an almost audible sigh travelled throughout the group.

They were all truly grateful.

They were refreshed and renewed.

They felt greater peace for having touched this Shining Soul's presence, and gratitude for receiving again her continued commitment to aid them with their spiritual work.

The perfect stillness came to an end when the silence was broken by Sheerah's final thought:

'Peace . . . ' she said, as the whole scene dissolved away before my gaze . . .

Epilogue

It formed itself and came to me in a dream, the kind of lucid picture-book experience that's full of moving kaleidoscopic images that remain long after waking.

Quietly, I yawned, stretched, wiped my brow, rose and set about making the vision a reality.

Opening the moisture-proof box, I carefully placed each item inside: first a poster, then a colour picture-programme, followed by a copy of my birth certificate, some inspirational poetry cards and a photograph of the portrait in pastels of White Owl and myself. Then I included an audio-tape I'd done, plus a letter and other bits and pieces.

On top of all this I laid my books: *Visions of Another World, Voices from Heaven* and the manuscript of *In Touch with Eternity*; a trilogy of psychic and spiritual adventures interwoven with spirit teachings, for discerning eyes to view.

I sighed, and closed the box.

After completely sealing it, I then gently loaded the precious booty into the car and drove alone for miles through country fields. I eventually stopped and walked into a misty afternoon which was kissing rolling fields, somewhere deep in the heart of Wales, the nation of my birth.

Silently, unseen, I carried the time-capsule far out into a peaceful green place where I thought it would never be discovered by the hands or machines of modern-day man. As a final precaution my attentive eyes meticulously scanned the horizon, seeking any sign of human life: there was none.

I was physically alone in the quiet field.

Deftly, I took the spade and dug a hole several feet deep and then knelt beside it on soft Welsh soil. I closed my eyes against the misty sun and spoke a few words of thankfulness to the Spirit People, without whom very few of the thousands of words I've written would have had any real meaning, for they'd been with me every step of the way.

'Thank you for the teachings, guidance and love. I gave you my promise and I kept it,' I said. 'I've shared the truth with others,' I murmured.

Then I opened my eyes to nothing but silence all around, though I did sense invisible presences quite near, watching, pensively thinking. In fact, it was they who had indicated the exact spot where this time-capsule should be entombed; this small piece of Yesterday, buried Today, to be found by someone of a distant Tomorrow.

'I'll never reveal its location,' I affirmed softly, heard only by a flock of singing birds.

The long drive home gave me plenty of time for reflection. Like an old-time flickering movie, I remembered dozens of different scenes: my pathway, gruelling work and public tours; perspiration and struggle; and secret spirit-guidance, when all earthly souls had deserted me.

Despite a sweeping melancholy, I remained grateful, for perhaps in centuries to come – in the next millennia – this capsule might suddenly be unearthed and its contents avidly studied by men of another time . . .

*   *   *

That night, lying in my warm bed, I pondered on the reaction of some future archaeologist as his trembling fingers smoothed my sealed container. I was fascinated.

Perhaps, in this remote future, our present form of English would no longer be used, or by then be unrecognizable? Our discoverer would have to painstakingly piece together fragmented writings, and carefully translate them as best he could – like his ancestors did after finding the Dead Sea Scrolls.

I turned out the bedside lamp and tucked myself further under the warm sheets.

In the darkness I could almost see his puzzled expression as a million questions galloped through the fields of his mind, wondering what in heaven he'd unearthed.

Who was this man? Was he a teacher? A reformer? A challenger of thoughts?
Could he have been a messenger who spoke with angels?
Was he a healer, a worker of wonders?
And if he was a man of God, where are the rest of his teachings hidden?

Under the soft blankets I wrapped my tired limbs in these distant thoughts, then smiled, thinking: 'Perhaps I'm all those things, possibly some. In certain eyes, maybe none.'

(Though I've loved the soul of Man, its expression through personality has frequently left much to be desired.)

Lying half-asleep I continued musing:

'There's plenty more to achieve: I haven't written about spiritual unfoldment or mediumistic development yet, or recorded my philosophy on the conduct of the soul. Then there's my poetry: yes, I've plenty more to share – if it's part of my Life-Plan.'

Wispy dreams threaded through the chasms of my mind, and I must have closed my eyes and gently drifted into peaceful reverie.

The faraway downstairs clock chimed out the hollow hour. It was now past midnight; tomorrow already, and the rain was pelting against the bedroom windows.

But before sleep fully embraced me, I remembered that in the coming evening – tonight, at 7.30 – I'd be standing again upon another stage, in another city, facing another thousand strangers desperately wanting news of their loved ones in the Next World.

They will have queued in the downpour, and then filled countless rows of seats with a sea of hopeful faces; eyes twinkling in the lights and brimming with expectancy.

They'll want me to succeed.

And, no matter how easy or difficult my work may be, through it all they'll expect me to smile, even if my spirit is racked with sorrow and my heart is breaking in two.

But then, I mustn't allow myself the luxury of complaining. The medium must deny this right, hide his despair, and serve.

Inside this darkness, the spotlight will pick me out and carry me through the meeting, high on a wave of love generated by the people . . .

Distant thunder cracked these images, then rolled like giant empty oil-drums around the skies, and the room lit up with sheets of lightning.

I curled up into a snug ball, pulled the bedclothes high up, further over my head, and wrapped myself in the velvet night, half-whispering as I fell asleep:

'Don't worry, I'll be there . . . and I'll do my best.

'God willing, I won't let you down . . .'

For further information on the life and work of Stephen O'Brien, e.g. bestselling audio cassettes on *'Life After Death, What Awaits Us in the Next World'*, full colour picture programmes, *'Portrait in Pastels'* (featured in this book), inspirational greeting cards, books and a full range of other quality items available by mail order – please write enclosing a stamped addressed envelope to:

VOICES MANAGEMENT
(Dept B3)
P O Box 8
SWANSEA
SA1 1BL
UK

Voices Management regrets it cannot reply without an sae.
Thank you.

ANGELS BY MY SIDE
BY STEPHEN O'BRIEN

As Britain's 'brightest young medium', Stephen O'Brien's extraordinary psychic gifts have comforted thousands of people and have silenced sceptics around the world.

Now, in *Angels By My Side*, his fourth volume of autobiography, Stephen O'Brien provides impressive evidence of the survival of the soul beyond death, and reveals:

* What awaits us after death and the secrets of the Next World

* Marlene Dietrich's first communication from the Beyond

* The secret powers of Light and Colour that enhance well-being and self-healing

* A compelling view of 'The One Living God'

Through more of his amazing out-of-body excursions into the Spirit World itself, Stephen O'Brien also shares with us timeless wisdom from the 'silent sentinels' who watch over us and unveils fascinating glimpses into mankind's future . . .

'Stunning clairvoyance . . . superb mediumship' *Psychic News*

A Bantam Paperback
0 553 40718 X

CLOSER TO THE LIGHT
BY MELVIN MORSE MD

Gathered from the testimony of children too young to have absorbed cultural attitudes to death, *Closer to the Light* offers evidence that consistently portrays the end of life as serene and joyous, to be welcomed rather than feared, an 'experience of Light'. Adults who almost died as children say that the effect of the Light has never left them. In a book that is both comforting and scientifically meticulous, Dr Morse asks whether children have different near-death experiences from those of adults; whether a particular area of the brain is involved or genetically coded. His answers may change your views about death and dying forever.

A Bantam Paperback
0 553 40449 0

A SELECTION OF NON-FICTION TITLES
PUBLISHED BY BANTAM AND CORGI BOOKS

THE PRICES SHOWN BELOW WERE CORRECT AT THE TIME OF
GOING TO PRESS. HOWEVER TRANSWORLD PUBLISHERS
RESERVE THE RIGHT TO SHOW NEW RETAIL PRICES ON COVERS
WHICH MAY DIFFER FROM THOSE PREVIOUSLY ADVERTISED IN
THE TEXT OR ELSEWHERE.